GCSE Physical Education

A Revision Guide

Tim Ferguson, BSc, PGCE
Physical Education and Outdoor Education Consultant

Human Kinetics

Cataloging-in-Publication Data is available.

ISBN: 0-7360-4014-5

Acquisitions Editor: Scott Wikgren; **Developmental Editor:** Diane Evans; **Managing Editor:** Amy Stahl; **Assistant Editor:** Derek Campbell; **Copyeditor:** Janet Pannocchia; **Proofreader:** Kathy Bennett; **Indexer:** Betty Frizzéll; **Permission Manager:** Dalene Reeder; **Graphic Designer:** Robert Reuther; **Graphic Artist:** Kathleen Boudreau-Fuoss; **Cover Designer:** Fred Starbird; **Photographer (cover):** © T. Hindley/Prosport/Newsport; **Art Managers:** Craig Newsom and Carl D. Johnson; **Illustrator:** Mic Greenberg; **Printer:** United Graphics

10 9 8 7 6 5 4 3 2 1

Human Kinetics
Web site: www.humankinetics.com

Europe: Human Kinetics, Units C2/C3 Wira Business Park, West Park Ring Road, Leeds LS16 6EB, United Kingdom
+44 (0) 113 278 1708
e-mail: hk@hkeurope.com

United States: Human Kinetics, P.O. Box 5076, Champaign, IL 61825-5076
800-747-4457
e-mail: humank@hkusa.com

Canada: Human Kinetics, 475 Devonshire Road Unit 100, Windsor, ON N8Y 2L5
800-465-7301 (in Canada only)
e-mail: orders@hkcanada.com

Australia: Human Kinetics, 57A Price Avenue, Lower Mitcham, South Australia 5062
08 8277 1555
e-mail: liahka@senet.com.au

New Zealand: Human Kinetics, P.O. Box 105-231, Auckland Central
09-523-3462
e-mail: hkp@ihug.co.nz

Contents

Preface

T his book provides both the student and teacher with a study resource for the theoretical components of GCSE Physical Education. The book covers the entire GCSE syllabus and provides both knowledge and a source of testing this knowledge by including two sets of questions in every chapter. These questions come in the form of "Quick Test" and past examination questions, which make the book unique in its field.

This book is a valuable resource to anyone sitting the GCSE Physical Education exam in England and Wales. It also provides those delivering the course an excellent resource for classroom content and some novel ways to teach GCSE Physical Education.

GCSE Physical Education: A Revision Guide is a valuable tool to help students and teachers alike successfully complete the GCSE syllabus; it acts as an ongoing course guide and a homework and revision aide.

Acknowledgments

Lots of people have helped in many ways in the long process of writing this book, giving me their help and support. In particular my Mum and Dad, and a BIG thank you to both of them and a bit extra for my Mum for help with the initial artwork and proofreading.

Special thanks to Lyn for her support and assistance, without which I would have missed countless deadlines, had no mind maps and had an uncompleted manuscript sitting on the floor. Thank you.

Also thanks to Diane, my editor, who must have sat in disbelief at the erratic way I worked over the last year. Thank you for getting this book to print.

Finally thanks to Science in Sport for their technical assistance, greatly appreciated, and also to High Adventure Outdoor Education Centre for giving your staff time and facilities so freely.

How to Use This Book

This book provides an easy approach to GCSE Physical Education so that readers can learn its components step by step. Each chapter presents key information logically using a "building blocks" approach. This allows readers to expand basic knowledge as they work through the book.

At the start of each chapter is a mind map which outlines the main points of the chapter. This is a key revision tool helping to summarise the main points of that chapter. Once readers have learned a chapter, they can refer back to the mind map and expand comprehensively on each part.

At the end of each chapter are two sets of questions. You will need a separate sheet of paper on which to list your answers. The "Quick Test" questions are included to allow formal or informal question-and-answer sessions. These are simple questions devised by the author for readers to find out what they have learned. Following the quick test questions is a set of questions taken from examination boards. The questions have been broken down so that only muscular system questions appear at the end of the chapter on the muscular system. The questions provide the readers with the opportunity to test themselves against the examinations they take at the end of their course.

Answers for both sets of questions are provided at the back of the book. The examination board answers are taken from the examination board mark schemes, giving readers an invaluable insight into the types of answers required in their examinations.

PART I

The Human Body

This part of the revision guide outlines the basic structure of the human body and how it functions. Chapter 1 looks at the skeleton, examining bones and joints before looking at how muscles combine with the skeleton in chapter 2. Chapter 3 explains circulation and the role of blood and the heart. Chapter 4 examines how breathing occurs and chapter 5 explains which systems control energy and movement and why they are important. Chapter 6 explains the differences between the body's aerobic (with oxygen) and anaerobic (without oxygen) systems. Chapter 7 consolidates the part by explaining what effect exercise has on each body system.

CHAPTER 1

Skeletal System

This chapter explains the bones the body contains and how these bones form joints to produce movement (see figure 1.1). There are different types of joints, which produce different types of movement, with synovial joints producing the most movement. Chapter 2 explains how muscles connect to the skeleton to produce movement.

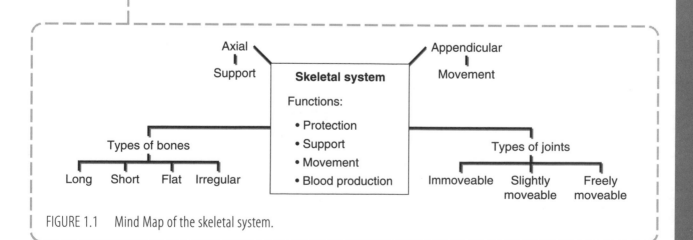

FIGURE 1.1   Mind Map of the skeletal system.

FOUR FUNCTIONS OF THE SKELETON

There are four main functions of the skeleton (figure 1.2):

1. **Protection.** The skeleton protects the delicate parts of the body (for example, the skull protects the brain and the rib cage protects the heart and lungs).
2. **Support.** Without the skeleton the body would be like a jellyfish. The skeleton gives shape. Some organs are suspended from the skeleton to keep them in an exact position.
3. **Movement**. The skeleton has joints, which provide a large range of movement.

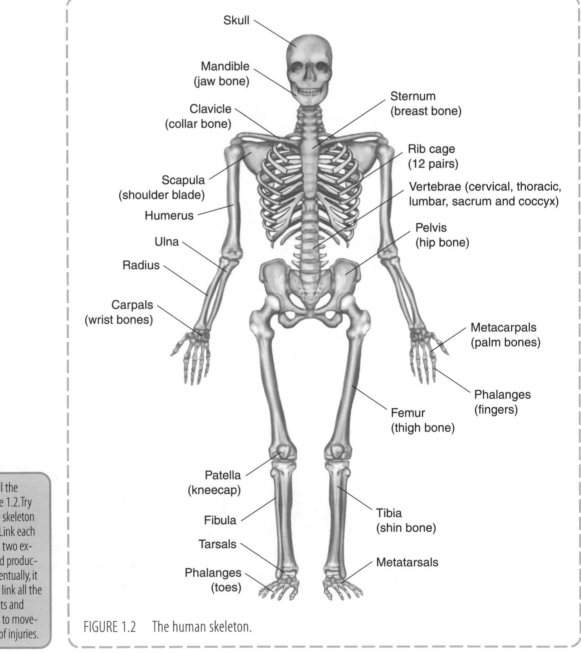

FIGURE 1.2   The human skeleton.

Learn the names of all the bones shown in figure 1.2. Try to draw and label the skeleton without using notes. Link each function with at least two examples (such as blood production in the femur). Eventually, it should be possible to link all the information with joints and muscles, and link this to movement and treatment of injuries.

4. **Blood production.** Red and white blood cells are formed in the marrow cavities of the larger bones (see figure 1.3).

The skeleton is divided into two main parts:

• **Axial.** This forms the support of the body.
• **Appendicular.** This is involved more with movement.

There are four types of bone:

1. Long, tubular bones (limbs)
2. Shorter, fibrous bones (wrist and ankle)
3. Flat, plate-like bones (skull and scapula)
4. Irregular bones (vertebrae and face)

FUNCTIONS OF JOINTS

A joint is where two or more bones meet and touch. There are over 100 joints in the body.

Three Types of Joint

There are three types of joint in the human body:

1. Immoveable (fixed) joints where movement is impossible (for example, the joints in the skull).
2. Slightly moveable joints where the bones can move slightly (for example, the vertebrae and the ribs).
3. Freely moveable (synovial) joints where bones rub together, so the ends are covered in a slippery shiny substance called cartilage. This, combined with synovial fluid, allows friction-free movement. The joint is held in place by the ligaments. The synovial membrane produces synovial fluid and also keeps the fluid sealed in (see figure 1.4).

checkpoint

✓ **Ligaments** attach bone to bone. They are strong, fibrous bands of tissue.
✓ **Cartilage** protects bone. It is a tough, smooth, slippery tissue that covers the ends of the bones, acting as a pad, buffer or shock absorber (for example, between vertebrae).
✓ **Synovial fluid** is like oil in an engine. It allows frictionless movement.
✓ **Synovial membranes** seal in the synovial fluid and also produce synovial fluid.
✓ **A capsule** surrounds the joint. Its inner lining is the synovial membrane.

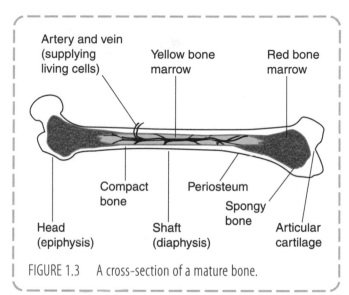

FIGURE 1.3   A cross-section of a mature bone.

Artery and vein (supplying living cells)   Yellow bone marrow   Red bone marrow   Compact bone   Periosteum   Spongy bone   Head (epiphysis)   Shaft (diaphysis)   Articular cartilage

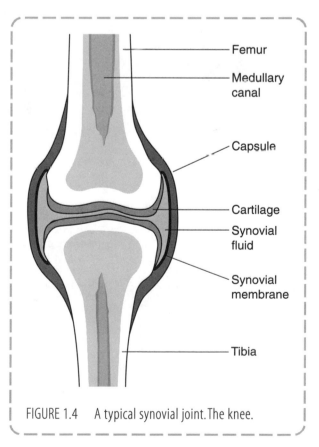

FIGURE 1.4   A typical synovial joint. The knee.

Femur   Medullary canal   Capsule   Cartilage   Synovial fluid   Synovial membrane   Tibia

Movement

Movement occurs at the joints (synovial joints) and each joint allows certain types of movement (see table 1.1 and figure 1.5). Learn which joints allow which movements and understand the way the muscular and skeletal systems combine to facilitate movement at the joints.

TABLE 1.1 Four Main Joints			
Type of joint	Actual joint	Bones of the joint	Types of movement
Ball and socket	Hip Shoulder	Femur and pelvis Humerus and scapula	Flexion/extension, rotation and abduction/adduction
Hinge	Knee Elbow	Femur and tibia Ulna and humerus	Flexion/extension
Condyloid	Wrist Ankle	Radius, ulna and carpals Tibia, fibula and tarsals	Flexion/extension and abduction/adduction
Pivot	Neck	Vertebrae	Rotation

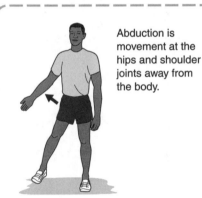

Abduction is movement at the hips and shoulder joints away from the body.

a Abduction

Adduction is movement at the hips and shoulder joints towards the body.

b Adduction

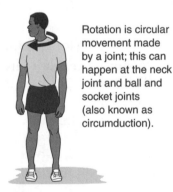

Rotation is circular movement made by a joint; this can happen at the neck joint and ball and socket joints (also known as circumduction).

c Rotation

Extension of all the joints is when the joints are extended (straight); to extend a joint means to increase the angle the bones make at the joint.

d Extension

Flexion of the knee and elbow joint is when the joint is flexed (bent); to flex at a joint means to decrease the angle the bones make at the joint.

e Flexion

FIGURE 1.5 Five types of joint movement. *(a)* Abduction; *(b)* adduction; *(c)* rotation; *(d)* extension; *(e)* flexion.

It is good practice to be able to name a joint, the bones that meet at the joint, the type of movements possible at that joint and the muscles involved in the movement. It is possible to build up a picture of how the body really works to produce movement. For example, the elbow joint is a hinge joint; the bones at the joint are the radius, ulna and humerus; the movements produced are flexion and extension; and the muscles involved are the biceps and triceps.

Quick Test

1. Where is the femur?
2. What is the anatomical (real) name for the shin bone?
3. Name two functions of the skeleton.
4. What is the largest bone in the body?
5. Where are the phalanges?
6. Name one bone in the arm.
7. Where is the fibula?
8. What is the anatomical (real) name for the hip bone?
9. Give another name for the patella.
10. Where is the scapula?
11. What protects the heart and lungs?
12. Name two types of bone.
13. What happens in the marrow cavity?
14. The skeleton is divided into axial and _____ parts.
15. What enables (helps) the skeleton to move?
16. What would the body be like without support from the skeleton?
17. Name two long, tubular bones.
18. The skeleton's function is to produce hormones. True or False?
19. The definition of a joint is where two or more bones meet. True or False?
20. The ulna is an irregular bone. True or False?
21. Name two components of a typical synovial joint.
22. What type of joint is the hip?
23. What does a ligament do?
24. What does synovial fluid do?
25. What does the membrane do?
26. The joints in the skull are immoveable joints. True or False?
27. Name one bone at the elbow joint.
28. What type of movement occurs at the neck?
29. Name one joint where flexion and extension occur.

From *GCSE Physical Education: A Revision Guide* by Tim Ferguson, 2002, Champaign, IL: Human Kinetics.

Examination Questions

The original numbering of the examination questions has been retained for ease of cross-referencing. Answers to these questions can be found at the end of the book.

MEG 1996 Paper 1 Q2

a. Give one example of a slightly moveable joint. (1)

c. Write the letters A, B, C and D on separate lines on your answer paper and state what part of the long bone they represent in figure 1.6. (4)

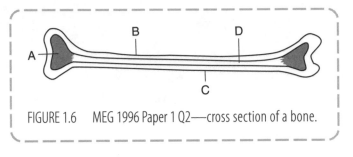

FIGURE 1.6   MEG 1996 Paper 1 Q2—cross section of a bone.

MEG 1995 Paper 1 Q2

c. Name two types of bone and describe their function. (4)

AQA(NEAB) 1999 QA3

a. Give one function of the skeleton. (1)

b. Name two synovial joints. (2)

c. Give three ways in which joints can be affected by exercise. (3)

AQA(NEAB) 1997 QA1

a. In which part of the body is the tibia? (1)

c. Name three parts of a synovial joint. (3)

AQA(NEAB) 1996 QA1

a. Give another name for the kneecap. (1)

b. Give two functions of the skeleton. (2)

c. Explain the following movements at a joint:

   i. flexion

   ii. extension

   iii. circumduction (3)

d. Describe ligaments and their function at synovial joints. (4)

AQA(SEG) 1998 Paper 2 Q1

b. Give one example of where each of the following joints is found in the body. State in each case which bones form the joint.

   i. Ball and socket (3)

   ii. Hinge (3)

AQA(SEG) 1997 Paper 2 Q4

a. State four functions of the skeleton. (4)

b. Long bones are one type of bone. State
  i. two other types of bone, and (2)
  ii. two examples of each of these types of bone. (4)
c. Immoveable is one type of joint. State
  i. two other types of joint, and (2)
  ii. two examples of each of these types of joint. (4)
d. Describe how muscle is attached to bone in order to allow movement, using the following words:
  tendons   origin   insertion (5)

London 1999 Q14

a. Table 1.2 refers to different types of joints found in the body. Complete the table by filling in the boxes. (8)
b. The shape of a joint affects the movement possible at that joint. Which of the joint types given in table 1.2 allows the greatest range of movement? (1)

TABLE 1.2 London 1999 Q14—Types of Joints		
Joint type	**Example 1**	**Example 2**
Gliding	Wrist	Spine
Hinge		
Ball and socket		
Pivot		

c. Flexion and extension are two types of movement possible at the joint you named in answer to question b. above. Give the three other movement possibilities. (3)

London 1998 Q11

a. Name the parts labelled A, B, C, D and E in figure 1.7. (5)
b. State the function of the part labelled B. (1)
c. Name the strong fibrous tissue that attaches bone to bone. (1)

London 1998 Q12

a. The knee is a hinge joint. Give another example of a hinge joint. (1)
b. What type of joint is found where the following bones meet?
  i. Atlas and axis (1)
  ii. Scapula and humerus (1)

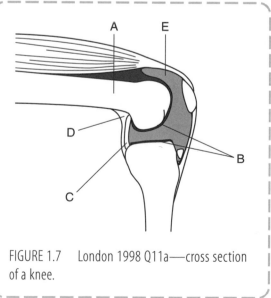

FIGURE 1.7   London 1998 Q11a—cross section of a knee.

CHAPTER 2

Muscular System

This chapter explains the muscles of the body and their function (see figures 2.1-2.3). It illustrates how muscles produce movement. Chapter 3 explains the importance of the circulatory system to the functioning of muscles.

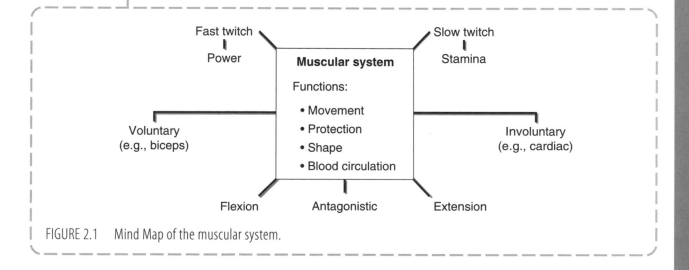

FIGURE 2.1   Mind Map of the muscular system.

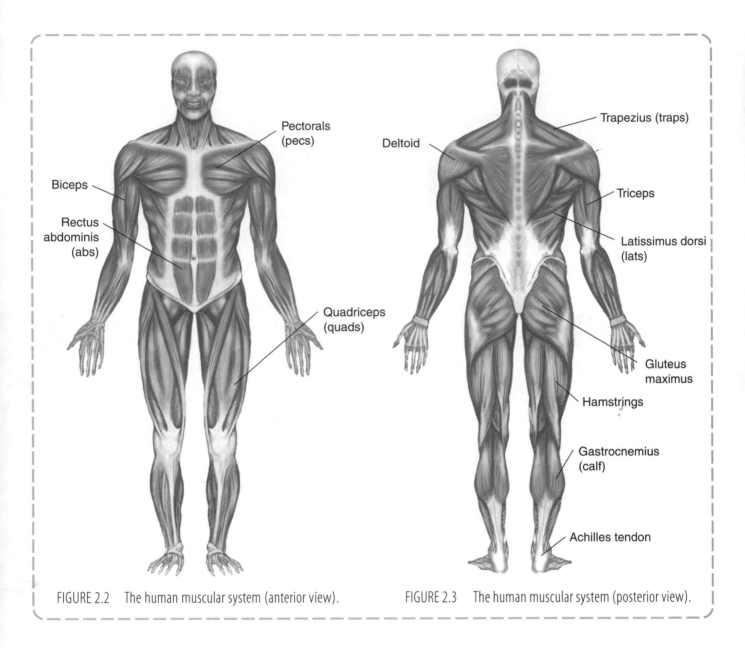

FIGURE 2.2   The human muscular system (anterior view).

FIGURE 2.3   The human muscular system (posterior view).

There are two types of muscle:

1. **Voluntary (skeletal) muscles** are under the brain's control (for example, the biceps).
2. **Involuntary muscles** work automatically, without needing conscious orders (for example, the heart [cardiac muscle]).

There are four functions of the muscles:

1. **Movement.** Muscles pull on the bones (they cannot push), causing movement.
2. **Protection.** Certain muscles help protect vital organs (for example, the abdominal wall protects the intestines).
3. **Shape.** Muscles give the body individual shape, size and muscle tone.
4. **Blood circulation.** Muscles squeeze the blood vessels.

Learn to link each muscle to the joints it helps to move (table 2.1).

TABLE 2.1 Muscles and Their Actions	
Muscles	**What they do**
Biceps	Bends (flexes) the arm at the elbow joint
Triceps	Straightens (extends) the arm at the elbow joint
Rectus abdominis	Bends (flexes) the trunk or spine so that you can bend forward
Trapezius	Maintains shoulder position, rotates the shoulder and moves the head
Deltoid	Raises the arm forwards, backwards and sideways at the shoulder
Pectoralis	Moves the shoulder, draws the arm across the chest
Latissimus dorsi	Pulls the arm down, draws the arm behind the back
Quadriceps	Straightens (extends) the leg at the knee joint
Gluteus maximus	Pulls the leg back at the hip when standing and climbing
Hamstrings	Bends (flexes) the leg at the knee
Gastrocnemius	Straightens (extends) the ankle joint

TENDONS

The function of tendons is to attach muscles to bones. The best-known example of a tendon is the Achilles tendon, which is found at the back of the lower leg and joins the calf muscle to the ankle.

HOW A MUSCLE PRODUCES MOVEMENT

Figure 2.4 illustrates how antagonistic muscles work together to bend and straighten the arm. A muscle goes through the following steps to produce movement:

1. The brain sends a message via the central nervous system (CNS) along the nerves to the muscle.
2. To bend the arm, the biceps contracts (shortens) and pulls the tendon, which pulls the ulna and radius up.
3. The triceps relaxes (lengthens) to allow the movement.

These muscles work together and are known as an antagonistic pair.

FAST- AND SLOW-TWITCH FIBRES

Some people are good at running 100 metres very quickly and others are good at running marathons at a slower, steady pace. People who run sprints utilise their fast-twitch muscle fibres, which are able to contract quickly and powerfully but

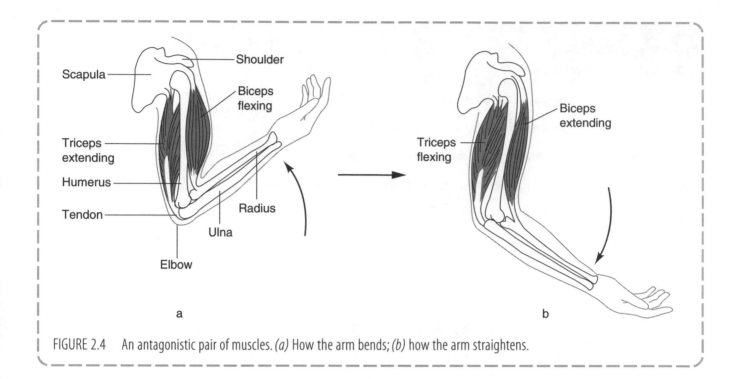

FIGURE 2.4   An antagonistic pair of muscles. *(a)* How the arm bends; *(b)* how the arm straightens.

tire quickly. People who run marathons utilise slow-twitch fibres, which contract much more slowly but have more endurance than fast-twitch fibres.

Everyone has a mix of both fast- and slow-twitch fibres, but different people have different amounts of each. The different amounts of fast- and slow-twitch fibres account for variations among people's sporting abilities.

- Someone with lots of fast-twitch fibres would be good at a sport that requires a lot of speed or power (for example, shot putting or sprinting).
- Someone with a lot of slow-twitch fibres would be good at a sport that requires a lot of stamina (for example, cycling or running marathons).

ROPE-LIKE VOLUNTARY MUSCLES

Each muscle, such as a biceps, consists of bundles of muscle fibres (see figure 2.5). The muscles are like a rope made up of hundreds of individual strands. These individual fibres combine to give muscles their strength. The muscle contracts when a message travels along the nerves from the brain to that particular muscle. This shortens the muscle. To lengthen the muscle the brain tells the muscle to relax.

Quick Test

1. Where is the triceps?
2. What is the anatomical (real) name of the "lats"?
3. Name two functions of the muscles.
4. Where are the "lats"?

From *GCSE Physical Education: A Revision Guide* by Tim Ferguson, 2002, Champaign, IL: Human Kinetics.

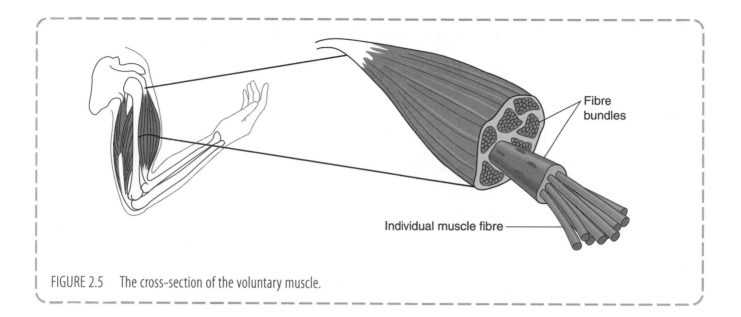

FIGURE 2.5   The cross-section of the voluntary muscle.

5. What movement does the biceps do?
6. What is the name of the chest muscles?
7. What is the function of a tendon?
8. The biceps and triceps are good examples of what?
9. What are the two types of muscle fibre?
10. What type of muscle fibre would a 100m sprinter have?
11. What is another name for "flexing"?
12. What is the real name of the "traps"?
13. Where is the gluteus maximus?
14. What does the triceps do?
15. Where is the Achilles tendon?
16. To bend the arm the biceps must do what?
17. What is the name of the muscle in the lower back?
18. Name the muscle going from the back of the knee to the gluteus maximus.
19. How do the muscles act on the bones to cause movement?
20. Why is the biceps called a voluntary muscle?
21. What is the other name for voluntary muscle?
22. What is the name of the stomach muscles?
23. What do the hamstrings do?
24. What tells the muscles to move?
25. Where are the deltoids?
26. What do the quadriceps do?
27. What type of muscle is cardiac muscle?
28. When the triceps flexes what does the arm do?
29. What is the anatomically correct name of the calf?
30. Why is it good for a long-distance swimmer to have mainly slow-twitch fibres?

From *GCSE Physical Education: A Revision Guide* by Tim Ferguson, 2002, Champaign, IL: Human Kinetics.

Examination Questions

The original numbering of the examination questions has been retained for ease of cross-referencing. Answers to these questions can be found at the end of the book.

MEG 1997 Paper 1 Q1

b. Name both muscles in the front of the body (indicated by the arrows) by writing the letters A and B on your answer paper followed by the correct name (see figure 2.6). (2)

c. Name and describe the function of two types of tissue (excluding muscular tissue) that are built up to form the human body. (4)

MEG 1996 Paper 1 Q1

d. Explain how skeletal muscles work to produce movement. (5)

FIGURE 2.6   MEG 1997 Paper 1 Q1—name the labelled muscles.

AQA(NEAB) 1999 QA1

d.   i. Give one type of muscle fibre.

d.   ii. Outline the benefits of this type of muscle fibre in sport and physical activity. (4)

AQA(NEAB) 1995 QA1

c. Name one muscle group in each of the following:

   i. Chest

   ii. Upper arm

   iii. Upper leg (3)

d.   i. What type of joint is the shoulder?

d.   ii. Give three types of movement possible at the shoulder. (4)

e. Jumping is an important action in many physical activities. Explain how the muscles of the leg work together to make a jump possible. (5)

AQA(SEG) 1999 Paper 2 Q1

c. Explain and describe how physical movement takes place through the combined actions of muscles and bones. (5)

AQA(SEG) 1996 Paper 2 Q4

c. Name the three different types of muscle and give one example of each. (6)

d. Describe what is meant by the following types of muscle movement. Give one example in each of your answers.

   i. Contraction (3)

   ii. Relaxation (3)

London 1999 Q15

Figure 2.7 is a diagram of the human muscular system.

    a. Name the muscles labelled. (4)

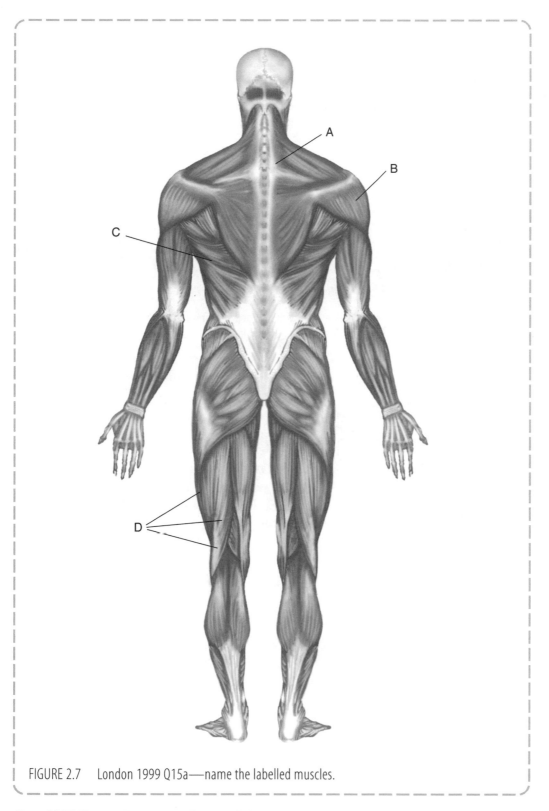

FIGURE 2.7   London 1999 Q15a—name the labelled muscles.

From *GCSE Physical Education: A Revision Guide* by Tim Ferguson, 2002, Champaign, IL: Human Kinetics. London questions reprinted, by permission, from Edexcel Foundation.

b. In table 2.2 name the main muscle contracting for each given action. (3)

TABLE 2.2 London 1999 Q15—Name the Muscle	
Action	**Main muscle**
Straightens the leg at the knee	
Pulls your leg back at the hip	
Flexes your trunk so that you can bend forward	

London 1998 Q13

Table 2.3 refers to the different types of muscle tissue. Complete the table by filling in the gaps. (6)

TABLE 2.3 London 1998 Q13—Fill In the Gaps		
Muscle type	**Identifying characteristic**	**Example**
	Involuntary muscle with a striped appearance which never tires or stops working	
Involuntary		
		Gastrocnemius

London 1998 Q15

Complete the following paragraph about muscle action:

The biceps and the _____ work together to move the forearm. One of these muscles will flex the forearm, whilst the other will extend it. When muscles work in this way they are said to be working _____. Two groups of muscles in the upper leg also work in this way. These muscles are the _____ and _____. (4)

From *GCSE Physical Education: A Revision Guide* by Tim Ferguson, 2002, Champaign, IL: Human Kinetics. London questions reprinted, by permission, from Edexcel Foundation.

CHAPTER 3

Circulatory System

This chapter provides an overview of the circulatory system (see figure 3.1), including the function of the heart (figure 3.2), blood and blood vessels. It also provides information about healthy circulatory systems. Chapter 4 deals with the respiratory system, which is closely linked to the circulatory system (see figure 3.3).

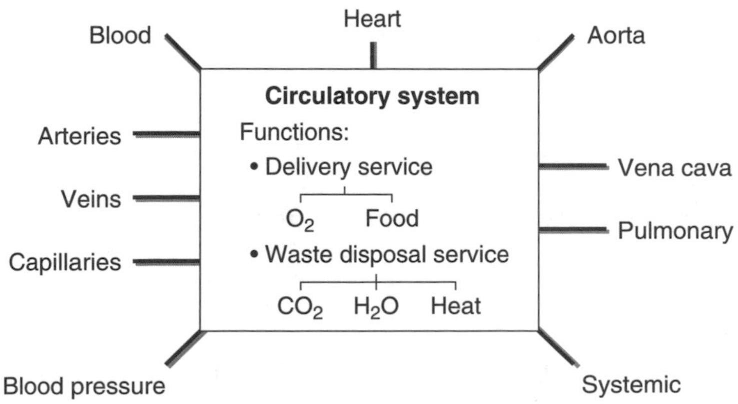

Blood   Heart   Aorta

Circulatory system

Arteries   Functions:
- Delivery service

     Veins O_2 Food   Vena cava

- Waste disposal service   Pulmonary

Capillaries CO_2 H_2O Heat

Blood pressure   Systemic

FIGURE 3.1   Mind Map of the circulatory system.

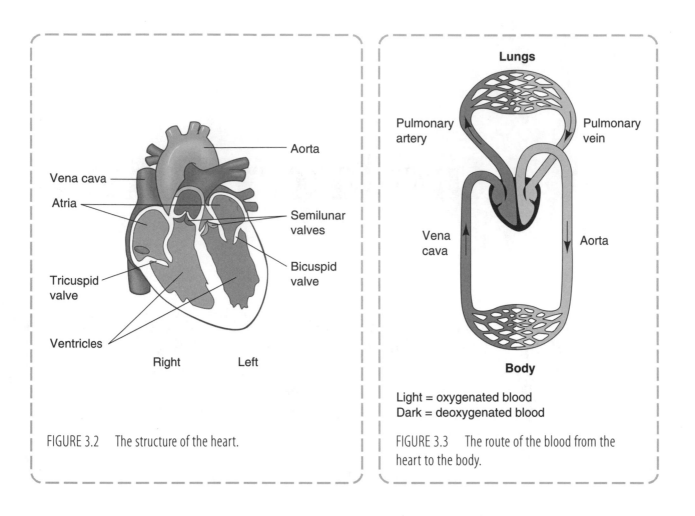

FIGURE 3.2   The structure of the heart.

FIGURE 3.3   The route of the blood from the heart to the body.

Light = oxygenated blood
Dark = deoxygenated blood

FUNCTIONS OF THE CIRCULATORY SYSTEM

The circulatory system performs two services. First, it performs a delivery service, taking oxygen (from the lungs) and food particles (from the digestive system) to the muscle cells. It also performs a waste-disposal service, taking carbon dioxide, water and heat (waste products from energy production) away from the cells.

THE HEART AND THE CIRCULATORY SYSTEM

The heart is key to the circulatory system. It is a hollow, muscular bag (cardiac muscle) that pumps blood around the body through a network of blood vessels. It contracts and expands to squirt blood out into the blood vessels. Each contraction is a heart beat. The heart has four chambers, an atrium and a ventricle on both the right and the left.

The body has two circulation systems known as the pulmonary and systemic systems:

- Blood is pumped to the lungs and back. This is known as the pulmonary circulation system.
- Blood is also pumped to the body and back. This is known as the systemic circulation system.

Actions of a typical heart are as follows:

- At rest the heart beats 50 to 80 times per minute. This is the pulse.
- In one minute 12 litres (30 pints) of blood will circulate around the body.
- During physical activity or in stressful situations the heart rate can increase to 180 to 220 beats per minute.
- The heart of a trained athlete can pump 45 litres of blood per minute.

BLOOD AND THE CIRCULATORY SYSTEM

Blood has three functions. First, it provides a **transport** system, delivering food and oxygen (O_2) and carrying away waste products. Second, it provides **protection**, as white blood cells fight disease. Finally, blood helps to control body temperature. It does this by absorbing heat, which is then carried to the lungs and exhaled or taken to the skin (vasodilation and sweat).

Blood is a fluid that contains plasma and cells. Cells are red and white. Red cells carry oxygen to the muscle cells. White cells fight disease and blood platelets help to clot the blood to help prevent bleeding. Haemoglobin is what gives the red cells their colour. Haemoglobin combines with O_2 to form oxyhaemoglobin. This is how O_2 is transported.

BLOOD VESSELS

Blood vessels consist of arteries, capillaries and veins. The best example of an **artery** is the **aorta**, which carries oxygenated (red) blood from the heart to the capillaries. Most arteries lie deep in the body for protection, as a severed artery can cause major blood loss. Some arteries lie near the skin surface. These are the places to find a pulse.

Capillaries are one cell thick. This is so they can allow O_2, carbon dioxide (CO_2), nutrients and waste products to pass through their walls.

The best example of a vein is the **vena cava**. This carries deoxygenated blood to the heart from the capillaries. They lie near the surface of the body so that excess heat caused by exercise can be lost more easily.

HEALTHY CIRCULATORY SYSTEM

To keep the circulatory system functioning efficiently, people need to take care of their hearts. There are a number of ways to measure the heart's performance to see how healthy it is.

Healthy Heart

There are two important measures of the heart that combine to show its capabilities.

1. How strong it is (stroke volume)
2. How quick it is (heart rate)

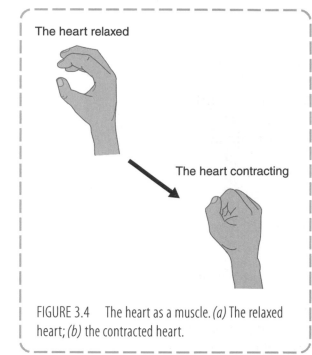

The heart relaxed

The heart contracting

FIGURE 3.4   The heart as a muscle. *(a)* The relaxed heart; *(b)* the contracted heart.

We call this the cardiac output. The dot in the following equation represents one minute:

$$(\dot{Q}) = SV \times HR$$

Imagine the heart to be a fist. As it contracts (beats) the fist closes, squeezing out all its blood (see figure 3.4). A strong heart can squeeze more powerfully, therefore injecting (pushing) more blood into the arteries. If the heart contracts quickly, that is more times in one minute, then the fist is opening and closing more often, so more blood is squirted out. This is cardiac output.

A healthy heart, such as the heart of a trained athlete, has a large stroke volume. A trained athlete can raise his heart rate to a high rate whilst exercising, but his heart rate is slow when resting.

Blood Pressure and Heart Disease

Blood moves around the circulatory system by the pumping action of the heart. To do this the blood has to be under pressure. The blood pressure (BP) must be higher in the arteries than in the veins because the blood starts its journey from the heart and arteries.

To calculate BP, measure the pressure required to stop the blood flow in an artery with a device called a sphygmomanometer. A sphygmomanometer puts pressure on an artery wall by squashing it. When BP is measured, there are two readings, such as 120/80. The biggest figure is the systolic pressure, or the pressure when the heart contracts (fist closes). The smaller figure is the diastolic pressure, or the pressure when the heart relaxes (fist opens). A typical BP range is 100/60 to 140/90. Most medical tests measure BP because it is a good indicator of general health.

Several factors can affect BP.

1. **Age**. BP is always much lower in children than adults because the artery walls lose some elasticity as they age.
2. **Sex**. BP readings vary between males and females.
3. **Stress and tension**. Stressful situations can cause BP to rise. Stressful situations include sitting an examination or taking a driving test. Extreme emotions are also a cause of high BP.
4. **Exercise**. As people exercise, the BP rises because the heart has to pump harder and faster.
5. **Any circulatory system disorders**. If the heart is weak, or there are problems with blood vessels, BP may increase.
6. **Smoking**. Smoking causes high BP.

Reducing High Blood Pressure

There are four ways to reduce high blood pressure:

1. Take regular exercise. Regular exercise also exercises the heart.
2. Stop smoking. Smoking causes coronary artery disease.

Stroke volume is the amount of blood forced out of the heart with each contraction. **Cardiac output** is the amount of blood forced out of the heart in one minute. **Heart rate** is the number of times the heart beats in one minute. This is also known as the pulse.

3. Avoid or reduce stress. Think about what situations are stressful and try to think of ways to adjust your lifestyle to manage stress.

4. Follow a sensible diet combined with exercise to control weight.

High blood pressure (hypertension) is linked to many serious cardiovascular diseases. These diseases include angina (temporary O_2 starvation of the heart), strokes (brain starved of O_2) and coronary artery disease (heart attack). Heart attacks are the biggest killer in this country.

How a Heart Attack Occurs

The mind map in figure 3.5 shows what happens in a heart attack, and it illustrates what factors contribute to a heart attack. Think about the risks around the outside of the mind map and think of ways to reduce the risk of a heart attack later in life.

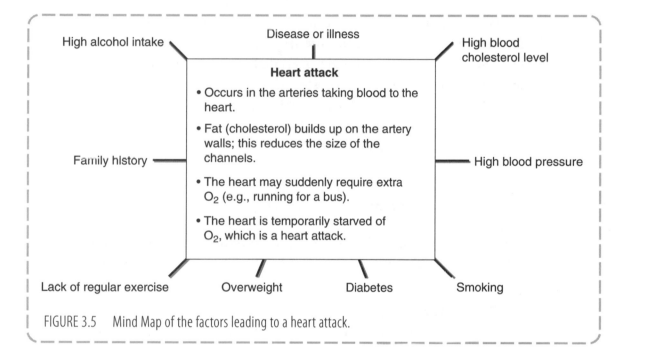

FIGURE 3.5   Mind Map of the factors leading to a heart attack.

Quick Test

1. Name the two functions of the circulatory system.
2. What type of muscle is the heart?
3. Name the upper chambers of the heart.
4. Blood is a fluid tissue. What does it consist of?
5. What do blood platelets do?
6. Name two types of blood vessels.
7. What gives red blood cells their colour?
8. Name a heart condition linked to high blood pressure.
9. What is the aorta?
10. Name two things that affect blood pressure.

From *GCSE Physical Education: A Revision Guide* by Tim Ferguson, 2002, Champaign, IL: Human Kinetics.

11. Name two things that can cause a heart attack.
12. Give a typical range for an average heart rate.
13. What do the white blood cells do?
14. What does the blood deliver?
15. Name one difference between the heart of an athlete and that of a non-athlete.
16. Name the lower chambers of the heart.
17. Does the volume of blood pumped around the body increase during physical activity?
18. Deoxygenated blood is carried in which vessels?
19. What is haemoglobin?
20. Name the largest vein in the body.
21. Name one thing that helps to reduce blood pressure.
22. What happens if the heart is temporarily starved of oxygen?
23. What type of blood do the arteries carry?
24. Name the very small blood vessels that carry blood to every cell.
25. What does the pulmonary system do?
26. Why is blood pressure lower in children?
27. What is meant by the term "pulse"?
29. How is blood pressure measured?

 # Examination Questions

The original numbering of the examination questions has been retained for ease of cross-referencing. Answers to these questions can be found at the end of the book.

MEG 1998 Q12

Describe three effects of exercise on the flow of blood through the heart. (3)

MEG 1996 Paper 1 Q1

b. Name one of the main components of blood and its function. (2)
c. Describe what happens when the left atrium and right atrium (L.A. and R.A. in figure 3.6) contract. (4)

AQA(NEAB) 1996 QA2

a. What are veins? (1)
b. Give two waste products carried in the veins. (2)
c. Give three features of an efficient heart. (3)

AQA(NEAB) 1997 QA3

a. What is the pulse? (1)
b. Give two places in the body where the pulse can be measured. (2)
c. Give three ways in which pulse rate can give an indication of physical fitness. (3)

From GCSE Physical Education: A Revision Guide by Tim Ferguson, 2002, Champaign, IL: Human Kinetics. MEG questions reproduced with the kind permission of OCR. AQA(NEAB)/AQA examination questions are reproduced by permission of the Assessment and Qualifications Alliance.

AQA(SEG) 1996 Paper 2 Q5

a. i. Name two substances delivered to a working muscle by the blood. (2)

a. ii. Name one substance removed from a working muscle by the blood. (1)

b. Using the descriptions given, name the parts of the heart which are described.

    i. The two chambers at the top of the heart (1)

    ii. The two chambers at the bottom of the heart (1)

    iii. The vessel through which the blood returns from the lungs to the heart (1)

    iv. The vessel through which the blood leaves the heart to be distributed to the body (1)

c. Name two places where the pulse can be located on the body. (2)

d. Name three disorders or diseases which can affect the circulatory system. (3)

e. Blood has two components.

    i. Cells are one; what is the other? (1)

    ii. Name the two types of blood cells. (2)

    iii. Where is haemoglobin produced and what is its function? (3)

    iv. What is the main function of platelets (thrombocytes)? (1)

f. State a simple way of calculating your maximum pulse rate. (2)

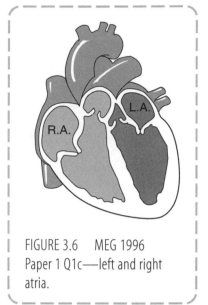

FIGURE 3.6   MEG 1996 Paper 1 Q1c—left and right atria.

London 1999 Q19

State the order of blood flow through the heart, starting with the return of deoxygenated blood.

a. Deoxygenated blood returns to the heart from the body via the _____.

b. From here blood enters the _____

c. and then passes through the _____ valve

d. into the _____.

e. The blood is then forced through the _____ valves

f. into the _____.

g. The blood then goes to the lungs to pick up oxygen and returns to the heart via the _____

h. and enters the _____

i. before passing through the _____ valve

j. into the _____.

k. The blood is then forced through the _____ valve

l. into the _____, which is the main artery. (12)

From *GCSE Physical Education: A Revision Guide* by Tim Ferguson, 2002, Champaign, IL: Human Kinetics. MEG questions reproduced with the kind permission of OCR. AQA(SEG) examination questions are reproduced by permission of the Assessment and Qualifications Alliance. London questions reprinted, by permission, from Edexcel Foundation.

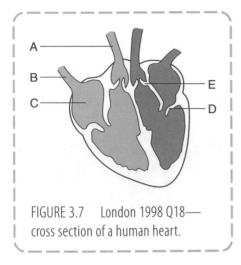

FIGURE 3.7   London 1998 Q18—cross section of a human heart.

London 1998 Q18

Figure 3.7 shows a section through the human heart.

a. In the space provided write the letter that labels each of the following parts

   i. bicuspid (mitral) valve _____,

   ii. vena cava _____,

   iii. right atrium _____,

   iv. pulmonary artery _____, and

   v. semilunar valves _____ (5)

b. On the diagram

   i. draw an arrow and label F to show where deoxygenated blood enters the heart, and (1)

   ii. draw an arrow and label G to show where the blood leaves the heart and goes to the lungs. (1)

London 1998 Q20

Use five of the words below to complete the following sentences relating to arteries, capillaries and veins:

   lower   higher   arteries   veins   thicker

   smaller   larger   smallest   largest   thinner

a. The muscular wall of an artery is _____ than that of a vein. Arteries have a _____ internal diameter than veins. This means that the blood in the artery will be at a _____ pressure than blood in the veins.

b. Capillaries are the _____ of the three types of vessels. Like _____, the capillaries do not have any valves. (5)

From *GCSE Physical Education: A Revision Guide* by Tim Ferguson, 2002, Champaign, IL: Human Kinetics. London questions reprinted, by permission, from Edexcel Foundation.

CHAPTER 4

Respiratory System

This chapter explains the respiratory system. It covers how oxygen enters and travels around the body, how to measure healthy lungs and different breathing rates (see figure 4.1). It shows how breathing is linked to exercise. Chapter 5 examines how the digestive, endocrine and nervous systems control energy and movement.

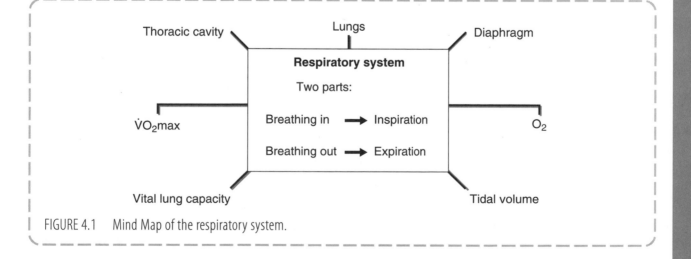

FIGURE 4.1   Mind Map of the respiratory system.

When the body breathes, or respires, it takes O_2 from the air to release energy from food. The lungs combine with the circulatory system to carry O_2 to all the cells in the body. Respiration has two parts:

- Breathing in is called **inspiration** or **inhaling**.
- Breathing out is called **expiration** or **exhaling**.

OXYGEN ROUTE

O_2 enters the body system through the nostrils, where it is warmed and filtered (see figure 4.2). It travels down the trachea (wind pipe) and into the two bronchi. The bronchi split into the bronchioles and then finally into millions of alveoli. The alveoli are small air sacs, which are surrounded by a vast network of small capillaries. It is here that a process called **diffusion** takes place.

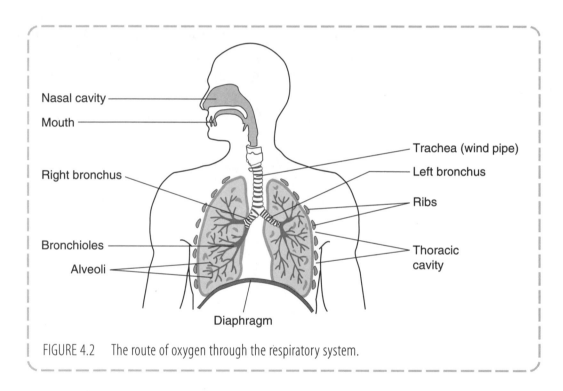

FIGURE 4.2   The route of oxygen through the respiratory system.

Diffusion is the constant movement of O_2 and CO_2 across the lining of the lungs. It takes place where the alveoli meet the tiny capillaries. When there is more O_2 in the lungs than in the bloodstream the O_2 moves across (this will be the case after breathing in), whilst the CO_2 moves from the blood stream to the lungs and is exhaled.

PURPOSE OF THE DIAPHRAGM

The diaphragm is a sheet of muscle which seals off the thoracic cavity. To get air (and hence O_2) inside the body, the lungs, ribs and diaphragm work together to increase the volume inside the thoracic cavity. Air then enters via the nose and

Picture the network of the lungs as a tree. The trachea is the trunk, and it has two main branches (bronchi), then smaller branches (bronchioles), finally dividing into the leaves (alveoli).

mouth. Breathing out eliminates CO_2 and H_2O, which are the waste products of the energy-making process. Figure 4.3 illustrates how the diaphragm relaxes and contracts when breathing in or out.

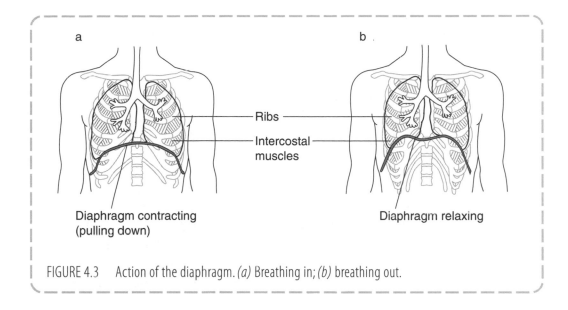

a

b

Ribs
Intercostal muscles

Diaphragm contracting
(pulling down)

Diaphragm relaxing

FIGURE 4.3   Action of the diaphragm. *(a)* Breathing in; *(b)* breathing out.

HEALTHY LUNGS

There are several lung measurements to take which give a good indication of a person's fitness and health.

1. $\dot{V}O_2$max is the maximum amount of O_2 a person can breathe in and use. A person cannot exercise indefinitely; she eventually reaches the point known as the $\dot{V}O_2$max. The greater a person's $\dot{V}O_2$max the "fitter" (stamina) she is.
2. Vital lung capacity is the largest volume of air which can be expired after the deepest possible inspiration. Larger vital lung capacities suggest a more healthy respiratory system.
3. Tidal volume is the volume of air breathed in and out normally.

RESTING AND ACTIVE BREATHING RATE

During rest a person breathes 13 to 17 times a minute. During vigorous physical activity this breathing rate can increase to 50 times a minute. This is called "forced breathing". A consequence of forced breathing for an untrained person is getting a "stitch". Experts believe that a stitch is a muscle cramp of the diaphragm, although there is no conclusive proof of this. Even the most highly trained athlete can get a stitch, although it does not happen as often. Excess stomach acids are also considered a possible cause of a stitch.

Quick Test

1. Why does the body need to breathe?
2. What are the two parts of respiration?
3. What protects the lungs?
4. What does the body use oxygen for?
5. What are alveoli?
6. Name one measure of lung capacity.
7. What is a stitch?
8. What waste products are breathed out?
9. What network surrounds the tiny air sacs?
10. Where does diffusion take place?
11. Nitrogen will not diffuse across the lining of the lungs. True or False?
12. Only the diaphragm can get a stitch. True or False?
13. The vital lung capacity is the normal volume of air breathed in and out. True or False?
14. Typically the body breathes 13 to 17 times a minute. True or False?
15. What is another word for breathing in?
16. What is the diaphragm?
17. What is the other name for the windpipe?
18. What does the windpipe split into?
19. What is at the end of the bronchioles?
20. What does the diaphragm do?
21. What is another name for breathing out?
22. Name two measures of lung capacity.
23. Give a typical breathing rate range.
24. What can happen to the diaphragm after continuous running?
25. What is the function of the nostrils?
26. What is the definition of diffusion?
27. Name five parts of the respiratory system.

Examination Questions

The original numbering of the examination questions has been retained for ease of cross-referencing. Answers to these questions can be found at the end of the book.

MEG 1996 Paper 1 Q1

e. How does the respiratory system cope with the increased demand made by the muscles during exercise? (8)

From *GCSE Physical Education: A Revision Guide* by Tim Ferguson, 2002, Champaign, IL: Human Kinetics. MEG questions reproduced with the kind permission of OCR.

MEG 1995 Paper 1 Q1

a. What happens to the size of the lungs when we breathe in? (1)

d. Describe the following basic lung capacities:

    i. tidal volume (1)

    ii. vital capacity (2)

    iii. residual volume (2)

AQA(NEAB) 1998 QA3

c.   i. What is $\dot{V}O_2$ maximum?

c.   ii. Why is it important in sport and social activity? (3)

AQA(NEAB) 1996 QA2

d.   i. What is vital capacity?

d.   ii. What can be its effect on performance? (4)

London 1999 Q22

Figure 4.4 is a diagram of the human respiratory system.

a. Give the anatomical names for the parts labelled.

b. What happens to the diaphragm and the ribs during expiration?

    i. The diaphragm

    ii. The ribs (2)

London 1998 Q21

a. Place the following three words in the correct order to describe the passage of air through the respiratory system. (3)

    bronchioles   trachea   bronchi

b. What other gases are taken into the lungs apart from oxygen? (2)

c. What happens to the oxygen immediately after it passes through the alveoli? (1)

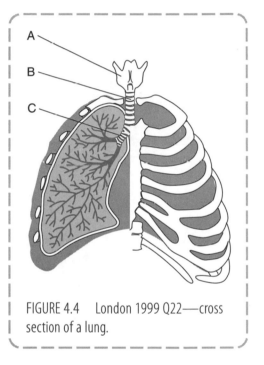

FIGURE 4.4   London 1999 Q22—cross section of a lung.

SEG. No direct questions about the respiratory system have come up between 1995 and 1999. There have been questions involving the respiratory system which can be found in chapter 7, "Effects of Exercise on the Body Systems". The questions are from papers 1997 Paper 2 Q7 and 1997 Paper 3 Q6.

From *GCSE Physical Education: A Revision Guide* by Tim Ferguson, 2002, Champaign, IL: Human Kinetics. MEG questions reproduced with the kind permission of OCR. AQA(NEAB)/AQA examination questions are reproduced by permission of the Assessment and Qualifications Alliance. London questions reprinted, by permission, from Edexcel Foundation.

CHAPTER 5

Digestive, Endocrine and Nervous Systems

This chapter investigates the digestive, endocrine and nervous systems (figure 5.1) to show how the body produces the right level of energy and movement to take part in sport and physical activity. Chapter 6 examines how aerobic and anaerobic systems produce energy.

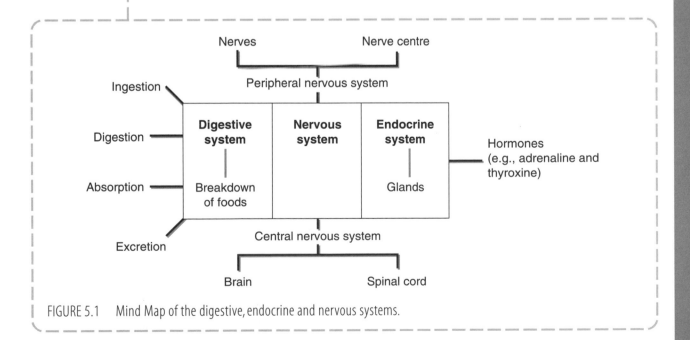

FIGURE 5.1 Mind Map of the digestive, endocrine and nervous systems.

FUNCTION OF THE DIGESTIVE SYSTEM

The function of the digestive system (figure 5.2) is to break down food into smaller particles. These molecules of food are absorbed into the body and used to produce energy.

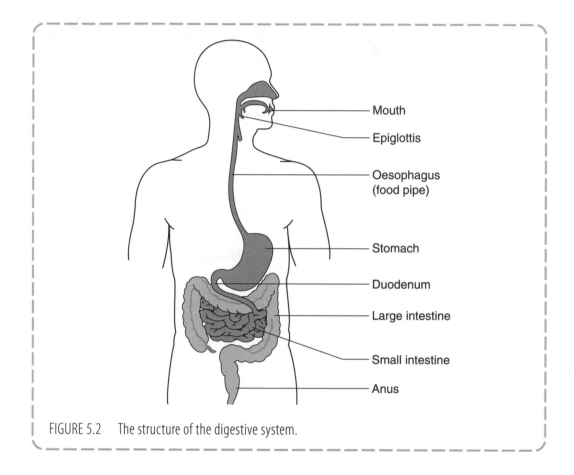

FIGURE 5.2   The structure of the digestive system.

Food is the main source of energy. Therefore, the digestive system is important to the sport scientist. There are four stages in the digestive process.

1. Ingestion
2. Digestion
3. Absorption
4. Excretion

Table 5.1 explains what happens at all four stages of the digestive system.

The digestive system would not be much use if the body could not control the rate it burned food, regulate blood sugar levels or use enough oxygen to produce more energy. These functions, and others, are controlled by the endocrine system.

ENDOCRINE SYSTEM

The endocrine system is composed of a number of glands. Each gland produces hormones which have a particular function. These hormones are released into the

TABLE 5.1   Areas of the Digestive System

Area	What happens
Mouth	**Ingestion** begins at the mouth, where food first enters the body. **Digestion** also begins here. The food is chewed into smaller pieces. During chewing, saliva is secreted into the mouth from the salivary gland. **Saliva** is a digestive juice and starts attacking the food. Saliva releases enzymes which break down carbohydrates.
Epiglottis	The epiglottis is found at the back of the throat. Its function is to keep food from entering the respiratory system.
Oesophagus	Once the food has been chewed into smaller pieces, it passes down the oesophagus (food pipe) and into the stomach. This is helped by a wave-like motion of the food pipe called peristalsis.
Stomach	The stomach is a muscular bag and is used to store food for periods of up to 5 hours. This means we don't have to eat all the time. Whilst the food is in the stomach the gastric juices start to break down the proteins.
Small intestine	Digestion continues here: The walls produce more enzymes which carry on breaking down the food. Absorption starts here: Food particles go through the intestine walls and into the bloodstream.
Large intestine	All undigested food passes to the large intestine and is prepared for excretion. Absorption of water, glucose and salts is still continuing. Once the undigested food has formed into faeces it is excreted through the anus.

bloodstream when the body requires them. They have particular effects on the body organs. Figure 5.3 shows where these glands are in the body.

checkpoint

✓ The **pituitary gland** secretes hormones which are responsible for controlling the other endocrine glands.

✓ The **thyroid** produces thyroxine, which controls the rate at which the body burns food to produce energy.

✓ The **pancreas** secretes digestive juices and insulin (which regulates blood sugar levels).

✓ The **adrenal glands** produce adrenaline and noradrenaline. Adrenaline, once in the bloodstream, causes the cells to use more oxygen, which produces more energy.

✓ The **ovaries** control the development of female sexual characteristics.

✓ The **testes** control the development of male sexual characteristics.

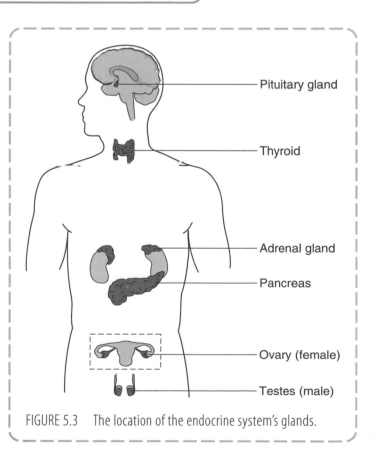

FIGURE 5.3   The location of the endocrine system's glands.

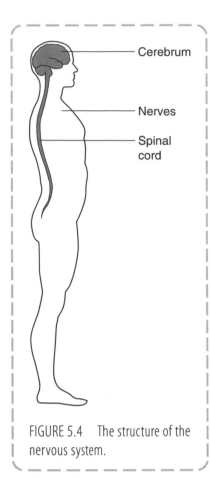

Cerebrum

Nerves

Spinal cord

FIGURE 5.4   The structure of the nervous system.

FUNCTION OF THE NERVOUS SYSTEM

The digestive and endocrine systems may be essential for producing the right amount of energy for the body to move at the right level of intensity, but the body still needs to be able to use that energy to move in a controlled manner. The nervous system plays an essential part in controlling movement.

The nervous system is made up of two parts:

1. The central nervous system consists of the brain and spinal cord (figure 5.4).
2. The peripheral nervous system contains the nerves.

The importance of the nervous system for the sport scientist is that the nervous system controls the muscular system and hence movement.

The Nervous System

The nervous system works in six steps:

1. The nervous system receives information through the sense organs (e.g., eyes, ears, nose).
2. Once the nervous system collects this information, it is sent to the brain for it to decide what movement to make.
3. When a decision has been made, the brain sends a message down the spinal cord to the nerve, which carries the message to the muscles.
4. Once the muscles carry out the task (e.g., walking) the nerves carry a message back to the brain informing it that the first step has been made.
5. Another message is then sent to the other leg.
6. These messages are sent very quickly and are constantly being sent and received by the brain.

Autonomic Nervous System

When completing any task, the body relies on the nervous system to help. The brain is the control centre; the nerves are the telephone lines.

The autonomic nervous system is the involuntary nervous system. The body does not have any control over it. This system controls the involuntary muscles such as the heart or lungs (so that the body never forgets to breathe). It is also responsible for reflexes such as the knee-jerk reflex or blinking. Reflexes are a good form of defence for the body. The body reacts quickly without having to first think about what decision to make.

Quick Test

1. Where does ingestion start?
2. Food is the main source of what?
3. Name two stages in the digestive process.

From *GCSE Physical Education: A Revision Guide* by Tim Ferguson, 2002, Champaign, IL: Human Kinetics.

4. What is secreted in the mouth?

5. What happens in the mouth?

6. What is the function of the digestive system?

7. What is saliva?

8. What are proteins used for?

9. What is the name of the food pipe?

10. Name three nutrients the body requires.

11. What is the function of the epiglottis?

12. Name the "wave-like motion" which helps move food down the food pipe.

13. How long is food stored in the stomach?

14. What are the juices in the stomach called?

15. How long before competition should people eat?

16. Where does digestion start?

17. Peristalsis is the wave-like, muscular movement in the abdomen. True or False?

18. What is the endocrine system concerned with?

19. What does CNS stand for?

20. What are the components of the CNS?

21. What are the sense organs?

22. Where is the pituitary gland?

23. What does the thyroid gland produce?

24. What is the function of the nerves?

25. What is the function of adrenaline?

26. Name four components of the endocrine system.

27. What is the autonomic nervous system?

28. The peripheral nervous system is made up of nerves. True or False?

29. The pituitary gland is responsible for controlling the other endocrine glands. True or False?

30. The cerebrum is not part of the CNS. True or False?

31. Adrenaline is released to help burn oxygen more quickly. True or False?

32. Reflex actions are controlled by the autonomic nervous system. True or False?

33. The thyroid produces the hormone thyroxine. True or False?

34. Hormones are released by glands into the bloodstream. True or False?

35. Once information is collected by the sense organs it is sent to the muscles. True or False?

36. The pancreas produces insulin and digestive juices. True or False?

Examination Questions

The original numbering of the examination questions has been retained for ease of cross-referencing. Answers to these questions can be found at the end of the book.

From *GCSE Physical Education: A Revision Guide* by Tim Ferguson, 2002, Champaign, IL: Human Kinetics.

MEG 1997 Paper 1 Q1

e. Describe the part played by the nervous system in the co-ordination of movement in physical activity. (8)

AQA(NEAB) 1998 QA3

e. How does the nervous system control muscular action? Use one example to illustrate your answer. (5)

CHAPTER 6

Aerobic and Anaerobic Systems

This chapter explains the aerobic and anaerobic energy systems. It discusses the creatine phosphate system, lactic acid system, glycogen and oxygen debt (see figure 6.1). Chapter 7 explains the effects of exercise on the body.

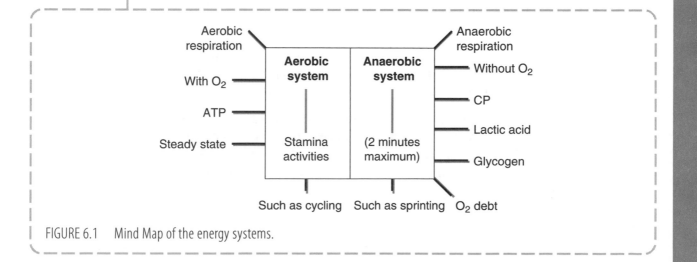

FIGURE 6.1   Mind Map of the energy systems.

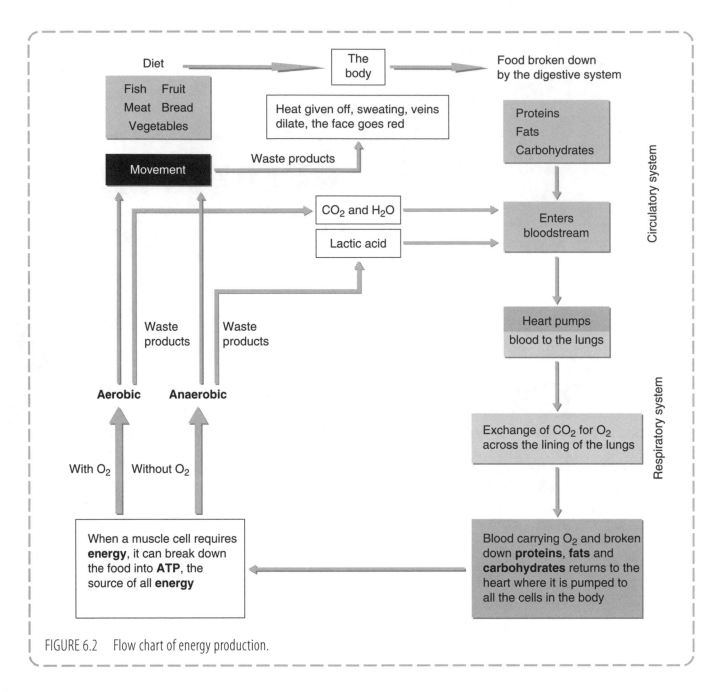

FIGURE 6.2   Flow chart of energy production.

Sport scientists are interested in movement. Movement requires energy. How the body produces energy is extremely important. There are two systems the body uses to produce energy (figure 6.2):

1. The **aerobic** system means the body uses oxygen from the outside environment. **Aerobic respiration means with O_2.**

2. The **anaerobic** system means the body does not use oxygen from the outside environment. **Anaerobic respiration means without O_2.**

The energy the body needs is used to help muscles contract. This energy is supplied by adenosine triphosphate (ATP), which is used in all the cells. ATP is broken down to give energy for muscle contraction, and this also produces adenosine diphosphate (ADP). Unfortunately, the body can only store a small amount of ATP in its cells; therefore, it needs to convert the ADP back to ATP to create more muscular contractions.

There are three ways of changing ADP into ATP. Two ways are part of the anaerobic system and the other way is the aerobic system.

AEROBIC SYSTEM

The aerobic system is used when the body does an activity for a long time (for example, running a marathon or cycling). A simple energy equation is as follows:

$$Food + O_2 \longrightarrow Energy + \underset{\text{waste products}}{CO_2 + H_2O + Heat}$$

The body requires a constant production of ATP (reforming ATP). Because the body does an activity for a long period, it needs to use the O_2 breathed to produce ATP. When using this system the body must work at a **steady state**. This means that the body is taking in and using enough O_2 to continue producing the energy required. If the body goes beyond the **steady state** then it has to switch systems.

ANAEROBIC SYSTEM

The body uses the anaerobic system when it cannot get enough O_2 from the outside environment. The body can only use this system for a maximum of two minutes. Examples of sports where the body uses the anaerobic system include shot putting and sprinting.

Two parts make up the anaerobic system:

1. Creatine phosphate (CP) system
2. Lactic acid system

The following is a simple energy equation:

$$Food \longrightarrow Energy + Lactic\ acid\ (waste\ product)$$

In anaerobic exercise a build-up of lactic acid leads to fatigue and eventually the body has to stop exercising.

Creatine Phosphate System

The body can use the creatine phosphate (CP) system for 30 to 60 seconds to produce energy without O_2. The problem is that stores of CP only last 30 to 60 seconds. After this point the body must change to an alternative system (lactic acid).

Lactic Acid System

The lactic acid system can last up to two minutes. Lactic acid builds up in the muscle cells and overflows into the bloodstream. With insufficient O_2 the body cannot remove lactic acid and eventually tires. This is how cramps occur. Lactic

> Whilst taking part in anaerobic exercise, the body produces energy without O_2, causing a shortage of O_2. This is known as oxygen debt. The oxygen debt must be paid off, so the body continues to breathe heavily after exercise to repay the oxygen debt.

acid will eventually be turned back into pyruvic acid and this in turn will be converted into CO_2, H_2O and heat.

Glycogen

Glucose is formed during the digestion of food. It is then changed into glycogen and stored in the muscles and the liver. Glycogen breaks down the ATP in the lactic acid system.

The limiting factors to the lactic acid system are

1. the amount of available glycogen,
2. the level of lactic acid the body can cope with, and
3. the amount of oxygen debt the body can cope with.

Quick Test

1. What is the aerobic system?
2. What does ATP stand for?
3. Where is ATP stored?
4. Name one waste product of the aerobic system.
5. Name one way of converting ADP to ATP.
6. What does ADP stand for?
7. Name one limiting factor of the lactic acid system.
8. What is anaerobic respiration?
9. How does the body get rid of lactic acid after exercise?
10. What does the body use ATP for?
11. What does ATP form after a muscle contraction?
12. In which system does the body work at the steady state?
13. For how long can the body work in the CP system?
14. Where is glycogen stored?
15. What happens to the muscles after lactic acid has built up?
16. What will pyruvic acid turn into if no O_2 is supplied?
17. For how long can the body work in the lactic acid system?
18. What is the simple aerobic energy equation?
19. What is "steady state"?
20. What is CP?
21. What is meant by the term O_2 debt?

Examination Questions

The original numbering of the examination questions has been retained for ease of cross-referencing. Answers to these questions can be found at the end of the book.

From *GCSE Physical Education: A Revision Guide* by Tim Ferguson, 2002, Champaign, IL: Human Kinetics.

MEG 1997 Paper 1 Q1

    d. Describe aerobic respiration and name one physical activity associated with it. (5)

MEG 1997 Paper 1 Q2

    e. Explain how anaerobic energy production systems produce movement in physical activity. (8)

AQA(NEAB) 1997 QA2

    d. Compare the energy production for short- and long-distance events. (4)

AQA(NEAB) 1995 QA2

    c.   i. What is aerobic respiration?

    c. ii. What is anaerobic respiration? (3)

    d. What would be the effects on breathing when taking part in

        i. a sprint race?

       ii. a long-distance race? (4)

    e. Explain how high altitude affects the performance of stamina-based activities. (5)

AQA(SEG) 1999 Paper 2 Q3

    d. Explain what is meant by the terms aerobic respiration and anaerobic respiration in relation to exercise. Give a specific example for each from a named physical game or activity. (6)

London 1999 Q23

    a. The body uses glucose and oxygen to help release energy. Complete the following equation:

$$\text{Glucose} + O_2 \rightarrow \text{Energy} + \underline{\hspace{2cm}} + \underline{\hspace{2cm}} \quad (2)$$

    b. The body can also release energy without the presence of oxygen. What harmful by-product is produced when performers work with insufficient oxygen? (1)

    c. What effect may this by-product have on the performers' muscles? (1)

    d. What is the term used to describe muscles working without oxygen? (1)

London 1998 Q22

    a. Define the following terms:

        i. Aerobic (2)

       ii. Anaerobic (2)

    b. Give a sporting example of an anaerobic activity. (1)

    c. Why is lactic acid produced during anaerobic work? (1)

    d. What happens to an athlete's performance as lactic acid builds up? (1)

CHAPTER 7

Effects of Exercise on the Body Systems

This chapter summarises the effects of exercise on major body systems discussed earlier in this part (see figure 7.1). It shows how essential exercise is to keep these systems functioning efficiently.

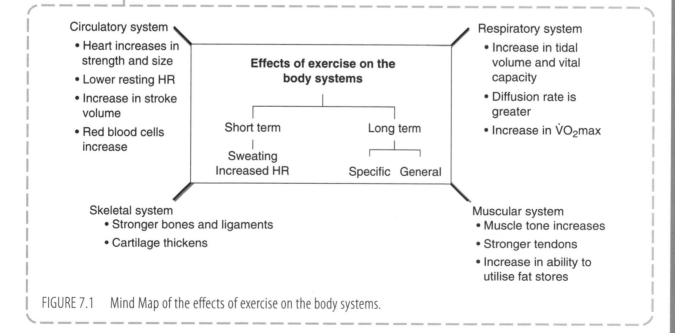

FIGURE 7.1   Mind Map of the effects of exercise on the body systems.

Remember the difference between STEs and LTEs. STEs are the changes which occur whilst the body exercises, whereas LTEs are more permanent changes to the body.

During exercise, the body systems are asked to complete tasks such as pumping the blood faster or contracting and relaxing certain muscle groups (e.g., the quads and hamstrings whilst running). This exercise causes the body to undergo two types of change:

1. Short-term effects (STEs)
2. Long-term effects (LTEs)

SHORT-TERM EFFECTS

STEs are the changes that occur whilst exercising. Some of these changes are visible (for example, sweating or going red), whereas some changes cannot be seen (for example, an increased heart rate). STEs affect the muscular system, circulatory system, respiratory system, endocrine system and digestive system. See figure 7.2 for more information on how these changes affect the systems.

LONG-TERM EFFECTS

Long-term effects are the more permanent changes that occur in the body systems of people who undergo training. As a result of training, different systems undergo general or specific changes. Marathon runners undergo both general and specific changes. Marathon runners develop increased cardiac output (general) and strong leg muscles (specific).

Skeletal System

The skeletal system can improve in three ways through regular training. Bones and ligaments become stronger and cartilage gets thicker, giving more cushioning from impact.

Muscular System

Long-term effects on the muscular system mean muscles can change over time if an individual trains regularly. With regular training, six changes occur:

1. Muscles become larger in size.
2. Muscle tone is enhanced.
3. The specific muscles used will be affected. Therefore a climber will have strong, toned upper-body muscles whilst a runner will have stronger muscles in the legs.
4. Tendons increase in strength.
5. Muscles improve at tolerating lactic acid. This means that an increased build-up of lactic acid can occur before fatigue sets in.
6. Muscles improve at burning (utilising) fat stores, increasing the body's ability to switch from using carbohydrate to fat stores. Through training the percentage body fat decreases.

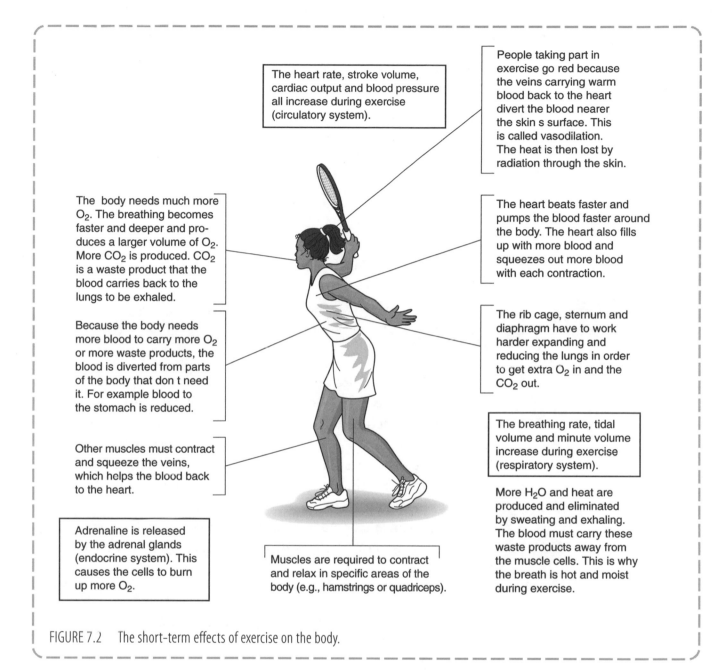

The heart rate, stroke volume, cardiac output and blood pressure all increase during exercise (circulatory system).

People taking part in exercise go red because the veins carrying warm blood back to the heart divert the blood nearer the skin s surface. This is called vasodilation. The heat is then lost by radiation through the skin.

The body needs much more O_2. The breathing becomes faster and deeper and produces a larger volume of O_2. More CO_2 is produced. CO_2 is a waste product that the blood carries back to the lungs to be exhaled.

The heart beats faster and pumps the blood faster around the body. The heart also fills up with more blood and squeezes out more blood with each contraction.

Because the body needs more blood to carry more O_2 or more waste products, the blood is diverted from parts of the body that don t need it. For example blood to the stomach is reduced.

The rib cage, sternum and diaphragm have to work harder expanding and reducing the lungs in order to get extra O_2 in and the CO_2 out.

Other muscles must contract and squeeze the veins, which helps the blood back to the heart.

The breathing rate, tidal volume and minute volume increase during exercise (respiratory system).

More H_2O and heat are produced and eliminated by sweating and exhaling. The blood must carry these waste products away from the muscle cells. This is why the breath is hot and moist during exercise.

Adrenaline is released by the adrenal glands (endocrine system). This causes the cells to burn up more O_2.

Muscles are required to contract and relax in specific areas of the body (e.g., hamstrings or quadriceps).

FIGURE 7.2 The short-term effects of exercise on the body.

Circulatory System

The circulatory system is altered in several ways through regular training. The heart (a muscle) increases in size and its walls get thicker. It holds more blood and is able to contract strongly. During exercise, the heart works for longer periods at a higher level. Yet the resting heart rate is lower. The heart rate also returns to normal at a faster rate after exercise.

The stroke volume (SV) also increases, which means that the cardiac output ($\dot{Q} = HR \times SV$) is greater. The body produces more red blood cells meaning there is more haemoglobin. This means the body will have a greater capacity to carry O_2. The arteries become larger and more elastic, which reduces blood pressure. The capillary network also increases, causing more efficient blood distribution to the cells.

Respiratory System

The respiratory system benefits in five ways from regular training:

1. Thoracic cavity size increases when breathing because the body develops a stronger diaphragm, rib cage and sternum.
2. Vital capacity and tidal volume are increased.
3. The increase in vital capacity and tidal volume leads to a greater diffusion rate. This is because the lungs can inhale increased levels of O_2 and the blood can deliver a larger volume of CO_2 back to the lungs for exhalation.
4. The network of capillaries surrounding the alveoli becomes more developed, further enhancing the diffusion process.
5. All these factors, combined with the improved circulatory system, help to increase $\dot{V}O_2$max.

 *Quick Test*

1. Name two visible, short-term changes due to exercise.
2. On which equations could the short-term effects be based?
3. Name three short-term effects of exercise on the circulatory system.
4. Name three changes to the respiratory system during exercise.
5. What changes, if any, occur in the skeletal system through time?
6. Name two long-term changes to the heart rate from exercising.
7. Why does blood pressure increase during exercise?
8. Name three factors that help increase the $\dot{V}O_2$max in the long term.
9. Name three long-term changes to the muscular system resulting from exercise.
10. A long-term effect of exercise is going red due to vasodilation. True or False?
11. Blood is diverted from areas of less need, such as the stomach, during exercise. True or False?
12. Adrenaline is released up to 12 hours after exercise. True or False?
13. Heart rate will increase dramatically during vigorous exercise. True or False?
14. A long-term effect of exercise on the muscular system is increased muscle size. True or False?
15. Stroke volume decreases because of years of vigorous exercise. True or False?
16. Long-term effects are permanent changes. True or False?
17. There are no long-term effects of exercise on the skeletal system. True or False?
18. During exercise, one effect is an increased network of capillaries. True or False?
19. Short-term effects are those that are immediate. True or False?

From *GCSE Physical Education: A Revision Guide* by Tim Ferguson, 2002, Champaign, IL: Human Kinetics.

Examination Questions

The original numbering of the examination questions has been retained for ease of cross-referencing. Answers to these questions can be found at the end of the book.

MEG 1999 Paper 1 QB2

e. Figure 7.3 shows the effects of moderate exercise on pulmonary ventilation (the amount of air breathed in and out in one minute).

Use the graph to help you explain the breathing changes that occur during and after 10 minutes of exercise. (8)

MEG 1998 QB2

d. The following graph (figure 7.4) shows the effects of a 10-minute run on heart rate.

With reference to sections A, B and C, labelled on the graph, explain the short-term effects of this exercise on the heart. (5)

AQA(NEAB) 1997 QB1

Outline the short-term effects and long-term benefits of exercise. (15)

AQA(SEG) 1997 Paper 1 Q7

a. What effect does exercise have at the time of activity on the following?

   i. Heart rate (1)

   ii. Breathing rate (1)

   iii. Body temperature (1)

   iv. Muscles being used (1)

b. Regular exercise is recommended.

   i. State three benefits of exercise. (3)

AQA(SEG) 1997 Paper 3 Q6

a. Efficient cardiovascular and respiratory systems are important in physical activity.

   i. Name two of the main components of the cardiovascular system and describe their function. (4)

   ii. Name two of the main components of the respiratory system and describe their function. (4)

   iii. Explain why improved efficiency of these systems is an advantage. Give an example from a physical activity to clarify your answer. (6)

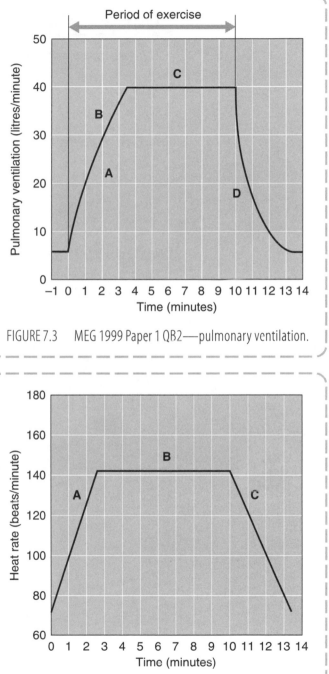

FIGURE 7.3   MEG 1999 Paper 1 QB2—pulmonary ventilation.

FIGURE 7.4   MEG 1998 QB2—the effects of a 10-minute run on heart rate.

London 1999 Q26

Fill in table 7.1, describing two examples of long-term changes to the cardiovascular system and two examples of long-term changes to the respiratory system as a result of regular aerobic training.

TABLE 7.1 London 1999 Q26—Results of Aerobic Training	
Long-term changes to the cardiovascular system	
(i)	(2)
(ii)	(2)
Long-term changes to the respiratory system	
(i)	(2)
(ii)	(2)

London 1998 Q29

Table 7.2 shows heart rate figures for two different athletes who completed a 1,500m race in 6 minutes. Minutes 7 to 11 were a rest period.

TABLE 7.2 London 1998 Q29—Heart Rate Figures												
						Time in minutes						
Athlete	0	1	2	3	4	5	6	7	8	9	10	11
A	75	80	95	120	130	130	130	130	120	105	100	90
B	65	75	85	115	135	135	145	130	115	100	95	80

From *GCSE Physical Education: A Revision Guide* by Tim Ferguson, 2002, Champaign, IL: Human Kinetics. London questions reprinted, by permission, from Edexcel Foundation.

a. Use the figures from table 7.2 to plot a graph to show the heart rate values (in figure 7.5). (4)

b. Which athlete started to recover from the exercise first? (1)

c. i. Did athlete A fully recover by the 11th minute? (1)

c. ii. Give a reason for your answer. (1)

d. i. According to these figures, who appears to be the fitter athlete? (1)

d. ii. Give a reason for your answer. (1)

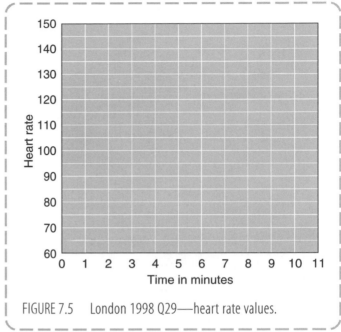

FIGURE 7.5   London 1998 Q29—heart rate values.

From *GCSE Physical Education: A Revision Guide* by Tim Ferguson, 2002, Champaign, IL: Human Kinetics. London questions reprinted, by permission, from Edexcel Foundation.

PART II

Training and Fitness

Part II of the revision guide outlines the importance of fitness and shows how training can improve fitness. Chapter 8 reveals the five factors that make up fitness, while chapter 9 examines the factors that can affect fitness and discusses whether they can be altered. In chapter 10, the factors people need to consider when undertaking training are examined as well as the effects of regular training on the body systems. Chapter 11 outlines different types of training and provides advantages and disadvantages of each method. Finally, chapter 12 details common injuries training creates, what causes these injuries and how to treat them.

CHAPTER 8

Fitness

This chapter examines the five S factors of fitness by describing each S factor and providing ways to measure each type of fitness (see figure 8.1). Chapter 9 outlines the factors that affect fitness.

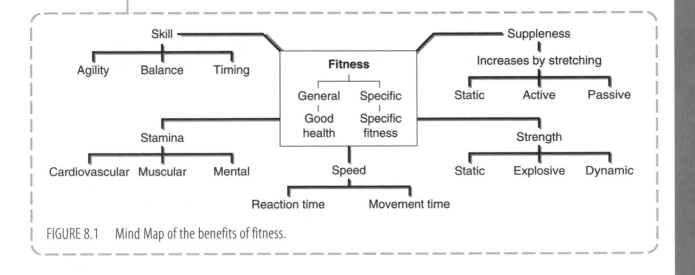

FIGURE 8.1   Mind Map of the benefits of fitness.

GENERAL FITNESS

General fitness can be described as "good health". It means the body has the ability to carry out everyday tasks such as light lifting or walking. General fitness ensures the body has enough energy to cope with emergency situations and can operate for a full day without tiring. The heart, lungs and muscles facilitate this. General fitness also provides enough energy for the brain to concentrate on simple tasks, such as driving to the shops.

SPECIFIC FITNESS

Specific fitness is an extension of general fitness. To take part in a particular sport, a person must be specifically fit. Specific fitness is made up of several key elements. It would be wrong to say, "A 100m sprinter is fit". The sprinter may be quick, yet may not be good at the other elements of fitness such as stamina.

FIVE S FACTORS OF FITNESS

Components of fitness are known as the S factors. There are five S factors of fitness:

1. **Strength**, or muscular power and endurance
2. **Speed**, or how quickly movement can be carried out
3. **Suppleness**, flexibility or the ability to bend at the joints
4. **Stamina**, also known as endurance, either muscular or cardiovascular
5. **Skill-related fitness,** connected with agility

The five S factors can be broken down again into different types.

Strength

There are three types of strength. These are static, explosive and dynamic strength. Learn what each sort of strength means and how to measure each type of strength.

Static Strength

Static strength is the greatest amount of force that can be applied to an immoveable object. In static strength the length of the muscle groups used does not alter. Examples of static muscle work include being in a rugby scrum or hanging from a beam.

checkpoint

Measuring Static Strength

✓ Static strength can be measured using a hand grip dynamometer or tensionometer. The person taking the test holds the dynamometer in one hand and squeezes as hard as possible. The device records how much pressure was exerted. Without specialist equipment, static strength can be measured by timing how long individuals can hang on a beam or perform a 90-degree squat with their back to a wall.

Explosive Strength

Explosive strength is the maximum force, or power, that can be exerted in one movement. Examples of explosive strength include a sprinter leaving the blocks or a weight (power) lifter performing a "clean and jerk".

checkpoint

Measuring Explosive Strength

✓ Explosive strength can be measured in two ways. The first way is to use a standing broad jump to measure the distance a person can jump horizontally from a standing start. Standing with feet in line, mark where the person's toes are. When the person jumps, mark where the back heel lands. Measure the distance between these two points to find out explosive strength.

✓ The second way to measure explosive strength is to use a sergeant jump to measure the vertical distance a person can reach up a wall. To measure the jump, the person taking the test must stand straight with both arms held outstretched above the head. Mark this height on a wall. Then mark the highest point on the wall that they can touch from the jump. Measure the distance between the two marks to record explosive strength.

Dynamic Strength

Dynamic strength is the muscular strength of a person and the ability to keep going. Dynamic strength means movement (for example, a rower uses dynamic strength in the upper body to keep rowing). Dynamic strength is similar to muscular stamina. For more information on how to improve strength, see chapter 10.

checkpoint

Measuring Dynamic Strength

✓ Dynamic strength can be measured by a cycle ergometer or rower. They measure power output by calculating how much work a person does in a period of time. Recently, an "abdominal bleep test" has been designed (see page 60).

Power is the maximum speed that can be produced combined with the maximum strength.

Speed

Speed has two elements:

1. Reaction time
2. Movement time

Reaction time and movement time can be improved and combined together to make response time.

Reaction Time

Reaction time is how long a person takes to start moving once they see or hear (sense) that they have to move. An example of reaction time is when a 100m sprinter sees the flag go down or hears the starter's gun. This information is sent to the brain and the brain decides to start running. The brain sends this decision via the nerves to the muscles telling them to contract or relax and start running. To improve reaction times, people need to practice.

To improve reaction time, a person can be taught to recognise things that indicate an action is about to happen (for example, a badminton player may recognise when her opponent is going to serve high). This allows more time to get close to the net to smash. This is known as anticipation. Often older, more experienced athletes have better reactions because of increased knowledge of sporting situations.

checkpoint

Measuring Reaction Time

✓ The "grab-ruler" test is an easy way to measure reaction time. A person places an arm on the edge of a table, with the hand over the edge of the table. A friend holds the ruler between the person's thumb and fingers. The friend releases the ruler without warning, whilst the person taking the test grabs it as quickly as possible. The distance down the ruler before it is grabbed is proportionate to the response time.

Movement Time

Movement time is the time taken to complete a task or movement from the time the person starts to move until they finish moving. In the case of a sprinter, this would be the time from the first movement to actually crossing the line.

Limb speed is the main factor in movement time. The ratio of fast- to slow-twitch muscles dictates a person's ability to have a fast movement time:

- Slow-twitch muscles contract slowly but are able to keep going for a long time.
- Fast-twitch muscles contract quickly and powerfully but soon tire.

A person's speed can be improved through training. Some individuals are better suited to certain sports than others. This is because of the ratio of muscle fibres people inherit.

checkpoint

Measuring Movement Time

✓ To measure limb speed, use the "plate-tapping" test. Use a table and three plates or discs placed 30 cm apart in a line. Place the non-preferred hand on the middle plate. Time how long it takes for the preferred hand or limb to tap the outside plate 25 times each. To measure the whole body speed, time sprints over short distances. This can involve turning, such as 5m or 10m shuttle runs.

Improving strength or any other fitness element can help avoid injury. Remember there are still injury risks from overtraining or poor technique.

Suppleness

Suppleness is also known as flexibility and refers to the amount the body can bend at the joints. Suppleness can be improved by stretching. There are three types of stretching.

1. Static
2. Active or dynamic
3. Passive or isometric

The more a body can stretch, the more supple it is. Suppleness is often undervalued as a component of fitness. The two advantages of suppleness are

1. a supple person has a greater chance of avoiding injury. When taking part in sport, a person may be forced into an awkward position (for example, a rugby player at the bottom of the scrum). Being flexible may help prevent tissue damage, and

2. skill is increased through suppleness (for example, footballers with a flexible leg will be more able to bring the ball under control when they receive a high pass).

Static Stretching

Static stretching is when the body stretches to its furthest point and holds this stretch. This means the muscle groups do not move.

Active or Dynamic Stretching

Active or dynamic stretching is when someone bounces into the stretched position. It is dangerous to bounce in stretches unless those exercising are warmed up properly and aware of the body's limits.

Passive or Isometric Stretching

Passive or isometric stretching is when two people work together to stretch. One person pushes or pulls the other person's muscle groups into the stretched position whilst that person remains relaxed. This can be dangerous if one partner does not know the flexibility limits of the other.

Imagine that muscles are elastic bands. If an elastic band is stretched when cold, it may snap or tear. If the band is heated up it will be able to stretch further without tearing.

Improving Suppleness

The best way to improve suppleness is through practice. Muscle groups must be warmed up first, stretched to their maximum point and held for six seconds. This needs to be carried out before and after exercise.

checkpoint

Measuring Suppleness

✓ Use the "sit and reach" test to measure suppleness. A person sits with their legs straight and heels flat against a bench or box. Position the ruler to extend from the feet. The score achieved is the distance touched beyond the toes with both hands.

Stamina

Stamina, also known as endurance, is the ability to continue a task for a period of time. Stamina is important because mistakes tend to be made when fatigue sets in. Often more goals are scored in the last quarter of a football match because the players tire and make mistakes. Injuries are also more frequent once stamina runs out. There are three types of stamina:

1. Cardiovascular stamina
2. Muscular stamina
3. Mental stamina

Cardiovascular Stamina

Cardiovascular stamina is also known as aerobic fitness or cardio-respiratory fitness. It is the ability of the heart and lungs to continue supplying oxygen to the muscles that need it. The more oxygen transported to the muscles, the better the cardiovascular stamina (see chapter 4, p. 29 for the definition of $\dot{V}O_2$max). A long-distance runner is an example of someone with good cardiovascular stamina.

see chapter 4, p. 29

checkpoint

Measuring Cardiovascular Stamina

✓ Use the bleep test (20m shuttle run) to measure cardiovascular stamina. This test begins slowly and gradually increases in speed. Individuals run faster between two points 20 metres apart. At every bleep candidates must reach one of the two markers. The bleeps get faster until the candidates cannot reach the markers in time.

Link stamina with aerobic respiration. Consider the energy-making equation,

$$Food + O_2 \rightarrow$$
$$Energy + CO_2 + H_2O + Heat.$$

Use a practical example to demonstrate each component of fitness.

Muscular Stamina

Muscular stamina is similar to dynamic strength. It is the muscles' ability to continue strenuous exercise over a period of time (for example, a canoeist will have good upper-body muscular stamina). The feeling of having "legs of lead" can be equated to the point where muscular stamina is exhausted.

checkpoint

Measuring Muscular Stamina

✓ Use the abdominal bleep test to measure muscular stamina. It can also be used to measure dynamic strength. The candidates sit up on one bleep and sit back on the next bleep. The bleeps continue and increase in frequency every minute. The length candidates keep up to the bleeps is proportional to their muscular stamina.

Mental Stamina

Mental stamina is the ability to concentrate for a long period of time (for example, a Formula One racing driver must concentrate continually). If athletes lose concentration, they may make a mistake.

How to Improve Stamina

Stamina can be improved through practice. It is important to take part in an activity that increases respiration. Being out of breath is a good measure of whether the body has been pushed. See chapters 10 and 11 for more information.

Skill-Related Fitness

Skill-related fitness can be improved through practice. Physical performance will improve at the same time skill-related fitness is improved. Skill-related fitness comprises three elements:

1. Agility, or the ability to change the body's position and direction quickly (for example, agility helps rugby players avoid being tackled).

2. Balance, or the ability of gymnasts to maintain body positions.

3. Timing, or knowing when to carry out an action (for example, when a diver knows at what point to extend out of a somersault to enter the water).

checkpoint

Measuring Agility

✓ The Illinois agility run is used to test agility. Although there is no direct test for balance and timing, the Illinois agility run tests a combination of speed and balance as well as agility. Candidates are timed while running through a series of cones in a small area. The quicker the candidates can run through the cones, the better their agility.

Quick Test

1. Name four elements of fitness.
2. Give an example of static strength.
3. What is explosive strength?
4. Give an example of dynamic strength.
5. What does reaction time plus movement time equal?
6. Why do many older people have quicker reactions?
7. Why is dynamic stretching potentially dangerous?
8. What does a person with good cardiovascular stamina have the ability to do?
9. Name one way of measuring dynamic strength.
10. Name one way of measuring cardiovascular stamina.
11. Name one way of measuring reactions.
12. What is passive stretching?
13. What is dynamic strength?
14. For how long should a stretch be held?
15. Name two types of stamina.
16. How would someone measure static strength?
17. What type of strength is required to perform a sergeant jump?
18. What does the plate-tapping test measure?
19. Name one way of measuring muscular stamina.
20. How can people measure suppleness?

Examination Questions

The original numbering of the examination questions has been retained for ease of cross-referencing. Answers to these questions can be found at the end of the book.

MEG 1997 Paper 1 Q6

e. Describe in detail how one of the following cardiovascular fitness tests would be administered and evaluated:

  i. Five-minute step test (Harvard)

  ii. National Coaching Foundation (NCF) multi-stage fitness test

  iii. Twelve-minute field run test (8)

MEG 1996 Paper 1 Q5

   a. What is general fitness? (1)

   c. List four reasons for maintaining a minimal level of fitness in sport. (4)

AQA(NEAB) 1999 QA1

   a. Name one organ in the body which is important for general fitness. (1)

   b. Give two physical activities for which general physical fitness is important. (2)

   c. Give three physical activities where the speed at which you can move your arms would be an advantage. (3)

   e. Choose one physical activity and describe the specific physical fitness requirements for effective performance. (5)

AQA(NEAB) 1998 QA1

   a. Give one physical activity that will improve general physical fitness. (1)

   b. Give two signs of fatigue. (2)

   c. Name three types of strength. (3)

   d. Describe a test for strength. (4)

   e. Which type of stamina is best suited for games such as football and hockey? Give reasons for your answer. (5)

AQA(SEG) 1996 Paper 2 Q6

   a. Apart from strength, state four factors of fitness. (4)

   b. Describe a physical activity which requires

      i. increased explosive strength, explaining how it is used, and (2)

      ii. increased static strength, explaining how it is used. (2)

   c. Explain how you would improve muscular strength using the principles of training. (4)

London 1999 Q28

Study the diagrams in figure 8.2.

   a. What aspect of skill-related fitness does each figure refer to? (3)

   b. Study figure 8.3. To work on the pommel horse, the gymnast will use different components of health-related and skill-related fitness. Complete table 8.1 by filling in the gaps. (7)

London 1998 Q27

   a. Define the following terms:

      i. Agility (2)

      ii. Reaction time (2)

      iii. Power (2)

   b. State an example of the following:

      i. Agility in a team game (1)

      ii. Reaction time in a swimming race (1)

      iii. Power in the high jump (1)

From *GCSE Physical Education: A Revision Guide* by Tim Ferguson, 2002, Champaign, IL: Human Kinetics. MEG questions reproduced with the kind permission of OCR. AQA(NEAB)/AQA examination questions and AQA(SEG) examination questions are reproduced by permission of the Assessment and Qualifications Alliance. London questions reprinted, by permission, from Edexcel Foundation.

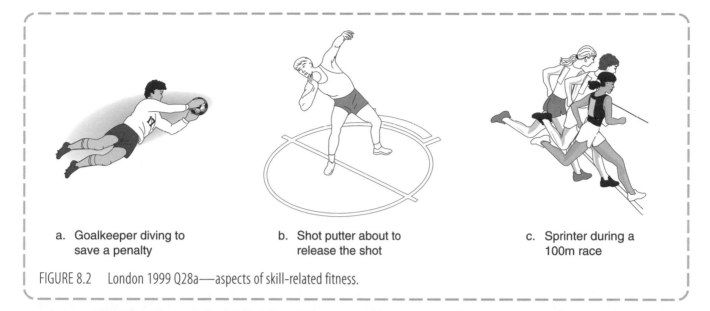

a. Goalkeeper diving to save a penalty

b. Shot putter about to release the shot

c. Sprinter during a 100m race

FIGURE 8.2   London 1999 Q28a—aspects of skill-related fitness.

TABLE 8.1 London 1998 Q28—Components of Fitness		
Component of fitness	**Skill related or health related**	**Use of component**
	Skill related	Change the body's position and direction quickly
Strength		
Flexibility		
		Accurate timing of movement of legs and hands

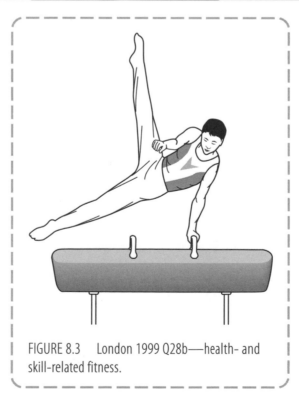

FIGURE 8.3   London 1999 Q28b—health- and skill-related fitness.

CHAPTER 9

Factors Affecting Fitness

This chapter examines what factors can affect individual fitness levels, such as age, sex and diet (see figure 9.1). Some of these factors cannot be altered, but others can be influenced. Chapter 10 examines the principles of training and discusses how the factors addressed in this chapter influence the development of individual training programmes.

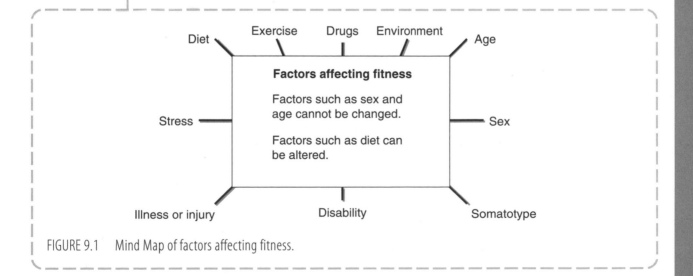

FIGURE 9.1   Mind Map of factors affecting fitness.

There are several factors that affect fitness and performance. Factors 1 to 5 of the following list are physiological factors that cannot be altered. Factor 6 is a psychological factor and factors 7 to 10 are factors that people can control.

1. Age
2. Sex
3. Somatotype
4. Disability
5. Illness or injury

6. Stress
7. Diet
8. Exercise
9. Drugs
10. Environment

AGE

Age affects fitness levels in several ways. Both males and females reach peak fitness in their 20s. Women reach peak fitness slightly earlier than men do. Fitness starts to decline from about age 30, although this varies from person to person. Certain fitness factors decline more quickly than others. Speed is affected more than stamina, which is why long-distance runners remain at the top of their sport for some years, whereas sprinters start losing their edge.

No matter what their age, all people can participate in sport. Old age just requires a steadier approach to sport. It is as important for a 60-year-old to exercise as it is for someone at her peak of fitness.

SEX

Sex, or gender, also affects fitness levels. Women are approximately 30 percent less physically efficient than men. Up to the age of 10, both sexes are on level terms, having both matured at the same rate. At age 11, this equality changes. Girls start adolescence at approximately age 11. They have a growth spurt, which means that they become taller and heavier than boys, and they reach physical maturity at about 16.

Boys start adolescence about two years after girls do, and they finish adolescence later than girls do. Males reach physical maturity around age 20. In international tennis, it is common to see girls aged 15 to 16 competing with the best women in the world, yet it is very rare to see men below the age of 20 competing with the best men in the world.

checkpoint

Physiological Differences

✓ The male bone structure is heavier, stronger and more robust than the female bone structure. It is also longer. The male bone structure is mechanically more efficient. Men can generate more power and speed than women can because they have longer limbs (see figure 9.2).

✓ Other differences can be seen in the pelvis. Women's pelvic girdles are wider and flatter to help with childbirth. This adds to an already reduced mechanical efficiency.

✓ Body fat percentages are also different. Men carry on average 15 percent fat, compared with 25 percent fat for women. Men are stronger than women, particularly in the upper body where there is approximately 50 percent difference in strength. There is also 25 percent difference between the lower-body strength of men and women. Men's capacity to get oxygen to the muscles is greater. Their heart and lungs are larger, so they can transport more oxygen. Women also have less haemoglobin in the blood than men do and they have a smaller blood volume percentage.

SOMATOTYPE

Somatotype means body type. We are all born with an inherited body type, although this can be altered, to an extent, through training. There are three somatotypes (figure 9.3):

1. Endomorph—fat
2. Ectomorph—thin
3. Mesomorph—muscular

FIGURE 9.2   Male versus female physique.

An extreme endomorph would have a rounded body shape with lots of body fat. He would have shorter limbs in relation to his trunk. An extreme ectomorph would be slim with longer limbs in relation to the trunk; she would have very little muscle and very little fat. An extreme mesomorph would be very muscular with broad shoulders and little fat.

These body types are not mutually exclusive, and most people are a mixture of the body types. For example, someone who is large and rounded but muscular could be described as a meso-endomorph (e.g., a modern-day forward in a rugby league or rugby union). Someone who is very thin and light but has strong muscles could be described as a meso-ectomorph (e.g., a high jumper).

People inherit their basic body characteristics. These characteristics mean that some people are more suited to certain sports than to others.

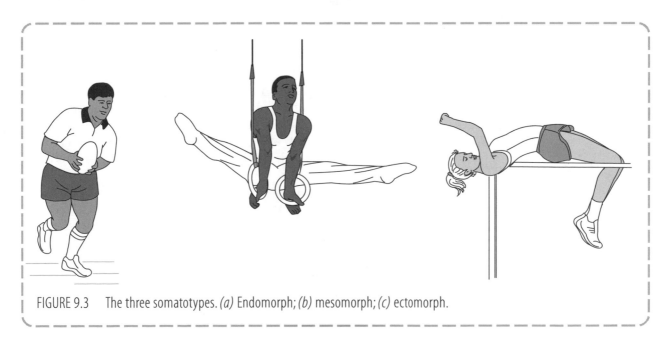

FIGURE 9.3   The three somatotypes. (a) Endomorph; (b) mesomorph; (c) ectomorph.

DISABILITY

There are many disabilities that have an effect on performance. Poor or no hearing may reduce a person's ability to participate in a team sport such as hockey, yet hearing would not have any effect on a person's ability to swim. It is important to realise that most people have disabilities, although not all are immediately obvious. Some disabilities are more of a hindrance than others and make certain sports harder. Yet part of sport is the challenge and having a disability adds to this challenge. A disability does not mean that someone cannot participate. The Paralympics are now one of the largest sporting events in the world.

ILLNESS OR INJURY

Performance can be reduced by either illness or injury. Fatigue, which is usually the result of an illness, reduces performance. If people are injured in sport, there are three points to remember:

1. It is better to allow time to recover before returning to sport.
2. It can be dangerous to continue training whilst injured. Further exercise can cause more damage to the current injury and may even damage other areas because of overcompensation.
3. Modern technology allows an athlete to return to action much sooner after injury, but medical advice should always be sought as to when to return.

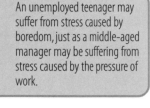

An unemployed teenager may suffer from stress caused by boredom, just as a middle-aged manager may be suffering from stress caused by the pressure of work.

STRESS

Stress is a psychological factor and has many components. Stress reduces fitness because it directly affects health. Exercise is a good "safety valve" and often helps reduce stress levels. Factors leading to stress include tension, anxiety, pressure, lack of motivation and boredom.

DIET

Energy is measured in KiloJoules (KJ). One Kilocalorie is equivalent to 4.18 KiloJoules.

To lead a healthy lifestyle, people need to eat a balanced diet. A balanced diet should contain all the right food groups and appropriate nutrients (see table 9.1). The pressure in society to look good means that dieting has become a big business. For many people, dieting means either eating fewer calories or less fat. If a person desires to lose weight, dieting is only half the answer. The other half of the answer is to take regular exercise.

When a person is resting, she requires energy to maintain the body's functions such as breathing and pumping the heart. This energy requirement is called the basal metabolic rate (BMR).

(1) Energy needed (from food eaten) =
(2) Individual's BMR +
(3) The amount of energy spent doing everyday tasks
such as washing up or playing football.

TABLE 9.1 Food Groups for a Balanced Diet

Nutrient	Food group	Function
Carbohydrate (simple/complex)	Bread, pasta, potatoes, rice	Provides energy, broken down into glucose which is stored as glycogen in the muscles and liver. This is why the technique known as "carboloading" has come about.
Protein	Fish, meat, milk, eggs	Can provide energy but the first function is to build or repair cells.
Fat	Cheese, butter, oils	Provides energy—trained athletes are able to utilise their fat stores better than untrained athletes, rather than using glycogen stores.
Vitamin A	Milk, fish	Healthy skin and bones, good eyesight.
B vitamins	There are several vitamin Bs, which are found in most foods. They help break down food.	
Vitamin C	Vegetables, citrus fruit	Heals wounds, good for teeth and gums.
Vitamin D	Fish, milk	Builds bones and teeth.
Vitamin E	Most foods	Protects cells.
Vitamin K	Green vegetables	Required for blood clotting.
Calcium	Milk, green vegetables	Bone and teeth strength, muscle contractions and blood clotting.
Iron	Meat, green vegetables	Production of haemoglobin in red blood cells.
Fibre*	Cereals, bread	Helps keep the digestive system healthy.
Water*	Essential for good health	

NOTE: *not nutrients

The preceding equation means

- we cannot alter (2) (BMR), but (1) (energy intake) and (3) (energy expended) vary,
- the amount of food eaten (1) will mean a person takes in more or less energy,
- whatever tasks a person does (3) will alter the amount of extra energy he requires, and
- to lose weight a person needs to reduce (1) the amount of food **and** increase (3) the amount of energy.

A balanced diet contains 15 percent protein, 35 percent fat and 50 percent carbohydrate (see figure 9.4).

Fat supplies roughly twice as much energy as protein or carbohydrate. This is why most diets involve reduced or zero fat intake. These diets should not be followed unless recommended by a doctor. Fats are a very important part of the body's nutrient intake.

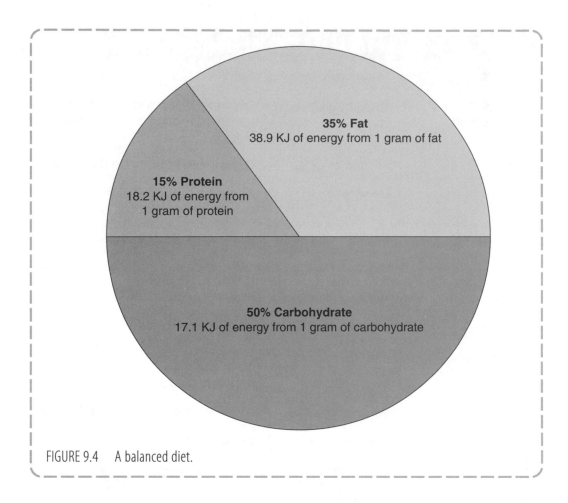

FIGURE 9.4   A balanced diet.

Diet and Performance

Different athletes require different diets. For example, weight lifting requires strength. A weight lifter has a high protein intake to help build muscle cells. Long-distance runners need a different diet to weight lifters because they require lots of energy over a long period. Long-distance runners need to utilise their fat and carbohydrate stores and need a high intake of carbohydrate.

"Carboloading" is a technique whereby athletes train very hard before an event whilst reducing their carbohydrate intake. This means that they use up all their glycogen stores. A few days before the event, they switch to light training and eat lots of carbohydrates. The muscles store more glycogen than normal. The end result is that their energy levels last longer.

Eating before an event requires careful attention. Athletes should not eat immediately before their event, and they should allow at least two hours between eating and competing. During activity, food should not be eaten, but fluids are very important and should be taken to prevent dehydration. After a competition (but not immediately) it is important for athletes to replace the energy used up. Athletes need to allow one to two hours before eating a large meal. Usually exercise suppresses the desire to eat immediately.

Two Dietary Problems

Two dietary problems are obesity and anorexia nervosa. **Obesity** means severely overweight. Being overweight puts an extra burden on the heart and other systems, and it can result in heart attack, stroke, diabetes and death. **Anorexia nervosa**, or **anorexia,** means not enough fat. Anorexia is a mental illness which can cause problems such as organ failure, which results in death.

EXERCISE

Exercise is an important factor of fitness. Regardless of age, sex or any other element of fitness, taking regular exercise will vastly improve fitness and performance. See chapter 11 for more details.

DRUGS

Drugs and drug-related issues are part of international and national sport. These issues are looked at more closely in chapter 17. However, drugs can have both negative and positive effects on fitness.

- Social drugs such as alcohol and cigarettes contain chemicals which affect bodily functions.
- Social drugs reduce the body's capacity to perform, lowering fitness and damaging health.
- Performance-enhancing drugs can have the opposite effect to social drugs in that they improve the body's capacity to perform. See chapter 17 for details.

ENVIRONMENT

The environment people live in has an effect on their health. Four factors to consider are altitude, humidity, pollution and weather.

At **high altitude**, the air is thinner and less oxygen is available. To inhale more oxygen, breathing needs to increase in both rate and depth. This results in fatigue as a person becomes breathless. Athletes undergo altitude training by spending time training at altitude. When they return to sea level they have an improved ability to take in oxygen. A large region of Kenya is at high altitude. This explains why Kenya has produced so many good long-distance runners.

If the atmosphere is **humid** it means that warm air is holding more water. When a person does exercise, her body sweats to help release heat. The sweat lies on the skin's surface and evaporates. This cools the body down. If there is high humidity the process of evaporation will not occur. This makes it harder for the body to regulate its temperature.

Pollution affects air quality. It can be caused by industry or may come from a number of other things such as cars or people's smoking. Fumes released into the air mean that thousands of tiny particles of pollution are present in the air people breathe. These particles enter the respiratory system and can have a detrimental effect on performance.

Any extreme weather conditions will affect fitness. If it is too hot, the body will struggle to keep cool. If it is too cold, the body is more prone to injury. In extreme cold the body can suffer from hypothermia (see chapter 12).

 *Quick Test*

1. Name two physiological factors that affect fitness.
2. Name two factors people can control that affect fitness.
3. At what age should people stop exercising?
4. Approximately how much less physically efficient are women compared to men?
5. At what age do boys (men) reach physical maturity?
6. What is the average body fat percentage for men?
7. What does somatotype mean?
8. Give an example of a sport suited to endomorphs.
9. Name three nutrients.
10. Which nutrient has the most energy per gram?
11. What is the function of carbohydrate?
12. Name a source of protein.
13. How long before exercise should people eat?
14. Name two elements of the environment that affect fitness.
15. Name a source of fat.
16. What is hypothermia?
17. What is altitude training?
18. What could be recommended to a person to help her lose weight?
19. What is the function of protein?
20. Describe an endomorph.
21. What is meant by the term meso-ectomorph?
22. Why does stress affect performance?
23. Why is fibre important?
24. What is carboloading?
25. Which mineral is important for bone growth and strength?
26. In what conditions would the body struggle to release heat through evaporation?
27. What does BMR stand for?
28. Which mineral helps with blood production?

Examination Questions

The original numbering of the examination questions has been retained for ease of cross-referencing. Answers to these questions can be found at the end of the book.

From *GCSE Physical Education: A Revision Guide* by Tim Ferguson, 2002, Champaign, IL: Human Kinetics.

MEG 1998 QB1

b. Ectomorph is one body type. Name two others. (2)

MEG 1996 Paper 1 Q5

d. Describe the functions of five of the main components of a performer's diet. (5)

AQA(NEAB) 1999 QA2

c. Give three physical disabilities that may affect performance. (3)

d. In what ways can illness affect performance? (4)

AQA(NEAB) 1998 QA2

d. How does age affect performance? (4)

e. Use examples to show why the performance of women in sport and physical activity can be different from that of men. (5)

AQA(SEG) 1998 Paper 2 Q2

c. Describe fully what is meant by a balanced diet. Explain how dietary needs can vary between two different types of performers in physical activities which clearly have different needs. (7)

AQA(SEG) 1998 Paper 2 Q3

a. Name three different body types, or somatotypes. (3)

d. What is the difference between a physiological factor that can affect performance and a psychological factor? In your answer give one example for each and describe the effect it can have. (7)

London 1999 Q32

Jan's coach was explaining the need for élite performers to think carefully about diet. Seven food groups make up a balanced diet.

a. List the four food groups which would NOT provide Jan with energy. (4)

b. Which of the remaining three food groups would provide Jan with her main source of energy if she was

    i. competing in the 100m sprint, (1)

    ii. jogging for five minutes, (1)

    iii. cycling for three hours, (1)

    iv. running in a marathon, and (1)

    v. resting? (1)

London 1998 Q37

Jenny has been using the gym at the local sports centre regularly for several months.

a. Which of her body systems would have been most affected if she had just been using

    i. the weights, and

    ii. the cardiovascular equipment? (2)

b. Whilst training for a swimming competition, Jenny was very careful about the food she was eating. Name one food group that Jenny should eat if she wants sufficient energy. (1)

From *GCSE Physical Education: A Revision Guide* by Tim Ferguson, 2002, Champaign, IL: Human Kinetics. MEG questions reproduced with the kind permission of OCR. AQA(NEAB)/AQA examination questions and AQA(SEG) examination questions are reproduced by permission of the Assessment and Qualifications Alliance. London questions reprinted, by permission, from Edexcel Foundation.

    c. Pete is an apprentice jockey. Give a reason his diet may be different from Jenny's. (1)

    d. Of the food groups that give us energy, which should Pete try to eat less of in his diet? (1)

    e. During Jenny's last training session someone suggested she could improve her performance by taking drugs. Jenny refused for two reasons. Her first reason was that it would be cheating. What might the second reason have been? (1)

From *GCSE Physical Education: A Revision Guide* by Tim Ferguson, 2002, Champaign, IL: Human Kinetics. London questions reprinted, by permission, from Edexcel Foundation.

CHAPTER 10

Principles of Training

This chapter covers the basic components of training, individual differences and the effects of training (figure 10.1). Chapter 11 discusses various types of training.

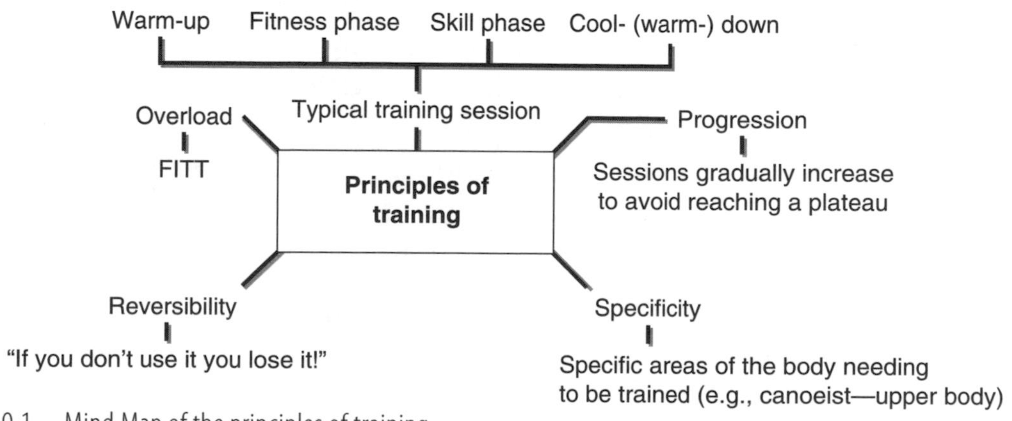

Warm-up   Fitness phase   Skill phase   Cool- (warm-) down

Typical training session

Overload

FITT

Principles of training

Progression

Sessions gradually increase
to avoid reaching a plateau

Reversibility

"If you don't use it you lose it!"

Specificity

Specific areas of the body needing
to be trained (e.g., canoeist—upper body)

FIGURE 10.1   Mind Map of the principles of training.

IMPROVING BODY SYSTEMS

Training is "a set of conditions the body is put under to improve one or more of its fitness characteristics". If the body is regularly trained, the body systems will undergo change to cope with the extra demands placed on them.

THRESHOLD OF TRAINING

As everyone is different, each individual's training programme needs to be different. The threshold of training is the amount of exercise needed to improve fitness. Factors to consider when training include age, gender, physique, disability, injury and illness, diet, and smoking or drinking.

Sport-related factors to consider when training include

1. which sport is being done,
2. present level of fitness,
3. experience, and
4. any special aims.

One common problem to avoid when training is overtraining. If people are struggling to reach a certain level of fitness, sometimes it is better to rest or change training methods rather than continually train. Overtraining can lead to injury or illness.

FOUR PRINCIPLES OF TRAINING

When training, no matter who is training or what sport they are training for, four principles apply:

1. **Overload.** The principle of overload is to make the body work harder than usual, thus overloading it. The body responds to this (through time) by improving its fitness characteristics to meet the demands placed on it.

checkpoint

Four Elements of Overload

The four elements of overload are also known as FITT:

✓ Frequency. How frequently the training sessions are held

✓ Intensity. How hard (or intense) the training session is

✓ Time. The length of each training session

✓ Type. The type of activity performed in the training session

2. **Progression.** The principle of progression means that over time, training sessions need to increase in intensity. Each session must be gradually harder than the previous one, requiring the body systems to work slightly harder. If a person exercises at the same level then fitness levels will plateau. This means there will be no improvement. To prevent this, those training must alter training methods.

3. **Specificity.** All exercise must be specific to individuals' needs and to the actual sport they are training for. Improvements will only occur in the areas

of the body that undergo training. Therefore a 100m sprinter would want to train to improve leg speed, whilst a 5000m rower would want to train to improve muscular endurance in the arms.

4. **Reversibility**. Fitness is reversible. When training, fitness will improve, yet if training is stopped, fitness declines (reverses). Generally fitness levels are lost three times as fast as they are gained.

TYPICAL TRAINING SESSION

A typical training session has four phases. Sessions generally comprise a warm-up, fitness phase, skill phase and cool-down (or warm-down).

Warm-Up

All the muscles and joints need to be warmed up. Do this by starting with light exercise, building slowly to moderate exercise. Once the muscles are warm they need to be stretched. Warm-ups help to prevent injury and prepare the body and mind for action. They should last at least 15 minutes and should be specific to the sport or tasks to be covered in the training session.

Fitness Phase

Work should be done on the aspect(s) of fitness that need to be improved. This will vary from one sport to the next, but most sports will require some training of each S factor. Usually it is best to do speed and strength training first and stamina training last. The main aim is to get close to fatigue, therefore overloading the body systems. Refer to chapter 8 for a description of the five S factors.

Skill Phase

The skill phase is where people learn skills important to the specific sport they play. Individual skills should be practised in a way that resembles the game or event being trained for. This is also known as specific training.

For a team sport it is important to practise teamwork and set pieces. At the top level it is often the "well-practised" teams that win rather than the most skilled (a good example of this is the success of the German football team over the last two decades).

All skill practices should be done under pressure. It would be silly to practise shooting in basketball without a defender present. In basketball it is rare for players to have no defender in front of them.

Cool-Down

The cool-down is just as important as the warm-up yet is often overlooked. Cooling down requires the reverse principles to warming up. Moderate exercise should lead to light exercise with gentle stretching. This prevents soreness and aching muscles and joints. It helps the body remove lactic acid. After training, taking a hot shower or bath can form part of the cooling down process. The cool-down should last at least 15 minutes.

> Imagine the body is a car. A car would not go from being parked straight to fifth gear. Warming up is the body's way of moving through the gears safely. The same principle (in reverse) also applies to cooling down.

EFFECTS OF TRAINING

For more detailed information on the effects of training, see chapter 7. Training will help to improve all five S factors:

1. **Strength**. Training will improve muscular endurance, muscular strength, power and muscle bulk.
2. **Speed**. Training will improve limb speed, whole body movement and reaction time, and provide an increased ability to maintain speed for longer.
3. **Suppleness**. Training will allow a larger range of movement. The range of movement leads to greater strength and speed, and better technique and skill level.
4. **Stamina**. Training will improve all aspects of stamina, including mental stamina.
5. **Skill**. Training will improve general motor skills and precise skills. Team cohesion will be increased. This means team moves and skills will be improved and team members will understand each other better.

Quick Test

1. Why should people warm up?
2. Name two elements of overload.
3. What should people do at the end of a training session?
4. Name three principles of training.
5. Explain the term "reversibility".
6. Name five factors to consider when training.
7. Why does the body change as a result of exercise?
8. What is the aim of the fitness phase of a training session?
9. What does cooling down prevent?
10. What changes may occur to strength as a result of training?
11. A hot shower can be considered part of the cooling down process. True or False?
12. Training should lead to increased fitness levels. True or False?
13. A typical training session should have a warm-up, fitness phase, skills phase and a cool-down. True or False?
14. Reversibility occurs if people stop training for a number of weeks. True or False?
15. Reaching a fitness plateau is good for motivation. True or False?
16. What is the threshold of training?
17. What is overtraining?
18. What is a fitness plateau?
19. Explain the term "specificity".
20. What is the aim of the skills phase of a training session?

From *GCSE Physical Education: A Revision Guide* by Tim Ferguson, 2002, Champaign, IL: Human Kinetics.

Examination Questions

The original numbering of the examination questions has been retained for ease of cross-referencing. Answers to these questions can be found at the end of the book.

MEG 1996 Paper 1 Q5

e. Specificity, overload, progression and reversibility are four guiding principles that can help us to decide on the most effective training for a physical activity. Describe how two of them can be applied to the problem of increasing strength. (8)

MEG 1995 Paper 1 Q6

b. What is stamina? (2)

c. What does reversibility mean? (4)

d. i. Define power. (1)

d. ii. Describe a test you would carry out to determine muscular power. (4)

AQA(NEAB) 1999 QA4

a. Give one principle of training. (1)

d. Outline the reasons for warming down after taking part in exercise. (4)

e. Choose one physical activity. Explain one training session designed to improve performance in the selected activity. (5)

AQA(NEAB) 1998 QA4

e. Define the principle of overload. How can it be applied through weight training? (5)

AQA(SEG) 1998 Q2

b. A suitable warm-up is important before taking part in a physical activity. Provide

  i. two reasons why a warm-up is necessary, and (2)

  ii. an outline of a suitable warm-up. (2)

London 1999 Q29

Mohammed is an "up and coming" badminton player and is told that his standard of play will improve if he increases his level of fitness. He starts training three times a week, for an hour each session (table 10.1).

a. Name which aspect of the FITT principle relates to each of the following:

  i. An hour each session

  ii. Three times a week

  iii. Speed work on court with shuttle (3)

There are several other principles of training in addition to the FITT principle. Answer the following questions relating to these other principles:

b. Which principle of training needs to be applied to the programme to ensure that his fitness continues to improve? (1)

From *GCSE Physical Education: A Revision Guide* by Tim Ferguson, 2002, Champaign, IL: Human Kinetics. MEG questions reproduced with the kind permission of OCR. AQA(NEAB)/AQA examination questions and AQA(SEG) examination questions are reproduced by permission of the Assessment and Qualifications Alliance. London questions reprinted, by permission, from Edexcel Foundation.

TABLE 10.1 London 1999 Q29—Badminton Training			
Week no.	Session 1	Session 2	Session 3
Week 1	Running session	Speed work on court with shuttle	Weights session

c. Which principle of training should be applied to his programme to reduce the chances of injury? (1)

d. Which principle of training will apply if he stops training for a couple of months? (1)

e. Which principle of training needs to be considered if he takes up basketball instead of badminton and wants a fitness programme for this activity instead? (1)

London 1998 Q28

a. Match the following definitions to the principle of training by putting the correct letter in table 10.2:

A: How long you exercise

B: Start slowly and increase the amount of exercise

C: How hard you work during the session

D: How often you train (4)

TABLE 10.2 London 1998 Q28—Definitions of the Principles of Training	
Intensity	
Frequency	
Duration / time	
Progression	

b. The FITT principle is made up of four separate principles. Which of these four is not referred to in the table earlier? (1)

CHAPTER 11

Types of Training

This chapter describes and evaluates various types of training (figure 11.1) and links training to critical thresholds. Chapter 12 deals with injuries and how they should be treated.

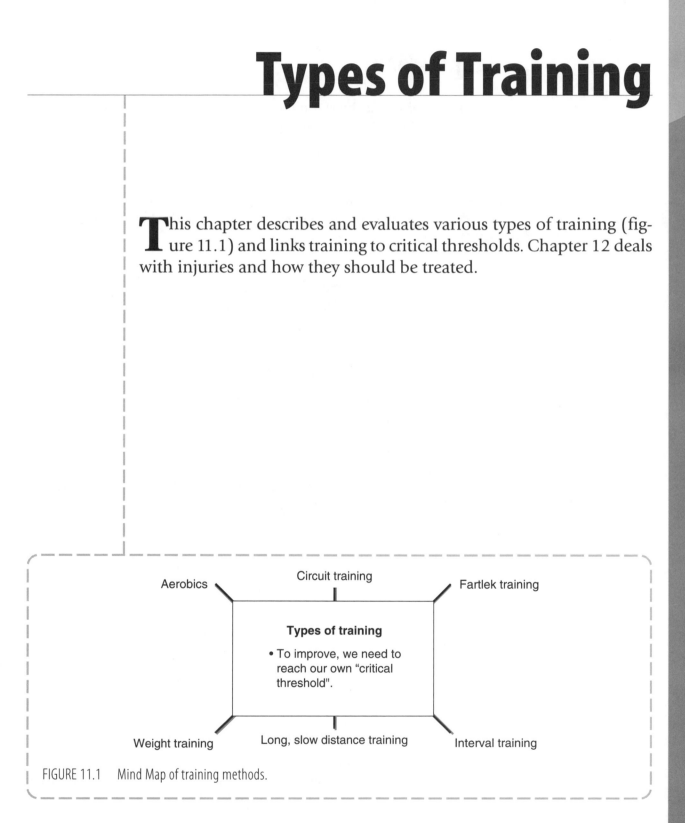

FIGURE 11.1   Mind Map of training methods.

Use a practical example to explain each type of training. (For example, Fartlek training is an aerobic training method and involves walking, jogging, running and sprinting. Fartlek training tones the legs, exercises the cardio-respiratory system and improves cardiovascular fitness. Sessions could be adapted for swimming, cycling or rowing.)

There are a variety of training types, each with its own advantages and disadvantages. The training type used depends on the individual's fitness requirements. The following types of training mainly work the aerobic energy system or anaerobic energy system, although some methods train both systems. Before concentrating on different types of training, an individual needs to calculate how hard they need to work (overloading).

CRITICAL THRESHOLD

The threshold of training is the amount of exercise each individual needs to improve fitness. To improve fitness, individuals need to reach "critical fitness".

Critical threshold =
Resting heart rate + 60% of (Maximum heart rate − Resting heart rate)

Resting heart rate (HR) is the body's HR (pulse) taken at rest. To be measured accurately, this should be done as soon as a person wakes up in the morning after a full night's sleep.

Maximum HR = 220 minus age
Bob is aged 30. Therefore Bob's maximum HR is 220 − 30 = 190.
Bob's resting HR is 70. Bob's critical threshold is 70 + 60% (190 − 70)
= 70 + 60% (120)
= 70 + 72
= 142 heart beats per minute.

This formula means it is possible to produce a training threshold zone. The training zone has a lower limit of 60 percent and an upper limit of 85 percent of the maximum HR.

Therefore at age 20:

60% of Maximum HR = 60% of (220 − 20) = 120.
85% of Maximum HR = 85% of (220 − 20) = 170.

Therefore at age 80:

60% of Maximum HR = 60% of (220 − 80) = 84.
85% of Maximum HR = 85% of (220 − 80) = 119.

To produce any aerobic effects of training a person needs to train at least three times a week for at least 20 minutes, working within their own training zone (see figure 11.2). For anaerobic training, they should do short bursts above the 85 percent limit.

SIX TYPES OF TRAINING

Six types of training are discussed in this chapter, although there are other methods available.

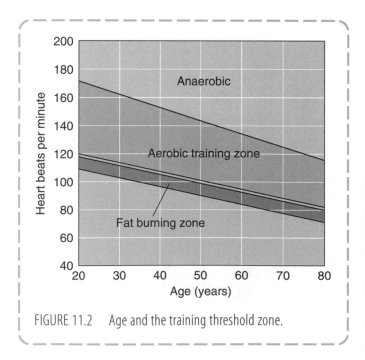

FIGURE 11.2   Age and the training threshold zone.

1. Aerobics
2. Circuit training
3. Fartlek training
4. Interval training
5. Long, slow, distance training
6. Weight training

Aerobics

As the name suggests, aerobics means working aerobically to train the cardio-respiratory system. Aerobics is a series of exercises performed continuously (usually to music) and the session becomes harder, increasing the heart rate. The exercises are designed to work out all body parts. A session always involves a lengthy warm-up and stretch and cool-down and stretch. Aerobics improves cardiovascular fitness, muscular stamina (this increases muscle tone), timing, balance and co-ordination.

checkpoint

✓ Aerobics is enjoyable and sociable. Participants do not need expensive equipment and it improves the cardio-respiratory system. The disadvantages of aerobics are that it has a high impact on the leg joints and all participants work at the same level, thus not allowing for those who are above or below the average fitness level of the class.

Circuit Training

Circuit training is usually an aerobic workout but can be adapted to be more anaerobically oriented. Circuit training

- exercises all parts of the body;
- involves performing different exercises at a series of stations;
- improves timing, balance and co-ordination;
- can be adapted to skills circuit training for specific sports (for example, all exercises are made to relate to dribbling and passing exercises in hockey);
- can be timed so that participants exercise for a minute;
- can have a fixed load (for example, participants perform 40 sit-ups then move to the next station and do 30 press-ups);
- means participants work at different exercises such as step-ups and sit-ups (see figure 11.3); and
- allows muscles to work aerobically and anaerobically to increase muscle size and tone.

checkpoint

✓ Circuit training is easily adapted and participants require no special equipment. It is suitable for all fitness levels within one session. The disadvantages of circuit training are that exercises need to be demonstrated to prevent misuse of technique or injury.

Fartlek Training

Fartlek is Swedish for "speed play". Fartlek training is a Swedish method of training. It is an aerobic training

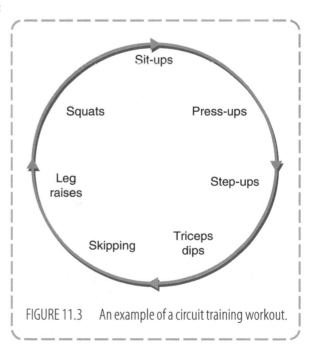

FIGURE 11.3   An example of a circuit training workout.

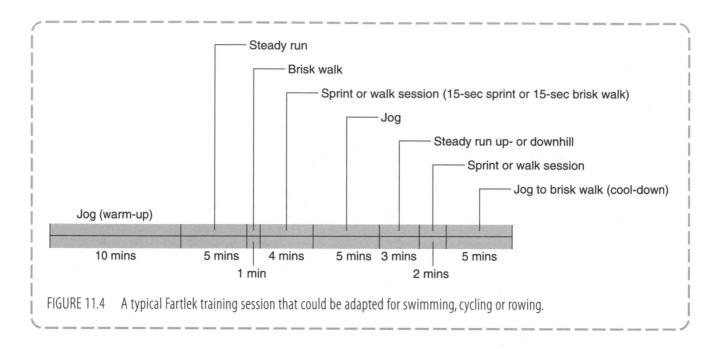

FIGURE 11.4   A typical Fartlek training session that could be adapted for swimming, cycling or rowing.

method that allows anaerobic bursts, similar to the type of exercise seen in field games such as football (jogging continuously intermixed with short bursts of sprinting). Fartlek training involves walking, jogging, running and sprinting. Participants run continually on a track or cross-country, varying the run with a variety of sprints, walks and jogs. Fartlek training tones the legs, exercises the cardio-respiratory system and improves cardiovascular fitness.

A typical Fartlek session is shown in figure 11.4. This session could be adapted for swimming, cycling or rowing.

checkpoint

✓ Fartlek training is advantageous in that participants require no equipment and can train both aerobically and anaerobically. The disadvantage of Fartlek training is that it does not increase muscular strength.

Interval Training

Interval training is similar to Fartlek training in that it works the body both aerobically and anaerobically. Interval training involves the following:

- There is a fixed pattern of slow and fast work.
- It encourages participants to work hard then rest. Participants perform one "rep" (repetition) of exercise.
- It involves performing a series of slightly different reps (for example participants perform 10 × 30m sprints, walk back to rest and then perform 5 × 200m sprints).
- It improves cardiovascular fitness.
- It improves upper- or lower-body muscular stamina depending on whether the activity is running, rowing, swimming or cycling).
- It can be either short or long interval training:
    1. Short interval training has a more anaerobic bias, requiring and improving speed and power, suitable for sprinters or racket sport.

2. Long interval training is more beneficial to middle distance runners or field sport.

checkpoint
✔ Interval training is advantageous in that participants require no equipment and can train both aerobically and anaerobically. The disadvantage of interval training is that it can be boring.

Long, Slow Distance Training

Long, slow distance training is also known as continuous training. It involves exercise without rest intervals and only works the aerobic energy system. Long, slow distance training requires participants to work at approximately 70 percent of the maximum heart rate for a constant (sustained) period of time over 30 minutes. Key benefits are that it trains the cardio-respiratory system and improves muscle tone of legs in running and arms in rowing. This type of training also helps train the body to burn fat rather than carbohydrate.

checkpoint
✔ Long, slow distance training means participants need no equipment. It burns fat stores and it is excellent for aerobic training. The disadvantages of long, slow distance training are that it does not train the anaerobic system or increase muscle strength.

Weight Training

The main aim of weight training is to increase strength, although there are several ways of increasing strength and also several different types of strength (see chapter 8, p. 56). Weight training can **increase muscle size** and strength, and can **increase muscle tone** and muscular stamina (a good example is an aerobics instructor).
There are three methods to increase muscle size and tone.

1. **Isotonic** training is when the muscles contract, therefore the body is moving whilst working (for example, performing a press-up is isotonic weight training).
2. **Isometric** training is when the muscle length remains the same—this is static strength, which is explained in chapter 8 (e.g., in a rugby scrum the players' muscles are under tension but are not moving).
3. **Isokinetic** training is when there is a high amount of tension put on the muscles throughout the range of movement. It is only due to recent advances in technology that designers have produced weight-training equipment capable of ensuring isokinetic contractions (e.g., multi-gym equipment rather than free weights).

To create a basic weight-training programme, first consider the two characteristics of strength: muscle size and muscle tone. A different programme needs to be adopted depending on whether someone wants to increase muscle size and bulk or muscle tone.
For each muscle group or each lift (for example, bench press [pectorals]) a person should find their maximum. The maximum refers to the maximum weight someone can push once. Before finding out their maximum, they should be completely

warmed up and stretched. When they perform a bench press, the maximum weight they can lift might be 100kg.

Because Bob pushed 100kg once it means he has done one rep (repetition). To increase muscle size Bob must do 10 reps at 65 percent of his maximum (for example, 10 × 65kg, but he must do three sets [do this three times]). To increase muscle tone Bob must do 20 reps at 35 percent of his maximum. This means lifting 20 × 35kg for at least three sets (or three times).

Bob must repeat this for all the different muscle groups (for example, lat pulls, quadriceps extension, biceps curl).

All the usual safety rules apply, such as the warm-up and stretch and cool-down and stretch. Also, as in circuit training, Bob should move from an arm exercise to an exercise on the legs or trunk. This gives his arms the chance to recover.

checkpoint

✓ Weight training improves the anaerobic system. It is easy for participants who are weight training to work with a partner at two different levels. Participants can easily record performance and measure improvement. The disadvantages of weight training are that participants need special equipment and it is not as effective for the aerobic system as other forms of training.

Seasonal Training

The main reason for seasonal training is to ensure the athlete's performance "peaks" at the best time of the year. Not all athletes work to a calendar year. A footballer works for approximately nine months of each year (season), whilst an athlete has various competitions. Important competitions for athletes come every four years (Olympics). This is why all athletes modify training to try and "peak" at the right moment. They reduce training at points in the year to allow the body to rest and recover and then intensify training leading up to a competition or to coincide with the start of a season.

Quick Test

1. Name two aerobic training methods.
2. Name two anaerobic training methods.
3. Name a training method that could be either aerobic or anaerobic.
4. Give one advantage of circuit training.
5. Give one advantage of long, slow distance training.
6. What does the term "seasonal training" mean?
7. Why is it good for training programmes to have variety?
8. What could be done to someone's training programme if they experience a plateau?
9. What is the training zone?

From *GCSE Physical Education: A Revision Guide* by Tim Ferguson, 2002, Champaign, IL: Human Kinetics.

10. Explain Fartlek training.
11. Explain interval training.
12. How is the maximum heart rate calculated?
13. What is the difference between working in the aerobic and anaerobic training zone?
14. With reference to heart rate, explain what might be a good indication of a person's fitness.

Examination Questions

The original numbering of the examination questions has been retained for ease of cross-referencing. Answers to these questions can be found at the end of the book.

MEG 1996 Paper 1 Q6

a. What is meant by cardiovascular fitness? (1)

MEG 1995 Paper 1 Q5

c. Describe how you would carry out a test with a partner to assess the endurance of a specific group of muscles. (4)

d. What does "resistance training" mean? (5)

AQA(NEAB) 1999 QA4

b. Give two physical activities for which interval training is suitable. (2)

c. Give three reasons why jogging may be good for aerobic needs. (3)

AQA(NEAB)1998 QA4

a. Give one physical advantage of training. (1)

b. Give two features of Fartlek training. (2)

AQA(NEAB) 1997 QA4

a. What component of fitness does aerobic training mainly improve? (1)

b. Give two types of aerobic training. (2)

d.   i. What is the training threshold?

d.   ii. How would you calculate the training threshold? (4)

e. Explain the factors you would take into consideration when designing a "circuit" to improve all-around fitness. (5)

AQA(SEG) 1997 Paper 3 Q3

a. For a named activity, give a detailed description of the warm-up to be performed immediately before the event or performance. Consider the following:

    i. The body parts to be prepared (2)

    ii. The types of exercises to be used (2)

    iii. The length of time it should take (2)

b. For a named activity or event, state the training method or programme which would be appropriate to follow. Give a detailed description of your chosen method or programme. (4)

c. For a named activity or event, explain how a coach, teacher or trainer can help a performer with the following:
   i. Mental preparation (2)
   ii. Physical preparation (3)

AQA(SEG) 1997 Paper 3 Q4

b. In weight training what is meant by the following terms:
   i. Repetitions (2)
   ii. Sets (2)

c. In weight training, give the following:
   i. A detailed description of the types of equipment available (4)
   ii. The benefits of following a weight training programme for a performer in a named physical activity (3)

London 1998 Q35

Figure 11.5 shows Sally's heart rate values recorded during a training session.

a. What happens to her heart rate during the training session? (1)

b. What causes her heart rate to alter in this way? (2)

c. What type of training method is she doing to give this result? (1)

d. For each set Sally is working close to her maximum heart rate. State a games situation when this type of training would be of benefit. (1)

e. Which principle of training is Sally applying by developing her training so that it meets the demands of one particular sport? (1)

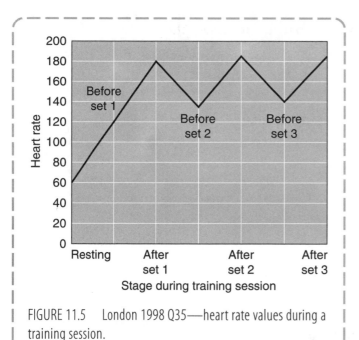

FIGURE 11.5   London 1998 Q35—heart rate values during a training session.

London 1998 Q36

Glen is a good gymnast. He is looking to improve by following a flexibility and speed training programme.

a. i. Suggest another component of fitness he might need to develop. (1)

a. ii. What type of training method could he use to develop this component of fitness? (1)

b. Why is it important that he trains regularly? (1)

c. The coach has given Glen a different training programme to that of his friend, who is also a gymnast. Why might he do this? (1)

d. In gymnastics Glen has to perform various balances. What type of muscle contraction is occurring when he holds a handstand? (1)

From *GCSE Physical Education: A Revision Guide* by Tim Ferguson, 2002, Champaign, IL: Human Kinetics. AQA(SEG) examination questions are reproduced by permission of the Assessment and Qualifications Alliance. London questions reprinted, by permission, from Edexcel Foundation.

e. If you were planning a training session for Glen it should be broken down into three sections. The middle section would be the main part of the activity.

   i. What should he do before the main activity?

   ii. What should he do after the main activity? (2)

From *GCSE Physical Education: A Revision Guide* by Tim Ferguson, 2002, Champaign, IL: Human Kinetics. London questions reprinted, by permission, from Edexcel Foundation.

CHAPTER 12

Injuries

This chapter discusses injuries in training. It describes how to treat injuries, and covers the basics of resuscitation, before briefly describing safe practice in sport (figure 12.1). Part III focuses on issues of coaching and performance.

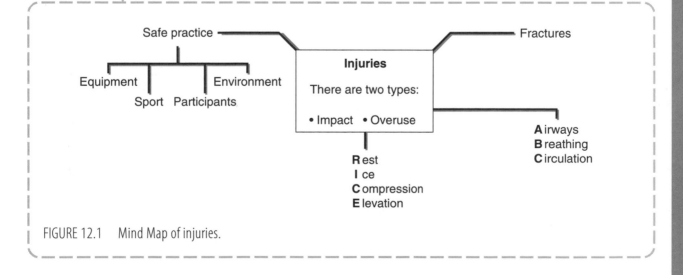

FIGURE 12.1   Mind Map of injuries.

Sport is good for people because it involves exercising to improve health. However, taking part in sport brings the risk of injury. All sports have an injury risk, although some sports have a greater risk than others. Rugby involves body contact. This means there is a higher risk of injury in rugby, whereas the risk is lower in a non-contact sport such as badminton. Other non-contact sports such as climbing or mountaineering carry even greater risks (possibly death). This element of risk attracts some people to the sport.

There are two explanations for the occurrence of sport injuries:

1. **Impact**. This is an injury through direct contact with something or someone (for example, a footballer being tackled or a jockey falling off the horse).
2. **Overuse**. This is an injury caused by constant stress on part(s) of the body. This happens through overtraining or playing too many matches or competitions. The body is like a car. Its parts wear away through overuse.

Table 12.1 shows a list of injuries common in sport, their symptoms, short-term treatment and how the injury occurs. Fractures (another word for broken

TABLE 12.1 Common Sport Injuries				
Injury	Description	How injury occurs	Symptoms of injury	Short-term treatment
Sprain (minor or major)	Ligaments and other tissues around the joint are torn	Usually due to a sudden blow forcing the joint to overstretch.	Movement is painful and difficult, the joint swells and bruising appears due to blood and other fluids spreading from damaged vessels.	RICE.
Dislocation	When one or more bones at a joint are forced beyond their normal position	Usually due to a large force making contact with the joint.	Severe sickening pain at the joint. The joint will look deformed due to the bones being out of place. Lots of swelling; no movement will be possible.	Send for medical help. Support the injured area, preferably with slings or bandages (practically: clothes or other soft objects). Take immediately to hospital.
Strained/ torn ligaments	Ligaments overstretched or torn	Due to a blow to the joint or through a large force exerted, forcing the joint to overstretch.	Swelling and lack of movement, localised pain.	RICE. If severe, take to hospital.
Torn cartilage (semilunar) knee	Tears in the cartilage (which is the buffer between bones at joints, most common in the knee)	This is a rotational injury caused by rapid turning at the knee or direct contact on the knee.	The knee joint locks into position or gives way. Some swelling and immense pain, especially if movement is attempted.	Send for medical help. Support the injured leg in the most comfortable position. Do not try to straighten the leg. Immobilise it. Take immediately to hospital.
Tendon (strained or torn)	Muscle exerts a large force which translates down to the tendon	Lack of warm-up or through fatigue, or through a larger force (overload) than the muscle or tendon can cope with. A bad landing, poor training methods or technique can also contribute.	Localised pain—extreme pain if badly torn and loss of movement.	RICE. If torn (ruptured) support the injured area and seek medical advice.

Injury	Description	How injury occurs	Symptoms of injury	Short-term treatment
Muscle (strained or torn)	Muscle fibres overstretched or torn (ruptured)		Localised pain—extreme pain if badly torn and loss of movement.	RICE.
Tendonitis	Inflamed tendons	Overuse, a repetitive action (e.g., tennis elbow).	Pain and swelling.	RICE.
Bruises (muscle or bone)	Internal bleeding from damaged cells and vessels	Muscle squashed against bone due to a direct blow from someone or something.	Painful to touch and when moving, swelling and discoloration.	RICE.
Fractures	A broken bone—open, closed, compound, greenstick	Contact, direct blow from something (e.g., a fall, bad tackle).	Localised pain, swelling and bruising. Movement very difficult and increased pain.	Send for medical help. Stop any bleeding, do not move casualty, keep them warm and comfortable. Talk and reassure, do not allow food or drink. Take immediately to hospital.
	Stress	Overuse, repetitive movements.	Pain and swelling.	Stop exercising.
Concussion (uncon-sciousness)	Knocked out	Blow to the head or through severe shock or injury to another body part.	Eyes closed, no response, relaxed body, shallow breathing and dilated pupils.	Send for medical help. Keep warm, check pulse and breathing rate. If other injuries suspected do not move (spinal). No food or drink given if they come round.
Cramps or stitch (special type)	Involuntary contraction of the muscles	Through intense exercise, chilling of the body and a lack of body salts.	Pain and locked muscles.	Stretch the muscle group.
	Cramp in the diaphragm	Through intense exercise, usually running.	Sharp pain in the abdomen when trying to breathe.	Stop running, bend forward and push fist into the painful area.
Dehydration	Loss or lack of body fluid	Not enough water intake and losing too much fluid through sweating and breathing.	Dry, parched and thirsty feeling. Can feel faint and dizzy.	Drink water.
Hypo thermia	Severe chilling of the body	Extreme weather conditions and inadequate clothing.	Pale skin, shallow breathing. The casualty may feel weak, dreamy and want to lie down and rest.	Shelter the casualty, change into warm and dry clothing, hot bath and hot drinks (no alcohol).
Hyper-thermia	Overheating of the body	Extreme weather conditions.	Dehydrated, faint or dizzy and feeling of sickness.	Drink, stop exercising and cool down.
Shock	Lack of blood circulating around the body	Severe blood loss from injury or from severe pain.	Blue lips, feel cold and clammy. Quick, shallow breathing rate and weak pulse. Feel nauseated and concussed.	Send for medical help. Try to prevent blood loss. Comfort and reassure casualty.
Cuts	Broken skin	Contact with someone or something.	Bleeding, pain and feel faint and sick.	Direct pressure on the cut using a dressing. Elevate limb above the heart. Stitches or sutures.
Blisters	Skin layers part, gaps filled with fluid	Friction on skin.	Local pain.	

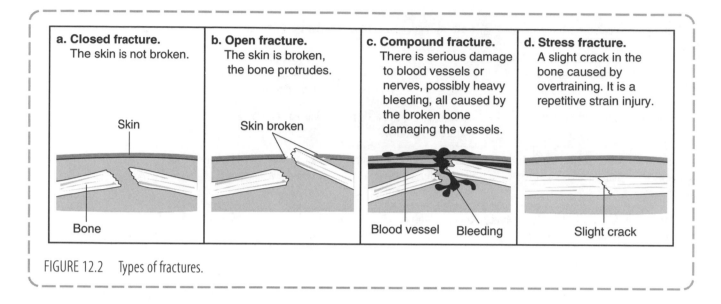

a. Closed fracture. The skin is not broken.	b. Open fracture. The skin is broken, the bone protrudes.	c. Compound fracture. There is serious damage to blood vessels or nerves, possibly heavy bleeding, all caused by the broken bone damaging the vessels.	d. Stress fracture. A slight crack in the bone caused by overtraining. It is a repetitive strain injury.
Skin Bone	Skin broken	Blood vessel Bleeding	Slight crack

FIGURE 12.2   Types of fractures.

bones) are one of the most complicated injuries to understand, as there are five different types of fractures. Figure 12.2 shows four of the different types of fracture in more detail. Greenstick fractures, where the bone bends rather than breaks, are not included. This is because greenstick fractures only occur in children.

TREATING INJURIES

With most injuries rest, ice, compression and elevation (RICE) will form at least part of the treatment. The following describes how to treat injuries using RICE:

checkpoint

1. **Rest.** Stop and rest the injured body part. This will help prevent further damage to the injury site.

2. **Ice.** Apply ice immediately to the injury. This causes the blood vessels to contract. This reduces the blood flow to the area and stops blood and other fluids spreading from the damaged vessels. The best method is to strap a bag of ice (or frozen food) to the injury. Application of ice to the injury should continue for approximately 4 hours with breaks every 15 minutes to allow some blood flow. This should help to limit the swelling and bruising.

3. **Compression.** Strap (support) the injury. This should be done in conjunction with ice but should continue for a longer period. Compression also limits the swelling and helps support the musculo-skeletal system in the period after the accident.

4. **Elevation.** Raise the injured body part above the level of the heart. This helps to drain the excess fluid and reduces the blood flow to the injury.

RICE treatment should continue for 48 hours after the injury occurred.

ABC OF RESUSCITATION

If a person collapses, he may have stopped breathing or his heart may have stopped. Usually if one stops the other will quickly follow. The main aim is to keep the injured person breathing (or restart his breathing) until an ambulance or medical assistance arrives.

To keep the injured person breathing, check his airways, breathing and circulation, or apply the ABC of resuscitation (figure 12.3):

checkpoint

Airways

Check the injured person's airways to make sure there is nothing obstructing breathing (for example, the tongue). Remove false teeth, gum shields, vomit or anything else blocking the airway. Loosen all tight clothing, particularly around the chest and neck. Raise the chin and tilt the head back to open the airway and straighten the trachea. If the injured person vomits during resuscitation, remove it from the airway.

checkpoint

Breathing

Check the injured person's chest to see if it rises and falls. Listen and feel for breath. If you cannot see the chest moving, or cannot hear anything, the injured person is not breathing. If the injured person is not breathing, force air into the injured person's lungs:

1. Pinch the nose shut, hold the mouth open at the chin, keeping the head back.

2. Take a deep breath. Firmly seal your mouth against the injured person's mouth and breathe out smoothly.

3. Remove your mouth, breathe in and repeat every six seconds.

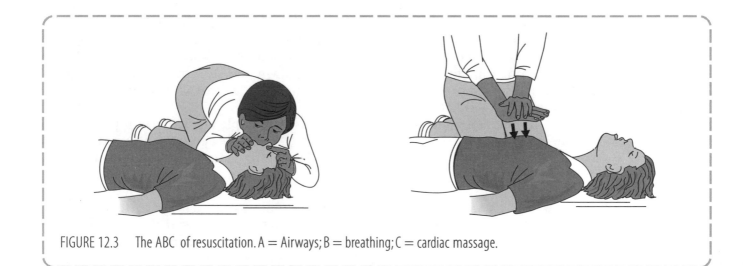

FIGURE 12.3   The ABC of resuscitation. A = Airways; B = breathing; C = cardiac massage.

checkpoint

Circulation

Check the carotid (neck) pulse and radial (wrist) pulse. If there is no circulation, force the heart to compress, imitating a contraction:

1. Place one hand on the other on the sternum (breast bone) and push down strongly.

2. Repeat this pumping action 12 times, then deliver two breaths in.

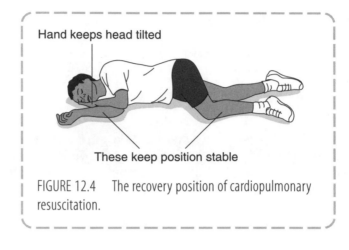

Hand keeps head tilted

These keep position stable

FIGURE 12.4   The recovery position of cardiopulmonary resuscitation.

If either B or C is stopped, artificially provide breathing and a heart beat. The ratio of breaths to chest compressions is 2 mouth-to-mouth ventilations to 15 chest compressions. If the injured person regains pulse or breathing, place them in the recovery position (see figure 12.4).

FOUR SAFE PRACTICE FACTORS OF SPORT

Some injuries will occur no matter what action is taken. Many injuries can be prevented through safe practice. Taking the right precautions goes a long way towards preventing or limiting the extent of an injury. There are several factors which influence safe practice in sport.

A person's characteristics influence safe practice. Participants should consider whether they have practised the skill requirements of the activity and whether they are trained for high or low levels of activity. They should be responsible for warming up and stretching, and cooling down and stretching. These are important factors in preventing injury. People should be aware that any illness, injury or disability could affect their safety.

The requirements of sport influence safety. People taking part in sport should make certain they consider certain factors before taking part. People need to know and understand the rules of the sport. They need to know the requirements of the sport and find out if it is a contact or non-contact sport. They should find out the standard of their opponents and compete against the appropriate level of opponents. They should find out if referees, umpires or coaches are officiating and check if the appropriate action has been taken before the event (for example, there should be a first aid kit available at a rugby match, or someone else should know the planned route or timing if people go mountain walking).

Equipment is important to consider when making sure sport is safe. Some sports require more equipment for safe practice than other sports do. Participants need to consider several factors. They need to wear appropriate clothing and have the correct safety equipment (for example, a gum shield in rugby or a helmet for canoeing). They need the correct footwear such as indoor shoe soles with sticky rubber, or outdoor shoe soles with spikes. All jewellery should be removed and long hair tied back.

Finally, the environment influences safe practice. Participants need to consider whether the sport takes place outside, inside or in an extreme environment. Safety factors to consider include the following:

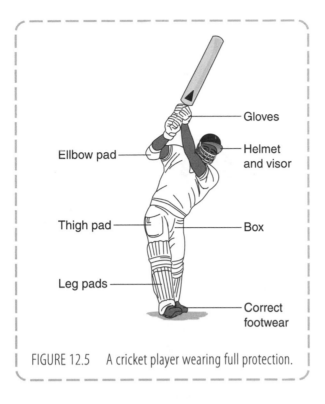

FIGURE 12.5   A cricket player wearing full protection.

- **Indoor courts**. Make sure there is no sweat or water on the floor, as this makes the surface slippery.
- **Outdoor pitches**. Make sure any glass or other debris is removed.
- **Outdoor pursuits**. Check the weather forecast to see if there is extreme heat, cold or fog.

The cricket player in figure 12.5 shows safe practice. Good practice before a cricket match includes warming up in the net wearing extra layers of clothing, practising skill requirements, preparing mentally for competition and wearing protective equipment such as pads, thigh pad, gloves, helmet, box and footwear.

Quick Test

1. What is a stitch?
2. What is a dislocation?
3. What is first aid?
4. Name three types of fracture.
5. Name the symptoms of a sprain.
6. What is the usual damage to cartilage at the knee joint?
7. What is a compound fracture?
8. Name three things to do immediately for a person with a suspected dislocated shoulder.
9. What is the long-term treatment for a broken bone?
10. What does RICE stand for?

From *GCSE Physical Education: A Revision Guide* by Tim Ferguson, 2002, Champaign, IL: Human Kinetics.

11. What is the treatment for cramp?
12. What is a pulled muscle?
13. What does elevating the injured part of the body help to do?
14. What is tendonitis?
15. How do stress fractures occur?

Examination Questions

The original numbering of the examination questions has been retained for ease of cross-referencing. Answers to these questions can be found at the end of the book.

MEG 1997 Paper 1 Q5

a. On an outdoor expedition an individual might suffer from exposure. What does this mean? (1)
d.   i. What is first aid? (1)
d.   ii. In an emergency what sequence of actions would a first aider carry out? (4)
e. What is stitch? How can it be treated or prevented? (8)

MEG 1997 Paper 1 Q6

b. Name one physical activity and write down the names of two pieces of correct safety equipment associated with that activity. (2)
c. What are the consequences of lack of water in physical activity? (4)
d. What are the probable causes of muscle cramp and how can it be treated? (5)

AQA(NEAB) 1999 QB2

People involved in playing sport are always under threat of injury. Outline a range of possible injuries arising from playing sport. Explain how the risks of injury might be reduced. (15)

AQA(NEAB) 1995 QA3

a. Give one example of a soft tissue injury. (1)
b. Give two symptoms of shock. (2)
c. What is the meaning of the following:
     i. Dehydration
     ii. Hypothermia
     iii. Hyperthermia
d. Injuries to bones occur in sport.
     i. Name one such injury.
     ii. What would be the first aid treatment? (4)
e. Choose a physical activity and outline the precautions, other than the wearing of protective clothing and equipment, that a performer can take to reduce the risk of injury. (5)

From *GCSE Physical Education: A Revision Guide* by Tim Ferguson, 2002, Champaign, IL: Human Kinetics. MEG questions reproduced with the kind permission of OCR. AQA(NEAB)/AQA examination questions are reproduced by permission of the Assessment and Qualifications Alliance.

AQA(SEG) 1998 Paper 2 Q2

 a. State what is meant by the term RICE when treating an injury which occurs during a physical activity. (4)

London 1999 Q37

Use the appropriate word from figure 12.6 to complete the following statements about sport injury:

 i. Tennis and golfer's elbow are _____ injuries.

 ii. Concussion results from injury to the _____.

 iii. Blisters are caused by _____ on the skin.

 iv. The blister _____ the injured area.

 v. A fracture is a break or _____ in a bone.

 vi. Dehydration is treated by giving the performer plenty of _____. (6)

Friction	Head	Scapula
Rest	Tendon	Brain	Protects
Crack	Water	Muscle sprain

FIGURE 12.6   London 1999 Q37—sport injury.

London 1998 Q38

Simon was watching a hockey match when one of the players slipped, fell over and injured his ankle.

 a. Apart from a sprain, what type of injury might they also have sustained? (1)

 b. If it was a sprain what treatment should be given to him? (4)

After the match Simon went back to the car park and found the umpire, apparently unconscious, by his car. Fortunately Simon was a first aider.

 c. What five steps should he follow? (5)

 d. If Simon found the umpire had no pulse, what should his next action be? (1)

From *GCSE Physical Education: A Revision Guide* by Tim Ferguson, 2002, Champaign, IL: Human Kinetics. AQA(SEG) examination question is reproduced by permission of the Assessment and Qualifications Alliance. London questions reprinted, by permission, from Edexcel Foundation.

PART III

Coaching and Performance

Part III of the revision guide outlines how athletes learn skills and how this knowledge can be applied to teaching. Chapter 13 examines how the brain processes information to create movement and how coaches apply this to training athletes. Chapter 14 looks at different personality types and the psychology behind the drive to succeed in sport.

CHAPTER 13

Skills and Information Processing

This chapter explains how skills are learnt in a sport and how having skills in a sport is different to having ability in a sport. To learn or teach skills, it is important to understand how information is processed or how it is passed from the senses, to the brain and to the muscles for movement to occur. The last part of this chapter explains how information processing occurs to improve skills in sport (see figure 13.1). Chapter 14 focuses on motivation and how it influences learning.

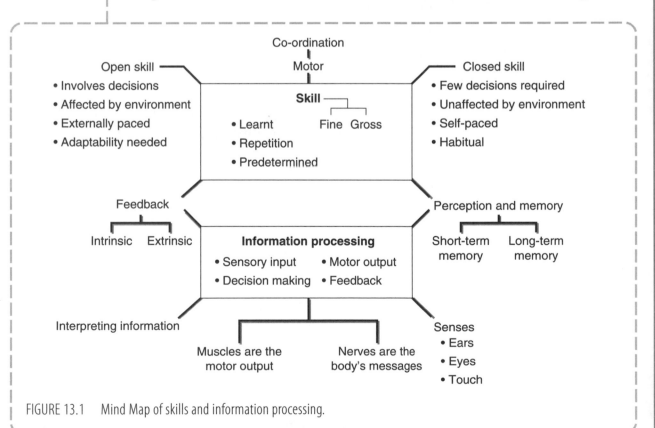

FIGURE 13.1   Mind Map of skills and information processing.

SKILLS

Think of a skill as co-ordinated, smooth and aesthetic (i.e., it looks good), goal directed (i.e., the brain consciously decides to carry a task out) and controlled.

Skills are learned; people are not born with skills. Skill means doing something efficiently and consistently and then having the ability to repeat it (e.g., in basketball, skill would mean scoring 8 out of 10 free throw shots, not 2 out of 10). Skill is predetermined. This means people decide in advance what they are going to do.

There are three types of skill.

1. **Cognitive skill** is intellectual skill (e.g., being good at maths).
2. **Perceptual skill** is observation, or being able to sense and interpret information (e.g., awareness of a games player).
3. **Perceptual-motor skill** is usually known as motor skill. This involves co-ordination (e.g., catching a ball). Motor skills are the skills associated with physical movement; they take time to learn and if they are not constantly practised can be forgotten. Motor skills are built up from a series of simple motor skills, forming complicated movement patterns. They can be gross or fine. Gross motor skill involves large muscle groups or limbs (e.g., throwing a javelin). Fine motor skill involves small muscle groups such as hands or fingers (e.g., achieving a spin action in cricket bowling).

All skills can be classified. This means taking a skill and putting it into a group. Skills are classified into three different continuums (areas). These three areas are the open or closed continuum, discrete or continuous continuum and the pacing continuum.

Open or Closed Continuum

The open or closed continuum is made up of open skills and closed skills (see figure 13.2). **Open skills** involve performing a skill in a situation that is constantly changing (e.g., making a pass in a game of football). Other key factors of open skills are that they

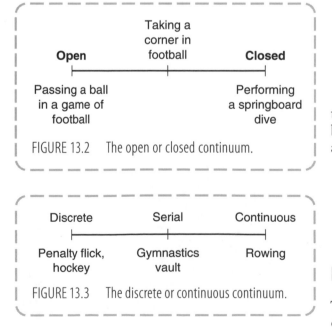

FIGURE 13.2 The open or closed continuum.

FIGURE 13.3 The discrete or continuous continuum.

- are affected by the sport environment,
- require adaptability,
- require that decisions be made, and
- are mostly externally paced.

Closed skills involve performing a skill in a situation that remains the same or stable (e.g., performing a basketball free shot). Other key factors of closed skills are that they

- are unaffected by the sport environment,
- are habitual,
- require few decisions, and
- are self-paced.

Discrete or Continuous Continuum

The discrete or continuous continuum is made up of discrete skills and continuous skills (see figure 13.3).

Discrete skills have a clear beginning and end (e.g., performing a basketball free throw shot is repeatable and must start again). It is a single, specific skill. **Serial skills** are made up of several discrete elements (e.g., in the triple jump the order of events is important). **Continuous skills** have no obvious beginning or end (e.g., cycling is timed by the performer, and consists of repetition of the same movement).

Pacing Continuum

The pacing continuum is made up of self-paced skills and externally paced skills (see figure 13.4). In **self-paced skills**, the performer controls the rate of execution. An example of a self-paced skill is when a player serves in tennis. In **externally paced skills**, the environment controls the timing of the skill (e.g., sailing).

Self-paced	Making a pass in rugby	Externally paced
Badminton serve		Wind surfing

FIGURE 13.4   The pacing continuum.

ABILITY

Ability is different from skill as a skill is something learnt. Ability is an innate physical characteristic which facilitates movement. Innate means a characteristic someone is born with (e.g., a rugby player may have the abilities of strength, speed and agility). Abilities are the building blocks of skill.

INFORMATION-PROCESSING MODEL

Now the difference between skills and ability has been explained, it is important to understand how the brain processes information to improve skills. Information processing is the structure and function of all the components that make up the process in the brain where information is received, dealt with and passed to our muscles for movement to be initiated (see figure 13.5). Figure 13.6 illustrates how someone processes information to catch a cricket ball. These are the steps of information processing:

- **Sensory input**. The senses (ears, eyes and touch) collect this information and send it to the brain.
- **Decision making**. The brain processes information about the cricket ball, makes a decision about which muscles are needed to move, and this decision is sent via the nerves to the muscles.
- **Motor output**. The muscles receive instructions about where and when to move, they carry out these orders and attempt to catch the ball.
- **Feedback**. Success or failure, all information about the catch or dropped catch is sent back to the brain, stored in the long-term memory so the player knows next time whether to adjust movement or repeat the same action. This is how skills are learned.

Ability is innate (people are born with it), the foundation of skills (it underpins skills development) and enduring (lasting). A simple way to remember the difference between skill and ability is:

Abilities + Practice + Experience or knowledge = Skilful performance.

Perception and Memory

Although the model has been simplified, it explains the route all information takes for our bodies to carry out a movement. There are two other elements to skill known as perception and memory.

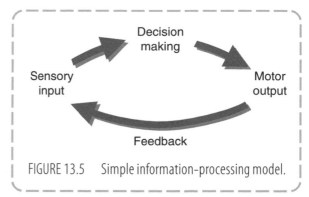

FIGURE 13.5   Simple information-processing model.

A cricket player uses a mixture of sensory input, decision making, motor output and feedback to catch a cricket ball.

He sees the ball, hears teammates shouting or hears how the ball sounded as it hit the bat. He calculates the flight of the ball and its speed. Then he decides how fast to move and where to stretch his arms and hands to catch the ball. He then feels the ball hit the palm of his hand.

Once the action is complete, the cricketer stores the result back in his long-term memory. He then uses his previous experiences to help him catch the ball next time.

FIGURE 13.6   Learning a skill: how to catch a cricket ball.

Perception occurs between the sensory input and the decision-making stage. It is the process of filtering the information coming in and picking out the important information. This is known as selective attention (e.g., goalkeepers focus on the ball coming towards them and ignore the background information such as the crowd or other players). This helps the keeper to concentrate on the speed and trajectory of the ball.

Memory could be considered to be in the centre of the model. At the decision-making stage, the brain refers to experience of the action. If the performer has any successful performances stored the brain refers to these and to any unsuccessful attempts. The brain uses this information to make the decision as to where to move.

There are two sections to the memory:

- **Short-term memory** (STM) has a limited capacity and can only store information for a short period of time. If the information stored in the STM is repeated and rehearsed it is passed into the long-term memory. If it is not rehearsed, this information is lost.
- **Long-term memory** (LTM) has an almost infinite capacity. Information can be stored in the long-term memory for a long time. Sometimes retrieval of information can be difficult if the information stored is not used often, but with a little practice it can be restored.

Feedback

The aim of feedback is to help improve the attempt at an action. Knowing whether a task was performed "right or wrong" helps the participant calculate how to do it right next time. Feedback can be intrinsic or extrinsic and can come from knowledge of results (KoR) or knowledge of performance (KoP):

- **KoR** is feedback that is specific about the success or failure of the action. For example, someone sees the penalty kick go in (intrinsic) or hears the crowd roar as it goes in (extrinsic).
- **KoP** is feedback informing the participant how the action felt. For example, they felt off-balance as they tried and failed to convert the rugby ball (intrinsic), or their coach told them that they did not have their head over the ball as they failed to convert the rugby ball (extrinsic).

Intrinsic (internal) feedback is information that performers feed themselves back. The performer may have felt the ball in her hands or watched the tennis serve go out. **Extrinsic (external) feedback** is information fed back to performers from someone else. The performer's teacher may tell her that she is gripping the racket incorrectly or that her serve went out.

The value of feedback should never be underestimated. Without feedback, it would not be possible to learn. A good coach has the ability to give athletes the correct amount of feedback in a form that is useful to them. The performer also needs to practise, using the feedback he is given. Feedback needs to be

- accurate;
- concise and to the point;
- immediate, not delayed; and
- in a form that is easily understood.

Reaction and Movement Time

Most sports require quick reactions. The ability to process information is the key to how quickly a performer reacts. To do a task quickly an individual must be able to react and move quickly. This is known as the response time.

Reaction time is the time taken from the signal to move until the first movement is initiated (e.g., the time from a 100m sprinter hearing the starter's gun to the point of first movement). **Movement time** is the time taken from first movement until last movement (e.g., the time from a 100m sprinter first starting to move out of the blocks to the point when the sprinter has crossed the finish line).

$$\text{Response time} = \text{Reaction time} + \text{Movement time}$$

Using the "grab-ruler" test is the best way of measuring response time without the use of expensive equipment. Also, because the "grab-ruler" test involves a small movement test, it is more indicative of someone's reactions, whereas performing a 100m sprint may only prove that the winner has a quick movement time not a quick reaction time (see chapter 8).

Quick Test

1. Define skill.
2. What does innate mean?
3. Name two abilities.
4. What are the three types of skill?
5. What is a gross motor skill?
6. Explain the open or closed continuum.
7. Name a discrete skill.
8. Name a self-paced skill.
9. Name a closed skill.
10. What is a perceptual-motor skill?
11. What is a fine motor skill?
12. Explain the pacing continuum.
13. Name a continuous skill.
14. Place the "triple jump" in all three continuums.
15. Name an open skill.

From *GCSE Physical Education: A Revision Guide* by Tim Ferguson, 2002, Champaign, IL: Human Kinetics.

16. Name two elements of the simple information-processing model.
17. What is selective attention?
18. Name two sensors in sensory input.
19. Explain the process of feedback.
20. What are the different memory stores?
21. What is extrinsic feedback?
22. What is KoR?
23. A coach informs her gymnast that she looked good although she didn't quite extend her toes. What type of feedback is this?
24. When should feedback be given?
25. What are the components of response time?
26. Name a way of measuring response time.
27. Define reaction time.
28. Explain the term "perception".
29. What information about a cricket ball someone is attempting to catch will the brain process?
30. What is motor output?
31. What is KoP?

Examination Questions

The original numbering of the examination questions has been retained for ease of cross-referencing. Answers to these questions can be found at the end of the book.

MEG 1998 Q9

Input (receiving information) is one component of the information-processing model. Name two other components. (2)

MEG 1998 QB1

c.   i. Explain what is meant by the term "closed skill". (2)

c.   ii. Give one example of a closed skill from two different physical activities. (2)

MEG 1997 Q3

b. Give two examples of feedback. (2)

d. Why do some skills in physical activity always have to be carried out in the same way and others do not? (5)

MEG 1997 Paper 1 Q4

a. What name is given to movements involving small muscle groups? (1)

b. What does being skilful mean? (2)

c. When performers receive too much information for them to cope with, performance declines. How can this be avoided? (4)

e. Describe extrinsic motivation and the effect performance awards might have. (5)

From *GCSE Physical Education: A Revision Guide* by Tim Ferguson, 2002, Champaign, IL: Human Kinetics. MEG questions reproduced with the kind permission of OCR.

MEG 1996 Paper 1 Q3

   a. What are motor skills? (1)

   b. Explain Poulton's open and closed skill continuum. (4)

   d. How should a performer practice open and closed skills? (5)

AQA(SEG) 1999 Paper 2 Q4

   d. Describe, and explain, what is meant by the term feedback in terms of skill acquisition. In your answer, give examples of how feedback can be used to improve performance in physical or game activity situations. (5)

AQA(NEAB) 1999 QB1

Define skill. Explain how skill affects performance, giving examples where necessary. (15)

AQA(NEAB) 1998 QA2

   b. Name two senses involved in physical activity. (2)

   c.   i. Why are quick reactions important?

   c.   ii. Give examples from two different physical activities. (3)

From *GCSE Physical Education: A Revision Guide* by Tim Ferguson, 2002, Champaign, IL: Human Kinetics. MEG questions reproduced with the kind permission of OCR. AQA(SEG) examination question and AQA(NEAB)/AQA examination questions are reproduced by permission of the Assessment and Qualifications Alliance.

CHAPTER 14

Psychology of Learning Sport

This chapter explains reasons people take part in sport to a high level, and it examines the drive behind winning (see figure 14.1). Personality type may also play a part in what sort of sport people take part in and how good at it they are. The latter part of the chapter discusses how anxiety affects arousal in sport and how traits such as aggression and assertion can affect performance. The chapters in part IV cover the social issues of sport, such as rules and organisations.

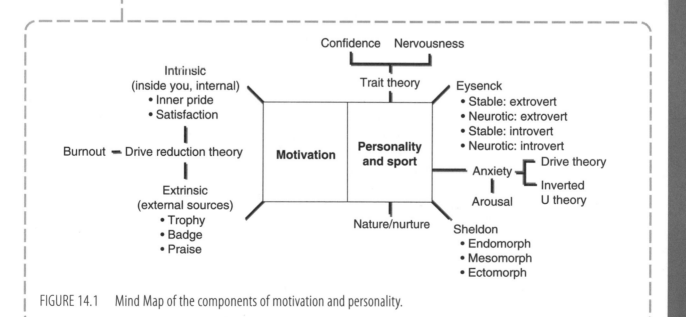

FIGURE 14.1   Mind Map of the components of motivation and personality.

MOTIVATED TO WIN

Motivation is goal-directed behaviour. It is the drive to achieve or the desire or will to win. This drive satisfies needs, which explains why people do what they do.

There are two types of motivation: intrinsic (internal) and extrinsic (external). **Intrinsic (internal) motivation** comes from inside. It is the inner pride and satisfaction people feel when completing a task. This is the best type of motivation and is the longest lasting. An example of this type of motivation is a novice (beginner) completing a marathon for their own sake.

Extrinsic (external) motivation comes from external sources such as winning trophies, badges, certificates or money. These are known as tangible rewards. Praise from coaches or friends and family is an external source, although this is non-tangible. Examples of extrinsic motivation include certificates for swimming 25m breaststroke or a professional footballer on a win bonus.

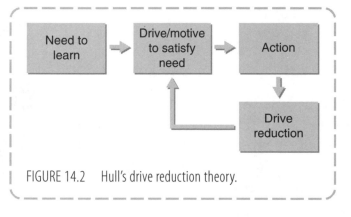

FIGURE 14.2   Hull's drive reduction theory.

Drive Reduction Theory

Drive reduction theory explains how the drive to succeed may be lost by people through success. In 1952 Hull worked on a theory as to why motivation can increase and decrease, shown in figure 14.2.

1. If people are given a task to do, a **need** for competence is generated, or there is a need to solve that problem.
2. The **need** in turn develops a drive and an incentive to learn to solve the problem.
3. People start to practise, and when **success** comes it is a perceived reward and acts as reinforcement.
4. The more often **success** comes and performance improves, the greater the drive reduction.
5. Eventually **motivation** is lost.

Burnout

Burnout can occur in young performers who have experienced a lot of competitive success; thus they gain tangible rewards easily. They lose their inner drive (internal motivation). Tangible rewards can be dangerous and should be used very carefully. Tangible rewards or external motivation are good to get people involved in an activity, but coaches and teachers should then try to get people involved in sport for their own sake (internal motivation).

PERSONALITY AND SPORT

"He was born a sprinter" is a frequently heard phrase, but what does it imply? And is there any truth in it? Everyone has his or her own distinctive personality. Many individual characteristics (traits) form someone's personality. Psychologists (people who study behaviour) have attempted to classify personalities into groups. Sport psychologists do this to see if particular personality types tend to choose certain sports and to see if different sports better suit certain personality types. Two attempts at classifying personality traits are explained later.

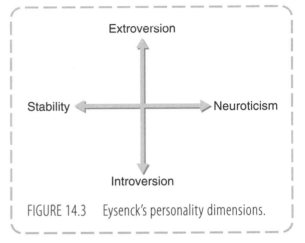

Personality is the individual's unique psychological make-up (Gill, 1986).

Trait Theory

Two psychologists, Eysenck (1947) and Cattell (1967), suggested that an individual personality is a collection of traits, or characteristics (for example, confidence or nervousness). Eysenck (1947) created a set of dimensions that everyone can be placed on (see figure 14.3).

Eysenck (1947) then conducted a questionnaire and from the results of these questions placed an individual within the dimensions. The theory was that if an individual demonstrated the trait of shyness then he or she would behave shyly in all settings such as the classroom, on the sport field, and in social situations. The flaw in this theory is that a person may act in a very assertive manner (one of her traits) whilst playing sport, yet never demonstrate this trait in any other social setting.

FIGURE 14.3   Eysenck's personality dimensions.

So far all work carried out on personality has not produced any conclusive evidence to show that a particular personality type is better suited to a particular sport.

Eysenck (1947) quotes four general personality types:

1. Stable / extrovert
2. Neurotic / extrovert
3. Stable / introvert
4. Neurotic / introvert

It is widely accepted that extroverts seem to prefer team games where there is a lot of interaction, whereas introverts prefer individual pursuits requiring sustained periods of practice and preparation. There are still exceptions to these rules.

Sheldon's (1940) Constitutional Theory

A second theory regarding personality was devised by Sheldon et al. (1940). His theory is based on an individual's somatotype (body shape and size, see chapter 9). Sheldon linked each of the three main somatotypes to a certain trait or temperament.

1. **Endomorph**: relaxed and happy
2. **Mesomorph**: aggressive and direct
3. **Ectomorph**: easily embarrassed, likes privacy

Further research into Sheldon's theory proved that his findings were unreliable and incorrect.

ANXIETY

Of more significance to a coach and athlete is the area of anxiety, and in particular competitive anxiety. Stress is "the non-specific response of the body to any demand made on it" (Seyle, 1976). Stress can make a person worry, which leads to a lack of concentration and a feeling of not being in control.

There are several factors that cause the athlete to become anxious. These factors are usually due to how an individual perceives a situation to be. This means anxiety is caused by the way an individual sees something rather than how the situation really is. Individuals may suffer from anxiety because of how they perceive

1. the demands of the situation (may be very high),
2. their own inability to cope with the situation, and
3. the expectations of those watching (e.g., their coach, the crowd, a scout, their friends and family, the opposition).

checkpoint

Two Types of Anxiety

There are two types of anxiety experienced by athletes:

✓ **State anxiety** is anxiety experienced by a specific situation (for example, a rugby player may only become anxious when faced with having to do a one-on-one tackle).

✓ **Trait anxiety** is anxiety experienced in all situations. It is a general disposition to be apprehensive. This is an individual trait or a person's more or less fixed behaviour.

Anxiety affects a person in two ways. **The cognitive affect is of the mind** and causes worry, irrational thoughts and results in a lack of concentration. **The somatic affect is of the body** and causes physiological changes such as sweating, raised heart rate and a release of adrenaline.

The reason that anxiety is important is that it has a very large effect on the performance of the athlete. Anxiety is closely related to arousal. If the coach is able to manipulate an athlete's arousal and anxiety levels then it is possible to improve performance.

EFFECTS OF AROUSAL

Arousal is an energized state of readiness to perform. If athletes are at their optimum arousal level then they are able to perform to their best ability. Arousal is the driving force behind motivation. Unfortunately, an athlete can become over-aroused as well as underaroused. The effects of arousal are therefore both positive and negative.

Arousal affects an individual in two ways. First there are physiological effects such as an increased heart rate, increased blood pressure, sweating, etc. Second, there are psychological effects such as worrying that lead to anxiety, which causes a loss of concentration. There are two theories regarding arousal.

Drive Theory

Hull (1943) developed an equation that explains the link between performance and drive (motivation) (see figure 14.4).

$$P = f(D+H) \qquad \text{Performance (P) is a function (f) of Drive (D) + Habit (H)}$$

Performance increases proportionally to the arousal levels. Drive theory has flaws and does not explain events that are often witnessed in sport. According to drive theory, if athletes are highly aroused then their performance will be at their own peak levels. Yet top athletes frequently make a simple mistake at a crucial point in their performance (for example, a tennis player at set or match point). If it were such a crucial point, the player would definitely be highly aroused and should be able to perform at a high level. This is known as the "bottling effect", whereby the athlete seems to have made a simple error due to overarousal, which affects concentration. This leads to a widely accepted theory regarding arousal and performance.

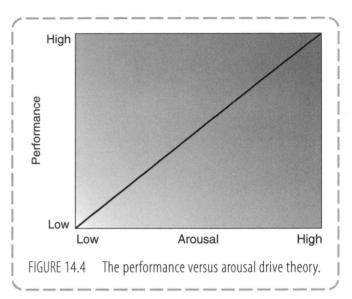

FIGURE 14.4   The performance versus arousal drive theory.

Inverted U Theory

Inverted U theory is so called because of the graph which shows the relationship between arousal levels and quality of performance (see figure 14.5).

According to the inverted U theory, performance increases with arousal but only to an optimum point (O), after which arousal starts to have a negative effect that leads to anxiety. Everyone is different, so therefore the optimum point will vary from one person to another. Inverted U theory also states that depending on the nature of the task or skill being attempted the arousal level will have a different effect on performance.

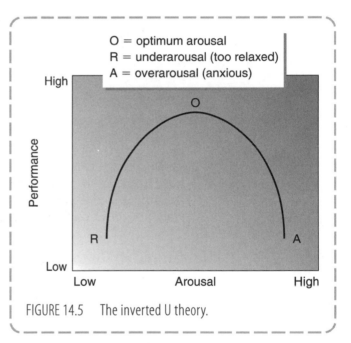

O = optimum arousal
R = underarousal (too relaxed)
A = overarousal (anxious)

FIGURE 14.5   The inverted U theory.

1. Gross skills (skills involving large muscle groups) require high arousal levels for increased performance (e.g., a tackle in rugby).

2. Fine skills (skills involving small muscle groups) require low arousal levels for increased performance (e.g., a shot in snooker).

3. Complex skills (skills needing more attention) require low arousal levels for increased performance (e.g., a gymnastic floor routine).

4. Simple skills (skills needing little attention) can tolerate high arousal levels for increased performance (e.g., a bench press).

Inverted U theory links arousal with personality, suggesting that introverts and extroverts can cope with different arousal levels. Extroverts can tolerate more excitement and can therefore concentrate whilst highly aroused, whilst introverts only require a small amount of excitement to become motivated and so perform better at lower levels of arousal. Finally a skilled performer (expert) can also cope with high arousal levels, whereas novices (unskilled) need to concentrate on the task they are doing and so require low levels of arousal only. High arousal levels for novices will affect their concentration.

ATTITUDES

The promotion of a positive attitude is important in sport. Coaches try to instil or develop a positive attitude to sport, which encourages individuals to maintain levels of skill and fitness. Attitudes are similar to traits. They are stable and enduring, but they are also different in that they are directed at an attitude object. This means they are specific.

Attitude has been defined as a permanent feeling or thought about a person, object or event. The theory behind attitudes is based on three components. This is known as the "triadic model".

1. The **cognitive component** (beliefs) is what a person thinks about another person, object or event (for example, "running ruins the joints"). Through the cognitive component, people learn from significant others (such as teachers, parents or coaches) about attitude objects.
2. The **affective component** (emotions) is how a person feels towards another person, object or event (for example, "he enjoys running"). Through the affective component of the triadic model, people learn to associate particular feelings with an attitude object. These feelings come from past experiences such as success and failure or pleasure and pain.
3. The **behavioural component** is what a person does, how they act regarding another person, object or event (for example, "he goes running three times a week"). The behavioural component is simply a person's actions towards running.

Attitudes can be positive or negative and are formed through either the cognitive or affective component of the triadic model. To illustrate this, consider the example of weight training (the attitude subject). From significant others a person will have been taught that weight training is good for them, but they may dislike weight training and find it boring, although they do think that a muscular physique looks good. Their behaviour towards weight training is to go three times a week.

Cognitive Dissonance

Challenging one of the attitude components creates conflict. For example, a person believes that everyone should exercise three times a week but they do not intend to exercise this week. This would create conflict. The dissonance (conflict) is reduced in several ways.

1. Change the cognitive element (i.e., people should exercise three times a week but only if they have time).
2. Reduce the importance of the cognitive element (i.e., exercise is not as important as I am a young, healthy person).
3. Seek additional cognitive elements (i.e., exercise causes injury).

Changing Attitudes

Using cognitive dissonance, a coach can influence attitude by creating opposing beliefs. For example, a footballer believes in fitness but thinks that dancers are effeminate; the coach tells his players that dancers are amongst the fittest people

TABLE 14.1 Strategies to Change Attitudes	
Strategies to change attitudes	**Examples of attitudes in sport**
Making it fun and enjoyable	Girls can't throw
Give easy success at first	White people can't jump
Use role models	Men are no good at aerobics
Highlight the benefits to health and fitness through education	Black people are poor swimmers

and that dancing is a real challenge. The players then try dance as a form of keeping fit (see table 14.1).

AGGRESSION VERSUS ASSERTION

Aggression is directed with intent to injure. It must also be outside of the rules of the game. Boxing is not an example of aggression as it is within the rules for opponents to punch each other. Aggression can be verbal, and this is often evidenced within sport. A good example of verbal aggression is "sledging" in cricket. Often a wicket keeper sledges in an attempt to put off the batsman.

Consider a tackle in rugby. If a player makes a very hard but legal tackle in rugby, this is legal and not an act of aggression. This is called being assertive. Assertion is forceful, decisive play within the rules of the game. If the tackle was high then it would be called aggression.

There are several types of aggression, but it is important to consider whether an individual is born aggressive or has learned to be aggressive. This argument is the nature versus nurture argument.

> Aggression is defined as "any form of behaviour directed towards the goal of harming or injuring another living being who is motivated to avoid such behaviour" (Baron, 1977).

checkpoint
Born Aggressive

✓ People are born with the traits that mean they act aggressively. Aggression is innate (born with) and an aggressive response is triggered by frustrating circumstances (for example, when a footballer is fouled but the referee does not give it. The player then makes an immediate foul on the nearest opponent).

checkpoint
Learnt Aggression

✓ Learnt aggression is based on social learning theory (Bandura, 1969) Aggression is learned from significant others (for example, a coach continually applauds someone for making bad tackles, telling him that his illegal challenge saved a goal).

 *Quick Test*

1. What are the two types of motivation?
2. Define the term "motivation".
3. Sum up drive reduction theory.
4. What is extrinsic motivation?
5. What is a tangible reward?
6. Which type of motivation is better in the long term?
7. Why is the coach interested in motivation?
8. Is praise from family or friends a form of motivation?
9. Give an example of a tangible reward given to a novice.
10. Give an example of a tangible reward given to a professional footballer.
11. Are intrinsic and internal motivation the same?
12. The more success comes and performance improves, the greater the drive reduction. True or False?
13. When performing, is success perceived as a reward?
14. Name three ways to help motivate someone.

Examination Questions

The original numbering of the examination questions has been retained for ease of cross-referencing. Answers to these questions can be found at the end of the book.

MEG 1999 QB1

e. "I have an incredible desire and ambition to succeed that has kept me going throughout my career. It has never left me and it is probably my greatest asset" (top performer in 1997).

Describe how this person, or any other performer, could make sure the desire (motivation) to do well stays with them. (8)

MEG 1998 QB2

e. i. Explain what is meant by the term "motivation". (1)

e. ii. Describe the different ways in which performers can be motivated to raise their levels of performance in physical activity. (7)

From *GCSE Physical Education: A Revision Guide* by Tim Ferguson, 2002, Champaign, IL: Human Kinetics. MEG questions reproduced with the kind permission of OCR.

PART IV

Sport in Society

Part IV examines the importance of sport in society and the effect society has on sport. Chapter 15 explains why sport needs rules and why society needs to organise sport so that rules can be applied easily throughout that sport at all levels. Chapter 16 describes where money goes in sport and how this money is used to provide better facilities to encourage high-level athletes. Chapters 17 and 18 look at the detrimental effect society has on sport. Chapter 17 outlines how the drive to succeed in sport can encourage athletes to take banned drugs to enhance their performance. Chapter 18 debates other issues such as politics, race and women in sport.

CHAPTER 15

Rules and Organisation of Sport

To function effectively and efficiently, sport needs to be structured in such a way that participants at all levels receive the benefit of support and guidance from a governing body. This chapter explains how sport is ruled and officiated; it then explains how sport is structured and run in the UK and how organising bodies enforce rules (see figure 15.1). Without these factors, sport would be disorganised, inconsistent and unprofessional. By understanding how sport is organised in the UK, it is possible to see how this eventually affects participation. These factors, combined with information on finance and facilities in the next chapter, make it possible to build a clear picture of how organisation, facilities and participation all intertwine to form the backbone of sport in society.

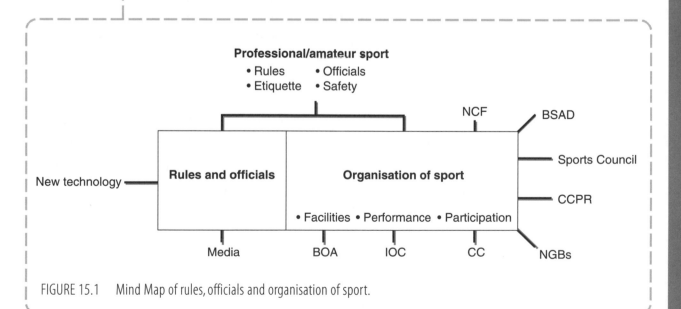

FIGURE 15.1   Mind Map of rules, officials and organisation of sport.

RULES

Almost all physical activities have rules (also known as laws or regulations). These rules cover how the activity should be carried out or played.

Each activity has a ruling body, which is the organisation that makes up the rules for that particular sport. For example, football has the Football Association; netball has the All England Netball Association; tennis has the Lawn Tennis Association; and basketball has the English Basketball Association.

Rules are necessary for

1. organisation of the sport (e.g., to sort out who plays in which division of a league),

2. administration of the sport (e.g., to arrange fixtures),

3. safety (e.g., not allowing high tackles in rugby), and

4. enjoyment (making a sport more entertaining for spectators).

checkpoint

Rules in Sport

There are many reasons rules have been developed in sport. The following list explains some of the reasons.

✓ Most rules have developed over the decades, evolving from very basic rules of some primitive games.

✓ Most rules are changed or developed to ensure safety and fair play and to increase the popularity of the sport. With professional sport becoming more important financially and socially, there is a greater desire for success. This has resulted in teams or coaches employing a greater variety of tactics to win at all costs.

✓ Changes are often made for big tournaments or events. There was a time that goalkeepers (in football) were allowed to pick up the ball from a back pass. This was altered to prevent time wasting.

✓ Rule changes are often tried out in smaller leagues first to see if they work. The football league in the Channel Islands introduced a rule to move a free kick back ten metres if a player complains (dissent) to the referee. It worked successfully, and this rule has been introduced into the major European football leagues. This rule came from rugby union, where it was successful in maintaining players' respect for officials.

If competitors do not obey rules, they are punished. Punishments can be in the form of expulsion from the game or event, suspension from subsequent games or events, a fine or a ban. A fine may be a fixed amount set by the governing body or a deduction in wages set by the club. For example, a club may deduct a week's or month's worth of wages from a player. A ban is usually set by the governing body. This could last for one or two years or may be permanent.

Some sports have other punishments:

• Football clubs have league points docked.

• Cricket teams have "overs" taken from them in limited overs cricket for slow bowling.

• Motor racing constructors or drivers may have points deducted for cheating. This happens if they use the wrong tyres or fuel type.

Within the different games there are differing levels of punishment according to the severity of the offence, which eventually lead to expulsion. For example, basketball players accumulate fouls (after five fouls they have to go off), rugby players can be "sin-binned" and then sent off, and football players are shown first a yellow and then a red card.

ETIQUETTE

Etiquette is a conventional rule, form of behaviour or moral or social rule that is not enforceable but is expected. In sport, etiquette is known as fair play. These social rules are not written down but are expected of competitors; if they are not observed, players can become unpopular. Incidents of poor etiquette become highly talked about sporting moments. The following are examples of etiquette:

- Rugby players shaking hands and forming a tunnel for their opponents to walk through.
- Footballers kicking the ball out of play if an opponent is injured. To restart, the ball is then thrown back to the opposition.
- In racket sports, players call their own fouls for shots that are double hits.

FACTS ABOUT OFFICIALS

Officials are the people who enforce (carry out) the rules for each sport and include referees, judges, umpires, linesmen, timekeepers, scorers, referees' assistants and, more recently, video referees.

The number of officials involved varies according to the sport. Some sports are relatively easy to officiate and only have two or three officials, whereas other sports require many more officials. Some officials have different names because of the job they do (for example, a "timekeeper" is an official who keeps time).

In general there are two groups of officials. **Senior officials** have different names but do the same job. They are the most visible of all officials because they are usually seen or heard on the field of play. Officials in charge of a competition include **referees**, **umpires** and **judges. Junior officials** are often unseen because they work behind the scenes. Junior officials usually outnumber the senior officials and their jobs are as crucial to running the sport. Officials that support the referee, umpire or judge include referees' assistants, linesmen, scorers and timekeepers.

Both sets of officials have to work together closely to officiate the activity in an organised and consistent manner. These officials are required to have a complete understanding of the rules (laws and regulations). They must be able to interpret these rules and enforce them as set out by the governing body. Rules are constantly changing, as are the expectations of players, coaches and spectators. Officials must keep ahead of these expectations.

checkpoint

Qualities of Officials

Officials need certain qualities to officiate a sport. These qualities are described in the following list.

✓ **Experience and knowledge of the sport**. Officials need knowledge about rules and should be experienced in methods of play. It would be unacceptable for the officials to stop an activity to check the rule book. All officials should work together to enforce rules.

✓ **Quick, decisive qualities**. Often officials only get a quick glance at a point in the game or activity that requires a decision to be made. Their decision can be crucial to the outcome. Officials must make a decision quickly and then stick to that decision.

✓ **Consistent and unbiased approach**. Officials must be unbiased (this means they cannot favour one team or player). They must also be consistent. If they can maintain consistency then players and spectators can see a fair and unbiased approach to the sport.

✓ **Good physical condition**. Any official on the field of play must be able to keep up with the action. Some officials are required to maintain a certain fitness level. The governing body tests fitness. It is also important for officials to have good eyesight and good hearing.

Payment for Officials

In some sports at the top level, officials are paid a lot of money. Currently the Football Association is considering making its referees professional. At amateur level, officials are not paid; they do the job because they love the sport.

Problems Associated With Officiating

Sport in general is gaining more prestige, increasing in popularity and becoming important to the nation. Often politicians quote the feel-good factor associated with a particular sporting success. It is widely accepted that success in important sporting events such as the Olympics or a world cup can lift a nation's spirits.

Because of the increasing importance of sport, problems encountered by officials are also increasing. For example, football is now an industry which involves vast sums of money. This means that in football, officials are in the spotlight whether they like it or not. The following are four reasons officials are under so much pressure:

1. Constantly changing rules are enforced to make sport more exciting for the spectator.
2. Minute differences in the quality of teams' or players' performance means that often a referee's decision can alter the outcome of the game.
3. Media analysis of every facet of an event puts every decision made by officials under the spotlight.
4. The outcome of an event is now worth millions of pounds and can involve people's livelihoods.

These reasons add to the pressure on officials. Whatever decision an official makes, someone will be unhappy about it. Officials are often cast as scapegoats.

New Technology

Because of the importance of sport and the amount of media scrutiny it undergoes, technology is being introduced into sport to assist officials. In recent years, there

Cricket umpires have their decisions scrutinised by TV pundits with the use of countless video playbacks, yet they only see every delivery once, at full speed, before making their decision. They are usually right, but occasionally they make mistakes. Pressure has increased on them because of the advances in camera technology. Now the viewer at home gets a better view than the umpire of any possible leg before wicket (LBW) decision.

have been advances to help officials in almost all sports. These include general improvements such as better timing devices to assist timekeepers. More significant advances in cricket include a third umpire, who can be called on to decide on run outs using video playback. In rugby league there is a video referee, who is called on to determine whether a try was scored. In the 1999–2000 football season, referees were "wired up" to their assistants to communicate more clearly. Eventually this communication will be available to the media so that they can hear what decisions have been made. The introduction of new technology is an attempt to reduce the number of officials' mistakes.

GOVERNING BODIES OF SPORT

There are a number of organisations that combine to help run sport in this country. Without these organisations controlling sport, there would be no improvements to rules, officiating would never improve and sport would be disorganised. The main organisations behind sport are the national governing bodies (NGBs), the UK Sports Council and its four national councils, and the Central Council for Physical Recreation (CCPR). Other organisations are the National Coaching Foundation (NCF), International Olympic Committee (IOC), British Olympic Association (BOA), British Sports Association for the Disabled (BSAD) and the Countryside Commission (CC). All these organisations function at one or more of the following levels of sport:

- International (e.g., the IOC)
- National (e.g., the BOA selecting a team)
- Regional (e.g., a NGB organising a league)
- Local (e.g., the NCF running courses)

National Governing Bodies

NGBs are responsible for running individual sports; for example, the HA (Hockey Association) runs all matters related to hockey. The following are responsibilities of NGBs:

1. Defining the rules, providing and training referees to uphold the rules
2. Organising leagues and other competitions or fixtures
3. Settling disputes between players, coaches, clubs and officials
4. Coaching, organising awards, and training coaches and officials
5. Promotion at all levels to increase participation and spectator numbers
6. Selection of representative teams for international competitions

NGBs need to find money to pay for the areas they are responsible for. Their money comes from various sources:

- Sports Council (SC) grants, such as the lottery fund
- Media rights where TV channels pay to televise matches
- Corporate sponsorship, such as the Nat West cup in cricket
- Ticket sales for events (80,000 watch most England football home games)
- Membership fees

Sports Council

The Sports Council (SC) was set up in 1972 to meet four aims. The first aim was to increase participation in sport and physical recreation. This was tackled in several ways, such as running campaigns (e.g., Sport For All Disabled People in 1980/1981, 50+ All to Play For in 1983/1984 and Ever Thought of Sport in 1985/1986). The SC also funded development staff such as a netball development officer. They focused on sport in school, as research has shown that if children play sport in school they are more likely to continue sport later in life. The SC helps schools' provision of coaches and training and encourages links with clubs.

The SC's second aim was to increase the quality and quantity of sport facilities. They did this through grants from the Lottery Sports Fund to help fund new facilities, improve existing facilities and provide equipment. They also provided National Sports Centres to become centres of excellence for all sport (see chapter 16 for more information).

Third, the SC aimed to increase the standards of performance in sport. They provided coaching, facilities, opportunities and education to help develop excellence in sport.

Finally, the SC provides information about all aspects of sport. This helps people's understanding of the social importance and value of sport and increases awareness of the health implications of sport.

The SC works closely with the Central Council for Physical Recreation (CCPR) and NGBs. It can be broken down into five components:

1. UK Sports Council, which is concerned with élite sport in the UK. The UK Sports Council's mission is "to help our athletes become winners". The UK Sports Council has four key directorates, including International Relations and Major Events, Ethics and Anti-Doping, Producing Winners and UK Sports Institute.
2. SC for England.
3. SC for Scotland.
4. SC for Northern Ireland.
5. SC for Wales.

The main aim of all four home countries' Sports Councils is to concentrate on sport for all through offering **participation**, **facilities**, **performance** and **information.**

Central Council for Physical Recreation

The CCPR has three main aims. These are to improve and develop sport and physical recreation, support and guide the governing bodies of sport, and act as an advisory body to the Sports Council.

The CCPR requires funds to promote British sport, provide legal and financial advice and represent sporting bodies in all issues related to sport. The CCPR consists of over 260 national sport organisations representing élite sportsmen and women. CCPR funding comes from corporate sponsorship, Sports Council grants and donations from its members.

National Coaching Foundation

The NCF was set up to provide a wide range of coaching, education and training services to the NGBs. The NCF works with the CCPR and the SC to maintain and improve the quality of coaching throughout sport.

International Olympic Committee

The IOC is in charge of the Olympic movement. Its main functions are to select hosts for the Olympic Games, liaise with the international governing bodies regarding rules and take action against drugs in sport.

British Olympic Association

The BOA is a member of the IOC. Its main roles include raising money for British athletes, selecting the British team and working with the IOC and NGBs to improve and prepare athletes.

British Sports Association for the Disabled

The BSAD provides assistance for all disabled people who wish to take part in sport. It provides financial support, expert coaching, tuition, facilities and equipment for disabled athletes. The BSAD also liaises with NGBs, the CCPR and the SC. Another of its roles is to select the British team for the Paralympics.

Countryside Commission

The CC is responsible for the conservation of the countryside for sport. Many sports, such as climbing and sailing, take place in the countryside. The CC's main aims are to improve and extend opportunities for people to enjoy the countryside. It does this by promoting outdoor recreation, providing grants for facilities and advice and expertise about the countryside. This helps people understand more about the countryside and what it has to offer.

Quick Test

1. Name three national governing bodies.
2. What does NCF stand for?
3. What does CCPR stand for?
4. Give two aims of the Sports Council.
5. Give two responsibilities of a national governing body.
6. Give two aims of the CCPR.
7. Where do national governing bodies get their money?
8. Name two things the Sports Council spends its money on.
9. Name one source of money for the CCPR.
10. How is the Sports Council broken down?
11. The UK Sports Council is more concerned with élite sport in the UK. True or False?
12. The UK Sports Council has four key directorates. Name two of them.
13. The Sports Council is keen to promote sport in school. Why?
14. The Sports Council acts as an advisory body to the CCPR. True or False?

From *GCSE Physical Education: A Revision Guide* by Tim Ferguson, 2002, Champaign, IL: Human Kinetics.

15. Name three different types of official.
16. Give two other names for rules.
17. Give an example of etiquette in sport.
18. Who makes up the rules in sport?
19. Give three punishments that can be given to players whilst they are competing.
20. Give three punishments that can be given to sportspersons after a competition or event.
21. Name two rule changes to any sport.
22. Give two examples of technology being used to assist officials.
23. What is etiquette?
24. Give two reasons why rules are necessary.
25. Who defines the rules for football and tennis in England?
26. Give two reasons why rules have changed in recent years.

Examination Questions

The original numbering of the examination questions has been retained for ease of cross-referencing. Answers to these questions can be found at the end of the book.

MEG 1999 QB3

e. The reasons and motives for participation in physical activity come from the individual.

Use figure 15.2 to help you describe the physical and social benefits of participating in physical activity during recreation and leisure time. (8)

FIGURE 15.2   MEG 1999 QB3—benefits of participating in physical activity.

MEG 1995 Paper 2 Q2

a. Choose one of the following national governing bodies of sport and write down its full name:
   i. ASA
   ii. FA
   iii. LTA
   iv. BAGA (1)

c. Identify the aims of the Sports Council. (4)

d. State how parents and the school can help develop a child's sporting talent. (5)

e. Define leisure and then explain leisure trends in recent years. (8)

AQA(NEAB) 1999 QA6

d. Explain how the national governing bodies promote sport and physical activity. (4)

AQA(NEAB) 1998 QA6

a. What do the initials NCF represent? (1)

From *GCSE Physical Education: A Revision Guide* by Tim Ferguson, 2002, Champaign, IL: Human Kinetics. MEG questions reproduced with the kind permission of OCR. AQA(NEAB)/AQA examination questions are reproduced by permission of the Assessment and Qualifications Alliance.

e. The Sports Council promotes sport and physical activity in different ways. How is this done? (5)

AQA(NEAB) 1997 QB3

"Behave or be banned". Use examples from different sports to show how and why foul behaviour on or off the field is punished. (15)

AQA(NEAB) 1995 QA6

d. Many of the laws and rules of a sport aim to ensure safety. Explain how laws and rules promote safe play. (4)

e. The results of some sports depend upon judgements by officials. Give examples to show how officials attempt to achieve fair results. (5)

AQA(SEG) 1998 Paper 2 Q5

c. Spectators are important at many sporting events. Describe the following:

i. three ways in which they can be of benefit to performers or organisers, and (3)

ii. three ways in which they can disrupt or cause problems for organisers. (3)

AQA(SEG) 1997 Paper 2 Q1

a. For a named activity

i. name the official in charge, (1)

ii. state three responsibilities of the official, and (3)

iii. name two items the official would need during the game. (2)

AQA(SEG) 1996 Paper 2 Q1

a. Name one activity and draw a diagram of its playing area. On this diagram, name four different pitch or court markings. (4)

b. For the same named activity

i. explain one rule or regulation, and (2)

ii. describe what action is taken by the official in charge if this rule or regulation is broken. (2)

From *GCSE Physical Education: A Revision Guide* by Tim Ferguson, 2002, Champaign, IL: Human Kinetics. AQA(NEAB)/AQA examination questions and AQA(SEG) examination questions are reproduced by permission of the Assessment and Qualifications Alliance.

CHAPTER 16

Finance and Facilities

Catering for sport participants of all levels involves a large amount of funding to provide adequate facilities and equipment for all activities to take place. This chapter explores the way money is distributed in sport and explains what sort of facilities need funding (see figure 16.1). Finally, the chapter looks at how money has encouraged the development of technology in sport. Chapter 17 examines how the desire for money and success leads people to cheat to become the best in their sport.

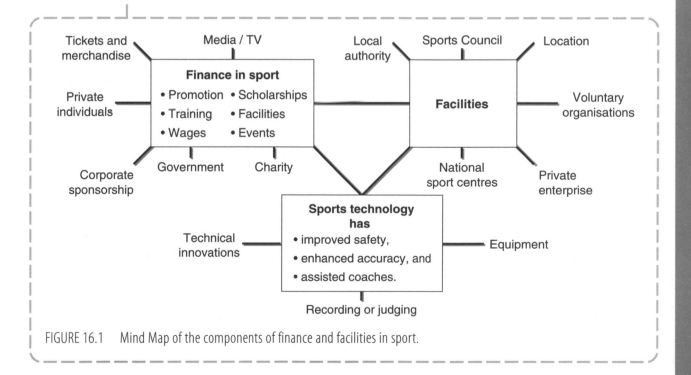

FIGURE 16.1   Mind Map of the components of finance and facilities in sport.

FINANCE IN SPORT

Sport receives money from several different sources. The **government** provides some funding via local councils from income tax, VAT and gambling tax. The National Lottery also provides the government with an income. The Sports Council distributes this money.

Corporate sponsorship (e.g., Cornhill Insurance sponsoring the cricket test series) provides some funding for sport, and TV or radio stations (**media**) will pay to obtain the broadcasting rights for certain games or matches. Some money may also come from **private individuals**. For example, Alan Sugar owns Tottenham HFC. Often, wealthy people buy large sport clubs because they love the sport rather than for financial gain.

Tickets and merchandise provide another source of revenue. Manchester United makes more money from selling replica shirts than from spectators at Old Trafford. This is possible because the club has a worldwide following. Most sport organisations depend heavily on paying spectators.

Finally, most amateur clubs depend on fund raising and donations (**charity**) to function. Most amateur teams have events such as annual raffles (with prizes donated) and other methods of raising money.

Where the Money Goes

Money in sport goes towards the following:

- **Promotion** or advertising the sport to encourage people to play, watch or help organise.
- **Facilities** at the top level of sport are hi-tech, whilst at amateur level facilities are more basic comprising a clubhouse or pitch.
- **Wages** of professionals are often high and support staff, such as physiotherapists, administration staff, groundsmen and coaching staff also need paying.
- **Scholarships** run by sport organisations. Schemes are set up to fund talented athletes of the future. As a future investment, football clubs often provide support if they spot talent at an early age.
- **Training** for coaches, officials and other support staff has to be funded.
- **Shareholders** invest money in professional clubs hoping for a return on this money. Manchester United is a limited company, and often decisions made by the club are purely financial.
- **Running events** requires money for prizes and other costs such as ticketing and promotion.

As mentioned earlier, some money in sport pays performers' wages. The amount performers earn depends on the sport and level they play at. It is important to understand the differences between amateur and professional sport before looking further at money in sport.

Professional and Amateur Sport

All sport started as amateur, but gradually money became more important. This created opportunities for those good at sport to make a living out of it. Both amateur

TABLE 16.1	Differences Between Amateurs and Professionals	
Area	**Amateur**	**Professional**
Definition	Someone who does not get paid for playing their sport.	Someone who plays sport full time; it is their job, they get paid for it.
Example	Swimming is an amateur sport. Playing football at amateur level for your local village team.	Cricket, tennis and almost every sport has some professional athletes; even obscure sports such as rock climbing have a few paid professionals.
Why do they do it?	For the satisfaction and enjoyment of taking part in the activity. People enjoy the challenge of competing against others; this involves training in their own time (after work and on weekends).	To earn a living, often professionals start in a sport because of the enjoyment they get from taking part. When they discover they are good, the rewards from turning professional are often high in terms of money, fame and glamour.
Problems	Amateurs choose to play when and where they want, but often are inhibited by lack of time or money. To achieve a high level of performance as an amateur requires a lot of dedication and devotion, which are often restricted due to other life commitments.	Professionals are employed athletes; they often work under contract and so have to fulfil commitments to their club or team and the public. Being in the limelight as a professional sportsperson is very stressful. With the ever-increasing media pressure that often intrudes into athletes' personal lives, the pressure to win and maintain form can lead professionals to perform poorly, cheat, lose motivation or confidence and act in an unsporting manner on the field (sometimes illegally off the field).

and professional players compete in sport, but have different reasons for competing and receive different financial support for competing (see table 16.1).

Olympic Ideal

The Olympic ideal brings the best athletes from around the world to compete in a friendly atmosphere to unite the world through friendship. The modern Olympics was originally designed for amateurs only, but today, this is not the case. Some competitors come from an amateur background such as rowing or boxing, yet there are also professionals who compete, such as tennis players or footballers. Originally competitors had to be amateurs but they avoided this by having trust funds or grants awarded to them. Some athletes competed for gifts, such as houses or cars. Now the Olympics is changing, and different sports are gradually allowing professionals to compete, such as football. Other sports such as boxing still only allow amateurs to compete.

Rugby League and Rugby Union

Originally there was only one game of rugby, called rugby union. In 1895, 22 teams in the North of England broke away from the rugby union, forming their own league. This happened because the players wanted to be paid money they missed from lost earnings. The league then gradually changed the rules over time to make it more entertaining. The players depended on spectators paying to watch, and used this money to replace lost earnings. Eventually rugby league became a full-time, professional game, whereas rugby union remained amateur. Recently, rugby union turned professional approximately 100 years after rugby league was introduced.

Scholarships

Scholarships, widespread in the American universities, are funds set up for individuals who excel in sport. They allow athletes to continue formal education whilst training in a lifestyle similar to a professional. The American college system provides the main arena for new, talented athletes soon to turn professional and involves a system of corporate sponsorship. In the UK, a few universities offer small sport scholarships to talented athletes. Because this financial aid is so small, the UK loses good athletes because they cannot fund academic qualifications and maintain a high level of training.

Media and Finance

The main forms of media are television, radio and the newspapers. Other forms of media include films, magazines, the Internet and books. The media offers advantages and disadvantages to sport.

checkpoint

Advantages of Media

1. Money—for most sport the largest part of their income comes from broadcasting rights.

2. Profile—with sport gaining more media interest, the profile of the sport, club, coaching staff and athletes is increased. This helps to maintain or increase the participation of the masses in sport.

3. Sponsorship—with a higher media profile, sport has more opportunity to gain bigger, more lucrative sponsorship deals (see the next section on sponsorship).

4. Personality—sport stars are "made" by the media. The media guides nations in finding heroes. Sport stars often go on to careers in a variety of fields. For example, Gary Lineker was a football player and is now a TV pundit, Vinnie Jones was a football player and is now a film star and Seb Coe was a long-distance runner and is now a politician.

5. Analysis—the media help sport analysis. People in sport use this information to improve coaching and teaching.

6. Technology—the media have played a major role in several areas of sport technology (see the next section on sport technology).

checkpoint

Disadvantages of Media

1. Lack of coverage—reduced or removed coverage of a sport can be damaging. Sport goes in and out of fashion and the media play a part in making sport fashionable or unfashionable.

2. Criticism—members of the media often take sport analysis too far. They find mistakes by officials and magnify them as controversy helps to sell their programme.

3. Pressure—sport stars are put under media pressure when the media probe into athletes' private lives. Pressure also affects action on the field as the media are constantly looking for incidents that may make headlines.

4. Rewards—the incentives to perform well are massive. Athletes in the spotlight often resort to foul play or underperform because of the importance of an event.

Sport Versus the Media

The relationship between sport and the media is complex. Both sides gain from the other, but often they are embroiled in conflict about money and coverage. The media usually pays sport for the right to cover an event or fixture and then makes a profit by selling this event to the public. The more contentious issues between sport and the media include intrusion and sponsorship.

Media Intrusion

The media pays money to cover sport and consequently demands things in return. Media companies insist on interviewing coaching staff at the end of premier league matches. Cameras intrude into the changing rooms of the rugby super league teams at half time. Members of the media try to dictate the timing of events to fit in with preferred broadcasting times. They pressure governing bodies to alter rules. Large media companies buy shares in premiership clubs so that they can have more say in future negotiations.

Sponsorship

Sponsorship forms another part of sport income. The media have helped encourage sponsorship by increased coverage. Companies find sport sponsorship attractive as millions of people watch various sporting events.

Companies can sponsor different groups, people or events. Individual athletes may have a sponsor (e.g., Michael Jordan is sponsored by Nike). The more successful athletes are, the larger the sponsorship deal. Some companies sponsor entire clubs or teams, such as Sharp sponsoring Manchester United. Companies often pay large amounts of money to teams to be the sole sponsor.

Sponsorship does not stop here. Actual events can be sponsored. For example, the Olympics have been sponsored by Mars and Coca-Cola although the hosts are forever finding other sponsors wanting to pay more to be associated with an event like the Olympics. Cornhill Insurance sponsors the England Test series, Green Flag likewise sponsors the England Football Team. Companies pay large amounts of money to be associated with success.

Sport itself may be sponsored. This is beneficial to more people as money is spread through the different levels of sport.

checkpoint

Forms of Sponsorship

For successful athletes, sponsorship usually comes in the form of money, although there are many other types of sponsorship:

1. Clothing—usually sponsors provide sport clothing, although they could supply other items not used by athletes whilst performing.

2. Transport—sponsors either pay whole or part subsidised travel costs, such as fuel costs or buying a minibus for an amateur club.

3. Equipment—sponsors usually pay for an athlete's sport equipment, such as cricket bags and golf bags.

4. Accessories—these can be anything (e.g., Shane Warne has worn a Nike ear stud whilst playing cricket, and tennis players can often be seen wearing a watch from a sponsor).
5. Training—provided by use of facilities or coaches.
6. Others—sponsors often supply food to athletes as well as energy supplements and drinks. Sponsors sometimes pay for entry fees to events.

The main reason for sponsorship is advertising. A sponsor may be seeking a certain image. Becoming associated with an individual or sport may help connect a product with excitement, good health and success. Tax relief is another benefit. Companies can claim money back from taxes paid through sponsorship. The whole effect of sponsoring something is improved sales gained through the accumulative effect of advertising and the association of a product with a personality, event or sport. Without finance, there would be no facilities or they would become very run down. Facility provision is dependent on the level of finance gained.

FACILITIES

Sport can require either indoor facilities (e.g., a fitness gym) or outdoor facilities (e.g., a hockey pitch, which is man-made, or a lake for sailing, which is natural). These sports need different, and often expensive, facilities.

Facility provision comes from four main areas. First, **local authorities**, via local councils, own most local facilities such as the sport centres, playing fields, swimming pools and school facilities. The two issues to be aware of are compulsory competitive tendering (CCT) and dual use (of schools). CCT was introduced to allow any group of people (usually managers) to compete to run sport centres. A management team under contract runs each sport centre. Dual use is the process where schools have their sport facilities enhanced so that they can function for the school in the daytime and as a sport centre on evenings and at the weekends.

Second, the **Sports Council (SC)** runs the five national sport centres (see chapter 15, p. 126). The SC also hands out grants to groups who apply for improvements to existing facilities or for new facilities to be introduced.

Third, **voluntary organisations,** which are not run for profit, can provide facilities. Village halls may provide facilities for keep-fit groups, badminton and scout groups. Charities such as the National Trust provide the environment for walking, climbing and outdoor pursuits.

Finally, businesses run **private enterprise** facilities to make a profit. These facilities tend to be very exclusive, with the latest sport equipment. Examples of private enterprise facilities are golf clubs and private health and fitness centres.

Location of Facilities

Location of facilities is important. Several factors need to be considered when making a decision about location.

• Facilities need to be built near to population centres so that they have the potential to be highly used.
• People need access to the facility, so a car park may be needed and the facility should be near to bus or train routes.

- The facility must meet a required demand. If the facility only serves one sport then it is important to check that there are enough people wanting to use it.
- If similar facilities already exist then demand for a new facility may be low.
- If the facility can be used for several different activities (dual use) then it will have more chance of being successful.

National Sport Centres

There are five national sport centres (for England). These are centres of excellence and are available to anyone, from beginners wishing to go on an introductory course to the NGBs' élite athletes who need training in their sport.

1. Bisham Abbey (Buckinghamshire) is a centre for tennis, football, hockey, squash and weight training.
2. Lilleshall (Shropshire) is a centre for football, cricket and gymnastics.
3. Holme Pierrepont (Nottingham) is the national water sport centre.
4. Crystal Palace (London) is a centre for athletics and swimming.
5. Plas y Brenin (N Wales) is the national centre for outdoor activities.

SPORT TECHNOLOGY

A combination of money in sport and the desire to be better has developed technology in sport. The centres of excellence listed earlier show there is a need for different specialist facilities and equipment for different sports. As technology develops, so equipment improves. New technology has a direct impact on sport. It is important to look at what technological changes have occurred, determine why these changes have occurred and identify which areas of sport they have affected (see table 16.2).

TABLE 16.2   Technology

New technology area	Advantage	Sports or items used for
Synthetic materials—playing surfaces	Strong, durable, consistent, all-weather, shock absorbent, safer, multi-purpose.	Astroturf—hockey, cricket, indoor gymnasia, martial arts floors.
Synthetic materials—clothing	Lighter and stronger, waterproof, breathable, energy-return systems.	Outdoor sports such as hiking, clothing for climbing. Running events have gained from improved footwear, including grip and shock absorbency.
Equipment—outdoor sports	Lighter and stronger.	Ski and snowboard bindings—moulded plastic boots, aerodynamic designs.
Equipment—racket sports	Lighter, stronger, more efficient.	Improved "sweet spot" and more powerful but with better control.
Equipment—motor sports	Quicker, better handling, more manoeuverable, better grip to the surface, aerodynamic.	Motor racing.

(continued)

TABLE 16.2 *(continued)*		
New technology area	**Advantage**	**Sports or items used for**
Equipment—personal protective	Safe, prevent injury, allow greater impact.	Contact sports make use of items such as gum shields, shin pads, gloves, protective glasses, helmets, scrum caps, shoulder pads.
Cameras	Still cameras with greater accuracy—allow to judge winners, aid performance through coaching and analysis. Video cameras used to aid coaching, and referees make use of the video referee. Smaller cameras placed in new, exciting locations and positions, giving a better insight into sport.	Still cameras used in sprinting and horse racing. Video cameras used in all sports for coaching. Video referees use cameras in rugby league and cricket as well as gymnastics, ice skating and diving. New camera locations such as stump cameras in cricket, attached to canoeists' helmets and attached to referees.
Timing	More accurate timing now takes place—helping to adjudicate and to assist in performance.	Events such as athletics, underwater timers for swimming, fastest lap times in motor racing. Assisting in false starts with timers situated in starter blocks.
Facilities and other innovations	Allow sport to be easier, more exciting and more appealing, aiding analysis, coaching, organisation, communication and performance enhancing.	Facilities with underground heating, heart monitors to record athletes' vital signs, ball-delivery machines in tennis, coaches and referees "wired up" for improved communication, magic eyes in tennis helping the umpire, food and drink designed to help refuel athletes, computers used to help collate statistics.

As shown in table 16.2, sport technology has made enormous advances in improving safety, enhancing accuracy and assisting coaching. Technology affects the equipment used and other materials, and how sport is measured, recorded and judged. The list of technical innovations in sport is endless. Technology means sport is constantly changing and improving.

 *Quick Test*

1. What does CCT stand for?
2. Explain CCT.
3. There are four main provider groups of facilities—name two.
4. Location of facilities is important. Name three factors to consider before opening any sport facility.
5. The national sport centres are also known as centres of what?
6. Name two national sport centres.
7. Name the national sport centre for water sport.
8. Why does private enterprise provide sport facilities?
9. Give an example of a sport facility run by or provided by a voluntary organisation.
10. Plas y Brenin is the national sport centre for which sport?
11. Define an amateur.
12. Define a professional.

From *GCSE Physical Education: A Revision Guide* by Tim Ferguson, 2002, Champaign, IL: Human Kinetics.

13. Give two problems amateurs may face.
14. Give two problems professionals may face.
15. Why did rugby league come about?
16. What is a scholarship?
17. Originally the Olympics were designed for amateurs. True or False?
18. Name an Olympic sport that does not allow professionals to compete.
19. Describe what the Olympic ideal is.
20. Name an Olympic sport that has recently changed to allow professionals to compete.
21. Name three sources of money for a chosen sport.
22. Who are the media?
23. What does the media do for the good of sport?
24. Give a disadvantage of media and their involvement in sport.
25. What does the term "sponsorship" mean?
26. Apart from money, name two other types of sponsorship.
27. Give two ways the sponsor gains.
28. Manchester United Football Club is a plc—what does this mean?
29. Where does the Sports Council get most of its money?
30. Name four things that sport in general spends its money on.
31. Playing surfaces have improved due to technology. Give three examples of this.
32. Other than becoming stronger and lighter, how else has clothing changed?
33. Give two other improvements to footwear apart from strength and weight.
34. Name four items of personal protective equipment in sport.
35. Cameras are now used to help officiate sport. Give two examples.
36. Other than rackets and general clothing, give two examples of technology used in professional tennis.
37. How are computers used to assist in sport?
38. Give two reasons why technology is used in sport.
39. Name a sport, an example of a technological innovation and the reason it was introduced in the sport.

Examination Questions

The original numbering of the examination questions has been retained for ease of cross-referencing. Answers to these questions can be found at the end of the book.

MEG 1998 QB3

d. Outline the differences between the amateur and professional performer. (5)

MEG 1997 Paper 2 Q2

a. Name one facility that members of the public can use for physical activity. (1)
b. Name two Sports Council campaigns. (2)
c. i. Copy and complete table 16.3. (2)

From *GCSE Physical Education: A Revision Guide* by Tim Ferguson, 2002, Champaign, IL: Human Kinetics. MEG questions reproduced with the kind permission of OCR.

TABLE 16.3 MEG 1997 Paper 2 Q2 National Sport Centres	
National Centre	**Activity**
Holme Pierrepont	
	Mountain activities

c. ii. Briefly describe the function of national sports centres. (2)

e. What are the benefits of media coverage to a lesser known physical activity? (8)

MEG 1995 Paper 2 Q1

b. Give two advantages of having dual use of local facilities. (2)

c. Write down four functions of national governing bodies of sport. (4)

d. Some British athletes take up sports scholarships in the United States. What benefits are there for the athletes and for British athletics in general? (5)

AQA(NEAB) 1999 QA6

a. State one local authority department that provides facilities for sport and physical activity. (1)

b. Give two types of sports facility provided by local authorities. (2)

AQA(NEAB) 1998 QA6

b. Give two places where excellence in sport and physical activity might be pursued. (2)

c. Give three factors that can restrict the provision of facilities at a local level. (3)

d. Explain the roles that volunteers play in the running of a local sports club. (4)

AQA(NEAB)1997 QA7

e. Many sports rely on sponsorship. What are the advantages and disadvantages of sponsorship for sport? (5)

AQA(NEAB) 1997 QB2

Sport makes good television. Is television good for sport? Give reasons for your answer. (15)

AQA(NEAB) 1996 QA7

a. What is a sponsor? (1)

b. Give two ways in which sponsorship can be used. (2)

c. Give three different but important sources of money (other than sponsorship) for sport. (3)

d. What are the advantages of being a professional sportsperson? (4)

e. In what ways has British sport been affected by our government and its policies? Give examples. (5)

AQA(NEAB) 1995 QA5

a. Give one function of a National Park Authority. (1)
b. Name two National Parks. (2)
c. Name three National Centres for Sport run by the Sports Council. (3)
d. What type of facilities for sport and physical activity might you find within a local government authority? (4)
e. What might be the advantages and the disadvantages of having one multi-purpose national sports venue? (5)

AQA(NEAB) 1995 QA8

a. What is an amateur sportsperson? (1)
b. Give two examples of professional sports. (2)
c. Give three different ways in which sport might be brought into disrepute. (3)
d. How might a performer benefit by winning a gold medal at the Olympic Games? (4)
e. In the Olympic Games of 1992, there were 28 sports involved. Why could this number change in the future? (5)

AQA(SEG) 1998 Paper 2 Q5

a. Name two different forms of media. (2)
b. State and describe three different types of sponsorship help which a performer could receive. (6)

AQA(SEG) 1997 Paper 2 Q10

a. Explain what is meant by the following:
   i. Professional sport (2)
   ii. Amateur sport (2)
   iii. Open sport (2)

AQA(SEG) 1996 Paper 2 Q9

a. The media can have an effect on sporting individuals. State
   i. one harmful effect, giving examples, and (3)
   ii. one beneficial effect, giving examples. (3)
   iii. State and describe two ways that sponsors and the media can affect sporting events. (4)

AQA(SEG) 1996 Paper 3 Q7

a. Changes have been made in sports, and technology has improved. Give examples of these under the following headings:
   i. Materials (3)
   ii. Equipment (3)
   iii. Facilities (3)

CHAPTER 17

Drugs in Sport

This chapter discusses social drugs, such as alcohol and nicotine, along with performance-enhancing drugs used in sport (see figure 17.1). It describes the effects of these drugs and discusses issues surrounding the use of drugs in sport. The final chapter covers wider social issues and their relevance to sport.

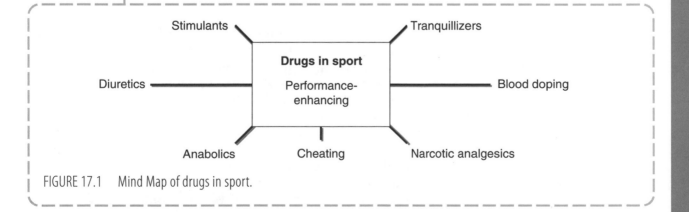

FIGURE 17.1   Mind Map of drugs in sport.

The use of drugs in sport (also known as "doping") is widespread. It exists because drugs can give athletes an advantage. There are two types of drugs: social drugs, such as alcohol and nicotine (drinking and smoking); and performance-enhancing drugs, which athletes take to improve their performance.

SOCIAL DRUGS

There are a number of legal and illegal drugs used by society. Illegal drugs include substances such as heroin, cocaine and marijuana. Legal drugs include alcohol and nicotine.

Alcohol is a widely used drug which acts as a depressant. Alcohol affects the brain, slowing reaction times and causing short-term muscular co-ordination problems. Also in the short term, speech and hearing gradually become affected, BP and HR increase, and vomiting can ensue. In the long term cirrhosis of the liver, which prevents the liver working efficiently, can develop. In extreme cases this can cause liver failure.

Tobacco contains thousands of harmful substances. Nicotine and tar are two of the most dangerous. Nicotine encourages dependence on tobacco, and tar coats the inside of the lungs, inhibiting breathing. Smoking reduces fitness levels and makes people more susceptible to colds and other chest infections. In the long term smokers are more likely to die of cancer and heart disease and suffer from angina, bronchitis and stomach ulcers. Smoking seriously damages health and is not compatible with sport.

PERFORMANCE-ENHANCING DRUGS

Performance-enhancing drugs can be classed into four groups:

1. Stimulants, or uppers
2. Tranquillizers, or downers
3. Narcotic analgesics, or painkillers
4. Anabolics, or body builders

Table 17.1 explains these drugs in more detail. There are also other ways of enhancing performance, such as blood doping.

Blood Doping

Blood doping first started in the 1960s, although scientists have now produced a drug which has the same effect of increasing the number of red blood cells. Blood doping is probably not practised as widely by athletes anymore.

Blood doping does not actually involve the introduction of a new substance into the body, although it is illegal. Scientists have researched athletes' oxygen-carrying capacity, which is connected to the number of red blood cells. Scientists remove a small volume of blood from athletes, and over the period of a month, the human body replaces this blood, bringing blood volume levels back to normal. Before competition, the blood is returned to the body, thus increasing the oxygen-carrying capacity of blood for about two weeks before the body finally reduces its volume of blood back to normal. The risks of blood doping include allergic

TABLE 17.1	Performance-Enhancing Drugs			
Drug	What it does	Examples	Sport performance it enhances	Risks
Stimulants	Reduce fatigue, pep the user up. They directly affect the CNS and cardio-vascular system. Stimulants speed up reactions, increase alertness and delay tiredness.	Amphetamines and caffeine	Cycling and other stamina-based sports	Death, high BP, brain and liver damage, overheating and anxiety. In cycling there have been two deaths from stimulants.
Tranquillizers	Reduce anxiety, slow the heart down and relax the muscles. Tranquillizers reduce limb tremors and palm sweating.	Valium and Beta blockers	Shooting and archery	Depression, insomnia and drowsiness, they also affect reaction times and co-ordination.
Narcotic analgesics	Kill pain (analgesics) and induce sleep (narcotic). These drugs give a powerful stimulating effect before giving a strong sedating effect, allowing an athlete to recover.	Morphine, heroin and codeine	Any athlete with an injury; cycling if it is a tour event	Pain is important, it tells you how your body is. Killing pain can lead to further injury. Narcotic analgesics are addictive and can lead to death.
Anabolics	Anabolics build and repair muscles, which allow athletes to increase muscle mass and to recover from training more quickly.	Testosterone (male hormone) and nandrolone	Sprinters and power lifters	Death through heart disease, high BP and cancer, also infertility and aggressive behaviour.

reactions, blood clots, kidney damage, hepatitis or AIDS and an overloaded circulatory system.

Other Drugs to Consider

There are two other drugs to consider:

1. Diuretics increase the amount of water eliminated from the body and promote weight loss for a short period of time. Therefore, weight-category sports such as boxing and martial arts would find them helpful. Effects of diuretics include dehydration, faintness and dizziness, muscle cramps and headaches and nausea.
2. Peptide and glycoprotein hormones and analogues stimulate the production of natural steroids, therefore helping to develop muscle mass in much the same way as anabolic steroids. The harmful effects of human-made hormones are unknown.

ISSUES CONNECTED WITH DRUGS IN SPORT

Drugs in sport are a serious problem. Athletes who take drugs are cheats, as they have not achieved the best at their sport by their own merit. In an effort to deter athletes from taking drugs, the International Olympic Committee (IOC) carries out drug tests on athletes. However, as new drugs are introduced, new tests are implemented to check athletes, and rogue scientists produce more new drugs. One

Classic cases

300 B.C.: Greek athletes use hallucinogenic mushrooms to enhance performance.

1908: Olympic marathon winner takes small dose of strychnine.

1962: IOC passes a resolution against doping. The war against the cheats begins.

1967: Tommy Simpson (British cyclist) collapses and dies on the Tour de France from an amphetamine overdose.

1968: Drug testing is introduced at the Olympics.

1988: Ben Johnson (Canadian sprinter), having won gold, has his medal stripped for cheating and is given a two-year ban.

1991: Katrin Krabbe (German sprinter) is surrounded by controversy over tampered urine samples. Eventually Krabbe is banned. East German coaches also confess to supplying their athletes with banned substances.

1995: Diane Modahl (British middle-distance runner) wins her appeal against her ban of 1994 over high levels of testosterone.

1999: Dougie Walker (British sprinter) wins appeal with the British athletics federation, only to have the IAAF turn it down; his appeal is still on-going. The substance is nandrolone, which is still causing consternation in the athletics world over doubts of the testing procedure and the natural existence of the drug in accepted food groups.

2001: Mark Richardson (400m sprinter) is allowed back into competition, having proved that food supplements he used had been contaminated with banned substances.

FIGURE 17.2   A timeline of classic cases involving drugs in sport.

argument is that all drugs should be allowed so that the best scientist wins rather than the best athlete. As shown in table 17.1, this could not be allowed because of the hazards of drug taking.

Athletes are put on a drug-testing register and can be notified at any time that they are to be tested. This may be out of season, during a competition or after a performance. The IOC tests athletes' urine with a mass spectrometer. If the sample has traces of a banned substance, the competitor is suspended whilst the IOC tests a second sample. The appropriate governing body decides whether to ban the athlete. The athlete does have the right to appeal as the process is not foolproof. Often athletes win their appeals and return to competition. There are notable cases of athletes who were banned for taking performance-enhancing drugs (figure 17.2).

 *Quick Test*

1. The use of drugs in sport is also known as what?
2. Define what a drug is.
3. There are two types of drugs to consider. One is performance-enhancing drugs; what is the other?

From *GCSE Physical Education: A Revision Guide* by Tim Ferguson, 2002, Champaign, IL: Human Kinetics.

4. There are four main categories of performance-enhancing drugs. Name two.
5. Alcohol is a widely used drug and is a depressant. True or False?
6. Give one effect alcohol has on the body.
7. Alcohol causes cirrhosis of what?
8. Name an actual drug ingested during smoking.
9. What is blood doping?
10. What does a stimulant do?
11. Give an example of a tranquillizer.
12. Give a sport in which stimulants help to enhance performance.
13. What is a narcotic analgesic?
14. Give an example of an anabolic steroid.
15. Give two risks of taking anabolic steroids.
16. What do diuretics do?
17. Taking drugs to stimulate the production of natural steroids is legal. True or False?
18. Give a year, event and name of a sportsperson who got caught taking drugs.
19. When athletes are tested, what sample do they have to give: urine or blood?
20. "Allow the use of all drugs and therefore let the best scientist win" is a view on drugs and cheating. What could happen if this were allowed?

Examination Questions

The original numbering of the examination questions has been retained for ease of cross-referencing. Answers to these questions can be found at the end of the book.

MEG 1999 QB1

c.   i. State two side-effects of misusing anabolic steroids to improve performance. (2)
c.   ii. How have governing bodies tried to stop the misuse of anabolic steroids? (2)

AQA(NEAB) 1999 QA2

a. What is a stimulant? (1)
b. Give two ways in which smoking reduces performance. (2)
e. How might alcohol affect performance?

AQA(SEG) 1996 Paper 3 Q6

a. Drug abuse is banned in sport.
   i. What is the difference between a social drug and a performance-enhancing drug? (2)
   ii. Name four types of drugs which are banned, other than steroids. (4)
   iii. Describe five side-effects which can occur through the continued use of anabolic steroids. (5)
b. Describe the harmful, long-term effects of smoking, and state how they would directly affect the sportsperson's performance. (5)

From *GCSE Physical Education: A Revision Guide* by Tim Ferguson, 2002, Champaign, IL: Human Kinetics. MEG questions reproduced with the kind permission of OCR. AQA(NEAB)/AQA examination questions and AQA(SEG) examination questions are reproduced by permission of the Assessment and Qualifications Alliance.

▶ **147**

London 1999 Q34

a. Which two socially accepted drugs are legal despite the possible health risks to those taking them? (2)

b. Some drugs, such as anabolic steroids, are on the International Olympic Committee's list of banned substances. State two physical dangers athletes may face if they take anabolic steroids.

c. State two reasons why an athlete might take anabolic steroids despite the risks. (2)

d. Some drugs stop the body from feeling pain. Why could this be dangerous for athletes when they are training? (1)

From *GCSE Physical Education: A Revision Guide* by Tim Ferguson, 2002, Champaign, IL: Human Kinetics. London questions reprinted, by permission, from Edexcel Foundation.

CHAPTER 18

Social Issues and Sport

Modern sport is to some extent a reflection of today's society. It is almost inevitable that sometimes society's problems spill over and affect sport. This chapter examines some social issues, such as why racial issues can affect sport and why women are not equally represented in sport (see figure 18.1). The chapter also explains why these issues have a detrimental effect on sport.

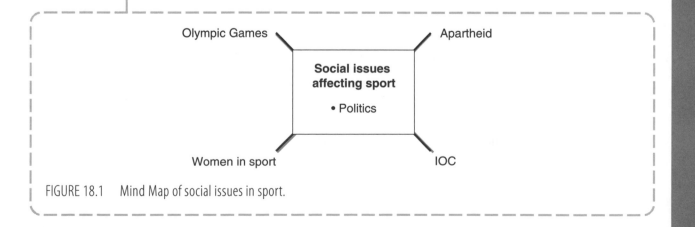

FIGURE 18.1   Mind Map of social issues in sport.

POLITICS IN SPORT

Sport is usually funded by governments and represents a whole country. Because sport is popular with millions of people throughout the world, it helps to unite nations. This is why sport is such a good vehicle for passing political messages from nation to nation.

There are numerous examples of sport used as a political tool. Apartheid and the Olympic Games are two examples of countries using sport as a political tool which have had a great impact on the world today.

Apartheid

Apartheid was a political system adopted in South Africa. Literally, apartheid means "separateness". It involves separating people of different races. South Africa has a predominantly black population, yet it was run by a white minority government. Over the years South Africa sent only white teams to represent their country, and they did not allow black athletes from guest countries to enter South Africa. See figure 18.2 for key dates in the controversy.

During the years of apartheid, nations around the world argued over the best method of forcing South Africa to change its political system. Some countries

1960: South Africa took an all-white team to the Rome Olympics; the IOC withdraws the invitation to the following Olympic Games.

1970: South Africa is expelled from the Olympic movement.

1976: Before the Montreal Olympics, the New Zealand rugby team tours South Africa. Many black African countries threaten to boycott the Olympics. The IOC refuses to bow to the pressure, so many of these countries carry out the boycott.

1977: The Gleneagles Agreement is made by the Commonwealth countries, who decide to allow individual governments to do everything possible to discourage contact or competition of their nationals with any sporting organisation from South Africa.

1981: The United Nations produces its first blacklist of sports performers who have worked in South Africa.

1984: Zola Budd changes nationalities from South African to British; people believe it was in order for her to run in the Olympics.

1986: Thirty-two nations boycott the Commonwealth games because of Britain s refusal to apply economic sanctions to South Africa.

1990: President De Klerk announces the unbanning of the African National Congress (ANC); Nelson Mandela is released from prison.

1991: The IOC readmits South Africa back to the Olympic movement.

FIGURE 18.2   A timeline of the key apartheid cases in sport.

believed that total isolation was the best method to change South Africa. Other countries thought that continuing to compete against South Africa may change their beliefs.

Olympic Games

Virtually every Olympic Games has seen sport used as a political tool. For as long as different nations continue to have disputes, it is likely that the Olympics will continue to be used for political reasons. The main reason for this is the magnitude of the Olympics. The Olympic Games are now the largest sporting event in the world, involving more athletes, countries and support staff than any other event. It is a big stage for a nation to voice their opinion. Figure 18.3 describes some political situations that have affected the Olympic Games.

The Olympic Games may be an obvious tool for voicing opinions through sport, but there are also more subtle ways that sport can reflect society's opinions. An example of this is women's participation in sport. Women still play a lesser role than men in society and this is mirrored in women's participation in sport. Changing both men's and women's attitudes to women's participation in sport has begun, but it will take more time and work for women to be treated fairly and equally, as the following section shows.

WOMEN AND SPORT

The traditional role women have played in sport has changed over the years. Initially women were given little opportunity to take part in sport. However, times have changed and now women have more roles to play within sport, and the level of involvement, access and opportunity for women has increased.

Lack of Involvement

Historically, women have been involved in all aspects of sport to a much lesser extent than men. The reasons for this are varied.

- There is a belief that some games could harm women (e.g., rugby).
- High levels of fitness, determination and commitment required clash with the feminine stereotype of women.
- A lack of role models in women's sport has been problematic. This is changing as more women take part in and improve at traditionally male-dominated sports. Examples of role models include Laura Davies in golf and Denise Lewis in the heptathlon.
- Prize money is lower for women, which means it is more difficult for them to make a living out of sport.
- There is a lack of sponsors who are prepared to sponsor women rather than men.
- Traditional values and attitudes have prevented women from being involved in all areas of sport such as running local teams and supporting a football match. Women were expected to look after the home, while men went out after work to play or be involved in sport.
- There are poor crèche facilities, lack of transport (one-car family) and lack of time.

1896: **Athens**—The first modern Olympics has problems: Greece cannot finance the games and has to be rescued by a wealthy businessman.

1909: **London**—Russia (who rules Finland) forces the Finnish team to parade without their flag.

1920: **Antwerp**—Germany and its wartime allies are not allowed to compete.

1936: **Berlin**—Hitler and the Nazis use the games to promote the supremacy of the blond, blue-eyed race. Hitler's plans are ruined by the success of the black American athlete Jesse Owens, who wins four gold medals.

1956: **Melbourne**—Spain and Holland pull out because of the Soviet invasion of Hungary, and China refuses because of the inclusion of Taiwan.

1968: **Mexico City**—IOC refuses entry to South Africa; 200 Mexicans die in rioting over the money wasted on the games whilst so many Mexicans are living in poverty; and demonstrations are made by black American athletes over the treatment of blacks in the USA.

1972: **Munich**—Eight Palestinian terrorists break into the Olympic village and kidnap nine Israeli athletes. A botched attempt to rescue them leads to the death of all nine athletes.

1976: **Montreal**—Over 20 African countries boycott the games because the IOC refuses to ban New Zealand from the games (New Zealand rugby had toured South Africa).

1980: **Moscow**—Several western countries led by the USA boycott the games over the Soviet Union's invasion of Afghanistan in 1979.

1984: **Los Angeles**—The Soviet Union and her allies boycott the games as payback for the 1980 games.

1988: **Seoul**—North Korea boycotts over the IOC's refusal to allow North Korea to host some events.

1992: **Barcelona**—German unification means that Germany is represented by one team; South Africa returns after 30 years in expulsion; the games are the first to be relatively politic-free.

1996: **Atlanta**—Terrorists attempt to ruin the games because of their anti-western feelings.

2000: **Sydney**—Worries regarding possible terrorist actions targeted at a local power plant prove to be unfounded. The games end in a complete success, the second games to be relatively free of trouble.

FIGURE 18.3 A timeline of social issues in the Olympic Games.

Women's Sports Foundation

The Women's Sports Foundation (WSF) was established in 1984. It is a charity and receives funding through grant aid, sponsorship, sale of resources, fund raising and membership fees. The majority of its grant aid is provided by Sport England.

The Women's Sports Foundation's vision is "To pursue and promote opportunities for women and girls in and through sport".

checkpoint

Eight Key Aims of WSF

1. **Equality.** To raise awareness of the contribution that women and girls in sport have made and make to society, to challenge instances of inequality in sport and seek to bring about change.

2. **Leadership.** To increase the number of female leaders at all levels in sport, to seek at least equal representation by women on decision-making bodies and to support the personal and career development of women at all levels in coaching, sports administration and management.

3. **Education, training and research.** To support those responsible for providing sport, recreation and physical education in schools and colleges, to deliver an equitable range of opportunities and learning experiences, and to increase the knowledge and understanding about women and girls in sport and physical activity through positive research.

4. **Young people.** To increase girls' and women's participation in a wide variety of sport and recreation opportunities and to generate girls' and women's positive attitudes about sport.

5. **Participation.** To increase girls' and women's participation in a wide variety of sport and recreation opportunities.

6. **High-performance sport.** To enable women and girls with the sporting ability and interest to excel in all sports, and to maximise the support to, and raise the profile of, top British sportswomen.

7. **Information and resources.** To increase and maximise the resources available for women's and girls' sport, and to provide valued and current information and resources on women and girls in sport.

8. **National and international co-operation.** To raise the awareness, support and understanding of the issues relating to women and girls in sport and to promote positive solutions and examples of good practice nationally and internationally.

Quick Test

1. Why is sport a good vehicle for passing on political messages?
2. What does apartheid mean?
3. Where does the apartheid system come from?
4. What was the Gleneagles Agreement?
5. Name a host city, year and incident involving politics that happened in the Olympic Games.
6. Why did the Soviet Union boycott the 1984 Olympics?
7. What is the main reason for using the Olympic Games as a sporting event to involve politics?
8. When was South Africa readmitted to the Olympic movement?
9. Nine Israeli athletes were killed by terrorists at the 1972 Munich games. True or False?
10. How did Jesse Owens ruin Hitler's plans in the 1936 Olympics?

From *GCSE Physical Education: A Revision Guide* by Tim Ferguson, 2002, Champaign, IL: Human Kinetics.

Examination Questions

The original numbering of the examination questions has been retained for ease of cross-referencing. Answers to these questions can be found at the end of the book.

MEG 1999 Paper 1 Q3

    d. Explain why fewer women take part in organised physical activity compared to men. (5)

MEG 1996 Paper 2 Q1

    e. With examples, explain how politicians and sportspersons have used sport for political purposes. (8)

MEG 1995 Paper 2 Q2

    b. Give the name and date of two summer Olympic Games affected by politics. (2)

AQA(NEAB) 1997 QA8

    a. Name one major sporting event. (1)

    b. Give two reasons why countries enter international events. (2)

    c. Give three examples of sport being used as a political tool. (3)

    d. Are medal tables a good way of showing the success of a country? Give reasons. (4)

    e. Explain how good citizenship can be promoted through sport. (5)

AQA(NEAB) 1996 QA8

    a. Name one city that has hosted the modern Olympic Games. (1)

    b. Name in full the following organisations:

        i. IOC

        ii. BOA (2)

    c. Give three major international incidents that have happened at the Olympic Games. (3)

    d. Why do some places find it difficult to bid as an Olympic venue?

    e. Why is it beneficial for some sports to be part of the Olympic Games?

AQA(SEG) 1997 Paper 3 Q8

    b. Describe, with examples, problems which have occurred at major international sporting events. (5)

Answers

The examination answers are taken from the relevant examination board mark scheme. All four examination boards would like to point out that although the answers are from their mark schemes, there is the question of interpretation. The examination boards do not accept any responsibility whatsoever for the accuracy or method of working in the answers.

Edexcel Foundation, London Examinations accepts no responsibility whatsoever for the accuracy or method of working in the answers given.

CHAPTER 1   QUICK TEST ANSWERS

Chapter 1 Quick Test questions are found on page 7. These are the author's own answers.

1. Upper leg
2. Tibia
3. Protection, support, movement, blood production
4. Femur
5. Fingers, toes
6. Humerus, ulna, radius
7. Lower leg
8. Pelvis
9. Kneecap
10. Back of shoulder / upper back
11. Rib cage
12. Long, tubular bones; shorter, fibrous bones; flat, plate-like bones; irregular bones
13. Red and white blood cells formed
14. Appendicular
15. Joints
16. Jellyfish
17. Humerus, ulna, radius, femur, tibia, fibula
18. False
19. True
20. False
21. Cartilage, synovial membrane, synovial fluid, capsule, the actual bones at the joint named
22. Ball and socket
23. Attaches bone to bone
24. Allows frictionless movement
25. Seals in the synovial fluid and produces it

From *GCSE Physical Education: A Revision Guide* by Tim Ferguson, 2002, Champaign, IL: Human Kinetics.

26. True
27. Humerus, ulna, radius
28. Rotation
29. Ball and socket, hinge, condyloid

CHAPTER 1   EXAMINATION QUESTION ANSWERS

The examination questions can be found on page 8. These answers are taken from the actual examination board mark scheme to provide an insight into the types of answers required.

MEG 1996 Paper 1 Q2

a. Joints of the spinal column, joints between the ribs and the sternum, the pubic bones
c. A: cancellous (spongy) bone, red marrow, epiphysis; B: shaft, periosteum, hard membrane casing, diphysis; C: compact bone; D: medullary cavity (yellow marrow) forms white corpuscles, bone marrow.

MEG 1995 Paper 1 Q2

c. Types of bone: **Sesamoid**; location: knee; function: to prevent hyperextension of knee joint. **Long, tubular**; location: limbs; function: movement and production of red blood cells. **Fibrous bones**; location: shorter bones of wrist and ankle; function: strength in support. **Flat, plate-like bones**; location: skull and scapula; function: protection and attachment. **Irregular bones**; location: vertebrae and face; function: movement, shape.

Type of bone and function award two marks; type of bone alone award one mark; name and correct function award one mark. Maximum two marks.

AQA(NEAB) 1999 QA3

a. One from protect, support, enable movement, produce red blood cells, attachment of muscles.
b. Either two from ball and socket, hinge, pivot, saddle, condyloid, gliding; or two from hip, shoulder, elbow, knee, ankle, wrist, neck.
c. Three such as arthritis, increased elasticity of ligaments, increased range of movements, increased suppleness of muscles, increased wear and tear on cartilage, inflammation or tennis elbow, possible sprained ligaments, fluid on the knee or torn bursa, possible injuries, displacement of cartilage, become stronger, become unstable.

NB Do not accept stiffness.

NB Accept both positive and negative aspects.

AQA(NEAB) 1997 QA1

a. The lower leg (accept the leg or the shin)

c. Three answers from ligament, synovial membrane, (articular) cartilage, bone, capsule, (synovial) fluid, disc cartilage (meniscus).

Accept, for one mark only, any three named bones. Do not accept tendons or muscles.

AQA(NEAB) 1996 QA1

a. Patella

b. Protection, support, movement, blood production

c. i. Decreasing of an angle between two bones (for example, bending the arm at the elbow)

c. ii. Increasing the angle between two bones (for example, straightening the arm at the elbow)

c. iii. Ability of a bone to move freely in a circle, rotation

d. Strong, fibrous bands of tissue, attach bone to bone, hold joints together, allow movement of bones at synovial joints, are slightly stretchy

AQA(SEG) 1998 Paper 2 Q1

b. i. Hip: pelvis and femur; Shoulder: humerus and scapula or clavicle

b. ii. Shoulder: humerus and scapula or clavicle (collar bone and shoulder blade); knee: femur and tibia or fibula.

AQA(SEG) 1997 Paper 2 Q4

a. Support, protection, movement, shape, blood cell production, mineral salts storage

b. i. Short bones; flat, plate-like bones; irregular bones

b. ii. Short bones: bones of feet or the wrist, ankles and hands (carpals and tarsals, phalanges, metatarsals, metacarpals); flat plate-like bones: skull, ribs, pelvis, scapula; irregular bones: face and vertebrae of the spine

c. i. Slightly moveable or cartilaginous, freely moveable or synovial

c. ii. Slightly moveable: vertebrae of the spine, pubic bones, joints between the ribs and the sternum; freely moveable: ball and socket, hinge, pivot, condyloid, gliding, saddle (any examples)

d. Tendons are strong, elastic-like cords which join muscle to bone. The point of the bone which is actually fixed in place is known as the origin and the insertion is the part of the muscle which actually moves the most. This is at the opposite position to the origin.

London 1999 Q14

a. See answers in table A.1.

b. ball and socket

c. abduction, adduction and rotation

From *GCSE Physical Education: A Revision Guide* by Tim Ferguson, 2002, Champaign, IL: Human Kinetics. AQA(NEAB)/AQA examination questions and AQA(SEG) examination questions are reproduced by permission of the Assessment and Qualifications Alliance. London questions reprinted, by permission, from Edexcel Foundation.

TABLE A.1 London 1999 Q14—Answers to Types of Joints		
Joint type	**Example 1**	**Example 2**
Gliding	Wrist	Spine
Hinge	Elbow	Knee
Ball and socket	Shoulder	Hip
Pivot	Atlas	Axis

London 1998 Q11

a. A: bone or femur; B: cartilage; C: synovial membrane; D: joint, capsule or ligament; E: synovial fluid.

b. Protects bone, prevents friction or rubbing

c. Ligament

London 1998 Q12

a. Elbow, phalanges: accurate location

b. i. Pivot

b. ii. Ball and socket

CHAPTER 2   QUICK TEST ANSWERS

Chapter 2 Quick Test questions are found on page 14. These are the author's own answers.

1. Back of upper arm
2. Latissimus dorsi
3. Movement, protection, shape, blood circulation
4. Lower back to under the arm
5. Bends (flexes) the arm
6. Pectorals
7. Attaches bones to muscles, pulls on the bone when muscles flex
8. Antagonistic pair of muscles
9. Fast and slow twitch
10. Fast twitch
11. Bending
12. Trapezius
13. Bottom
14. Straightens (extends) the arm
15. Back of the ankle

From *GCSE Physical Education: A Revision Guide* by Tim Ferguson, 2002, Champaign, IL: Human Kinetics. London questions reprinted, by permission, from Edexcel Foundation.

16. Contract (get shorter)
17. Latissimus dorsi
18. Hamstrings
19. Pull on the bones
20. It is under our control
21. Skeletal muscle
22. Rectus abdominus
23. Bend (flex) the leg
24. Brain or CNS via the nerves
25. Shoulder
26. Straighten (extend) the leg
27. Involuntary muscle, the heart muscle
28. Straightens
29. Gastrocnemius
30. Slow-twitch fibres contract slowly but do not tire easily

CHAPTER 2   EXAMINATION QUESTION ANSWERS

The examination questions can be found on page 16. These answers are taken from the actual examination board mark scheme to provide an insight into the types of answer required.

MEG 1997 Paper 1 Q1

b. A: pectoralis major (pectorals, pecs); B: abdominal muscle (abdominals, abs)

c. Epithelial tissue: lining organs, surfaces, skin, cells, etc. and is mainly protective; connective tissue: connects, fills out and supports body structures, and contains a contractile element; nervous tissue: confined to the nervous system and holds together and supports nerve cells and fibres; bone tissue (compact, cancellous); soft tissue: elastic tissue; white fibrous tissue (ligaments, tendons); adipose (fatty) tissue.

MEG 1996 Paper 1 Q1

d. Muscles can pull by contraction but they cannot push. If one muscle acts across a joint to pull bones closer, another pulls them apart. A joint must have two opposing (antagonistic) muscles crossing it (for example, biceps and triceps). One muscle is attached to a fixed point (origin) (tendon, bone), the other end of it is attached to the point to be moved (insertion). The insertion usually moves towards the origin. The main muscle used to produce movement is the prime mover. The antagonist relaxes to allow the movement to take place. Flexion and extension take place at a hinge joint. Fixation muscles steady one part of the body to give working muscles a firm base. Synergist muscles stabilise joints so that other joints can do their work. Actin and myosin molecules slide past each other to shorten the muscle fibre when stimulated by the central nervous system.

AQA(NEAB) 1999 QA1

d. i. Slow-twitch fibres, fast-twitch fibres

d. ii. Slow twitch: sustained tension, low-level work intensity, reduce tiredness, long durability, gradual response, important for stamina, receive good O_2 supplies, slow contractions

Fast twitch: immediate response (including reflexes), high-level work intensity, all-out effort, short but explosive, muscles work at quick rate, dynamic actions, contract quickly, important for speed and power

AQA(NEAB) 1995 QA1

c. i. Pectorals

c. ii. Biceps, triceps

c. iii. Hamstrings, quadriceps

d. i. Ball and socket

d. ii. Flexion, extension, rotation, abduction, adduction

e. Muscles work in pairs (antagonistic). The hamstrings and quadriceps are antagonistic. To jump the quadriceps must flex, and this straightens the leg, whilst the hamstrings relax (extend), allowing the leg to straighten at the knee. The brain or CNS sends message via the nerves to the muscles. The muscles act by pulling on the tendon, pulling on the bones.

AQA(SEG) 1999 Paper 2 Q1

c. Muscles are joined to the bone by tendons. Muscles can only pull, not push. The muscles are therefore arranged in pairs. One muscle contracts (shortens) and one relaxes (lengthens). Muscle movement is known as agonist and antagonist. The origin is where the muscle is fixed to the bone, and the insertion is the part of the muscle which actually moves. Bones are joined by ligaments.

AQA(SEG) 1996 Paper 2 Q4

c. Cardiac or heart muscle; smooth or involuntary muscle (for example, bowel, uterus, bladder); unstriated, voluntary, or skeletal muscle (for example, biceps, triceps, hamstrings, quadriceps, etc.); striated muscle.

d. i. The muscle shortens and gets fatter or bulges (for example, the biceps muscle as the arm is bent at the elbow).

d. ii. The muscle gradually lengthens and returns to its normal shape (for example, the biceps muscle as the arm is straightened).

London 1999 Q15

a. A: trapezius; B: deltoid; C: lats or latissimus dorsi; D: hamstrings.

b. See answers in table A.2.

TABLE A.2   London 1999 Q15—Answers to Name the Muscles

Action	Main muscle
Straightens the leg at the knee	Quadriceps
Pulls your leg back at the hip	Gluteals / gluteus maximus
Flexes your trunk so that you can bend forward	Abdominals / hip flexors / rectus abdominis

TABLE A.3   London 1998 Q13—Answers to Fill In the Gaps

Muscle type	Identifying characteristic	Example
Cardiac	Involuntary muscle with a striped appearance which never tires or stops working	Heart
Involuntary	Not controlled consciously	Blood vessels, gut, bladder, iris, intestines
Voluntary (striped, striated, skeletal)	Conscious control	Gastrocnemius

London 1998 Q13

See answers in table A.3.

London 1998 Q15

The biceps and the **triceps** work to move the forearm. One of these muscles will flex the forearm, whilst the other will extend it. When muscles work in this way they are said to be working **antagonistically**. Two groups of muscles in the upper leg also work in this way. They are the **quadriceps** (any order with hamstring) and **hamstrings.**

CHAPTER 3   QUICK TEST ANSWERS

Chapter 3 Quick Test questions are found on page 23. These are the author's own answers.

1. Delivery and waste disposal service
2. Involuntary, cardiac
3. Atria
4. Plasma and cells
5. Help with clotting
6. Veins, arteries, capillaries
7. Haemoglobin
8. Coronary heart disease, angina

From *GCSE Physical Education: A Revision Guide* by Tim Ferguson, 2002, Champaign, IL: Human Kinetics. London questions reprinted, by permission, from Edexcel Foundation.

9. Artery

10. Age, sex, stress or tension, exercise, circulatory disorders, smoking

11. High blood cholesterol level, high blood pressure, smoking, diabetes, over-weight, lack of regular exercise, family history, alcohol, illness

12. 65 to 85 beats per minute

13. Fight disease

14. Oxygen, food

15. Lower resting HR, higher working HR, larger stroke volume, larger cardiac output, stronger thicker walls

16. Ventricles

17. Yes

18. Veins

19. The component in red blood cells that attaches to oxygen, it carries oxygen

20. Vena cava

21. Relaxing situations, regular exercise, stop or don't smoke, sensible diet

22. Heart attack

23. Oxygenated blood

24. Capillaries

25. Carry blood to and from the lungs

26. Their arteries are more elastic

27. The number of beats per minute

28. With a sphygmomanometer

CHAPTER 3   EXAMINATION QUESTION ANSWERS

The examination questions can be found on page 24. These answers are taken from the actual examination board mark scheme to provide an insight into the types of answer required.

MEG 1998 Q12

Blood pressure is raised, stroke volume increases, cardiac output increases, volume of blood flow through the heart increases, blood flow speeds up (heart rate increases).

MEG 1996 Paper 1 Q1

b. Red blood cells carry oxygen and haemoglobin. White blood cells form antibodies against disease. Platelets are activated whenever blood clotting or repair to vessels is necessary. Liquid plasma transports the above and other nutrients, fats, glucose, etc. to tissues and is a medium for carrying away waste materials, and it controls temperature.

c. Right atrium: tricuspid valve opens, blood is forced into right ventricle, valve closes, right ventricle dilates. Left atrium: mitral valve opens bicuspid valve, blood forced into left ventricle, valve closes, left ventricle dilates.

AQA(NEAB) 1996 A2

a. Blood vessels that carry deoxygenated blood
b. Heat, carbon dioxide, water
c. Low resting HR, high working HR, large stroke volume, large cardiac output, strong or thick walls

AQA(NEAB) 1997 QA3

a. The beat of the heart (or contraction of the heart, or pumping of blood from the heart) (accept opening and closing of ventricles)
b. Two such as in the neck, groin, wrist, chest wall, thumb, head (accept named locations)
c. Three along the lines of the lower the resting rate, the fitter; the higher the maximum, the fitter; the higher the range, the fitter; the lower the cruise rate, the fitter; the quicker the recovery, the fitter

AQA(SEG) 1996 Paper 2 Q5

a.   i. Glucose and O_2 or glycogen
a.   ii. CO_2, lactic acid or lactate
b.   i. Atria
b.   ii. Ventricles
b.   iii. Pulmonary vein
b.   iv. Aorta
c. Radial pulse: inside of wrist; carotid pulse: side of neck; temporal pulse: temple or side of forehead; femoral pulse: groin
d. Increased cholesterol levels, heart attacks, thrombosis, cancers (leukaemia), high blood pressure, angina
e.   i. Plasma
e.   ii. Red blood cells (erythrocytes) and white blood cells (leukocytes)
e.   iii. Produced in the bone marrow, transports oxygen and carbon dioxide
e.   iv. Help the blood to clot and seal the skin
f. Maximum pulse rate is 220 minus your age

London 1999 Q19

a. Vena cava
b. Right atrium or auricle
c. Tricuspid
d. Right ventricle
e. Semilunar
f. Pulmonary artery
g. Pulmonary vein
h. Left atrium or auricle

From *GCSE Physical Education: A Revision Guide* by Tim Ferguson, 2002, Champaign, IL: Human Kinetics. AQA(NEAB)/AQA examination questions and AQA(SEG) examination questions are reproduced by permission of the Assessment and Qualifications Alliance. London questions reprinted, by permission, from Edexcel Foundation.

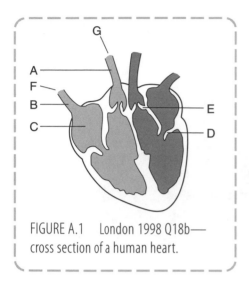

FIGURE A.1   London 1998 Q18b— cross section of a human heart.

i. Bicuspid or mitral
j. Left ventricle
k. Semilunar
l. Aorta

London 1998 Q18

a.   i. D
a.   ii. B
a.   iii. C
a.   iv. A
a.   v. E
b.   i. F: enters from vena cava (B). See figure A.1.
b.   ii. G: leaves via pulmonary artery (A). See figure A.1.

London 1998 Q20

a. The muscular wall of an artery is **thicker** than that of a vein. Arteries have a **smaller** internal diameter than veins. This means that the blood in the artery will be at a **higher** pressure than blood in the veins.

b. Capillaries are the **smallest** or **thinner** of the three types of vessels. Like **arteries**, the capillaries do not have any valves.

CHAPTER 4   QUICK TEST ANSWERS

Chapter 4 Quick Test questions are found on page 30. These are the author's own answers.

1. To obtain oxygen, to live, for respiration
2. Inspiration and expiration
3. The rib cage
4. To release energy by burning food
5. Tiny air sacs in the lungs
6. Tidal volume, $\dot{V}O_2$max, vital lung capacity
7. A cramp of the diaphragm
8. Carbon dioxide, water, heat
9. Small capillaries
10. In the network of capillaries surrounding the alveoli
11. False
12. True
13. False
14. True
15. Inhaling, inspiring
16. A sheet of muscle

From *GCSE Physical Education: A Revision Guide* by Tim Ferguson, 2002, Champaign, IL: Human Kinetics. London questions reprinted, by permission, from Edexcel Foundation.

17. Trachea

18. Bronchi

19. Alveoli

20. Decreases and increases the volume of the lungs or thoracic cavity

21. Exhaling, expiring

22. Tidal volume, vital lung capacity, $\dot{V}O_2$max

23. 13 to 17 times a minute

24. It gets a stitch

25. To warm the air and act as a filter

26. The crossing over of carbon dioxide and oxygen from the capillaries or alveoli

27. Nasal cavity, mouth, trachea, bronchi, bronchioles, alveoli, diaphragm, ribs

CHAPTER 4   EXAMINATION QUESTION ANSWERS

The examination questions can be found on page 30. These answers are taken from the actual examination board mark scheme to provide an insight into the types of answer required.

MEG 1996 Paper 1 Q1

e. When the body is at rest the movement of the diaphragm is sufficient to fill and empty the lungs. When at rest we breathe in and out about 16 times a minute. We take in 0.5 litres of air per breath. If there is a rise in the amount of CO_2 in the blood the rate of breathing increases, the depth of breathing increases. CO_2 concentration rises whenever the body is engaged in physical activity. The rate of breathing increases to 50 per minute, or according to severity of exercise. Greater upper-body involvement, surface area of lung increases, the amount of air with each breath can be 2.5 litres. Age and fitness affect how well the system copes with increased demand from the muscles. There is increased blood flow through the lungs, increased O_2 uptake, increased CO_2 expired, and gaseous exchange rate increases.

MEG 1995 Paper 1 Q1

a. The lungs increase in size or they get bigger.

d.   i. Tidal volume: during quiet breathing approximately 500ml of air (called the tidal volume) is taken per breath. With a resting breathing rate of approximately 12 per minute, the minute tidal volume is six litres (12 3 500ml).

d.   ii. Vital capacity: from maximum inspiration to maximum expiration is called the vital capacity, that is the total quantity of air which can be moved into and out of the lungs. Normal vital capacity = 4.5 litres; first-class athlete vital capacity = 5 litres; exceptional vital capacity = 7 litres.

d.   iii. Residual volume: after exhalation at any stage there is a volume of air remaining within the airways, composed of the unused expiratory reserve

From *GCSE Physical Education: A Revision Guide* by Tim Ferguson, 2002, Champaign, IL: Human Kinetics. MEG questions reproduced with the kind permission of OCR.

volume and a volume of air which is impossible to exhale called the residual volume.

AQA(NEAB) 1998 QA3

c. i. The amount of oxygen taken out of the inspired air and diffused into the bloodstream within one minute

c. ii. The higher the VO_2 the better the performer's potential for stamina events.

AQA(NEAB) 1996 A2

d. i. The largest volume of air that can be exhaled after the largest inhalation

d. ii. It aids performance if the vital lung capacity is large (a sign of a person with good cardiovascular stamina) and increases the ability to take oxygen in and use it, thus increasing the amount of energy that can be produced. If the vital lung capacity is low then the reverse can be applied.

London 1999 Q22

a. A: larynx; B: trachea; C: bronchi (right) or bronchus.

b. i. Relaxes, goes up or goes dome shaped

b. ii. Move down and in (must have both movements)

London 1998 Q21

a. Trachea, brochi and bronchioles

b. Carbon dioxide and nitrogen

c. It goes into the bloodstream, capillaries or pulmonary vein

CHAPTER 5   QUICK TEST ANSWERS

Chapter 5 Quick Test questions are found on page 36. These are the author's own answers.

1. Mouth
2. Energy
3. Ingestion, digestion, absorption, excretion
4. Saliva
5. Ingestion, digestion begins, saliva released
6. Breaks down food into smaller particles
7. Digestive juice
8. Building muscle tissue
9. Oesophagus
10. Vitamins, minerals, fibre, protein, fat, carbohydrate
11. Blocks food from entering the respiratory system

From *GCSE Physical Education: A Revision Guide* by Tim Ferguson, 2002, Champaign, IL: Human Kinetics. AQA(NEAB)/AQA examination questions are reproduced by permission of the Assessment and Qualifications Alliance. London questions reprinted, by permission, from Edexcel Foundation.

12. Peristalsis

13. Up to five hours

14. Gastric

15. Two hours

16. Mouth

17. False

18. Release of hormones

19. Central nervous system

20. Brain, spinal cord

21. Eyes, ears, nose, touch (skin)

22. Brain

23. Thyroxine

24. Carry messages

25. Causes the cells to produce more energy

26. Pituitary gland, thyroid, pancreas, adrenal glands, ovaries, testes

27. Involuntary nervous system

28. True

29. True

30. False

31. True

32. True

33. True

34. True

35. False

36. True

CHAPTER 5   EXAMINATION QUESTION ANSWERS

The examination questions can be found on page 38. These answers are taken from the actual examination board mark scheme to provide an insight into the types of answer required.

MEG 1997 Paper 1 Q1

   e. In any activity there is a need to be aware of what is happening. We need to be aware of all that is going on around us outside our body; we need to be able to sense events that impinge on our consciousness both inside and outside our body. We need to be able to hear, see, feel, smell and taste to survive and thrive in life and sport. The nervous system has overall control of these vital sections; the brain is the control centre for every body activity, including sporting movement, and is suspended in fluid (cerebrospinal fluid) and protected by the skull. The spinal cord passes from the brain to the bottom of the spinal canal. Nerve fibres carry messages to and from nearly every part of the body, and they enter and leave the spinal cord in bundles through gaps in the vertebrae. Sensory nerves carry information to the central nervous system from receptors. Effector, or motor nerves, carry information to effector organs from the central nervous system. Effector organs are the muscles and glands which only work when they receive information from the central nervous system. Receptor or sense organs are as follows: (a) exteroceptors (receive information from outside the body) eyes, ears; (b) interoceptors (receive information from organs inside the body including lungs); and (c) proprioceptors (are found mainly in muscles, tendons and joints). Proprioceptors respond to the degree of stretching in their particular body part and give information about the position of the limbs. Proprioceptors enable us to move limbs with accuracy and speed without the need to actually watch them. Involuntary muscles control our breathing, digestion, heart rate, adrenaline, without our conscious knowledge or control. Co-ordination is a combination of thought, effort and practice until it becomes almost automatic. Reflex actions and reaction times should be considered accordingly.

AQA(NEAB) 1998 QA3

e. The nervous system controls muscular action by receiving information via receptors in the senses, processing information and making decisions in the brain, transmitting instructions to the responding muscles, activating motor units appropriate to an action, stimulating slow- or fast-twitch fibres appropriate to an action, controlling the timing and the graduation of impulses, and co-ordinating the contractions of agonist and antagonist muscles. Examples could include the co-ordinated action of the biceps or triceps muscles, or a reflex action.

CHAPTER 6   QUICK TEST ANSWERS

Chapter 6 Quick Test questions are found on page 42. These are the author's own answers.

1. System for producing energy with O_2
2. Adenosine triphosphate
3. Muscle cells
4. CO_2; H_2O; heat
5. + glycogen; + creatine phosphate
6. Adenosine diphosphate
7. Amount of available glycogen; level of lactic acid an athlete can cope with; amount of oxygen debt an athlete can cope with
8. Producing energy without oxygen
9. Converted into pyruvic acid and then into CO_2, H_2O and heat by oxygen
10. Supply energy
11. ADP
12. Aerobic
13. 30 to 60 seconds
14. Liver and muscles
15. Cramp or fatigue

From *GCSE Physical Education: A Revision Guide* by Tim Ferguson, 2002, Champaign, IL: Human Kinetics. MEG questions reproduced with the kind permission of OCR. AQA(NEAB)/AQA examination questions are reproduced by permission of the Assessment and Qualifications Alliance.

16. Lactic acid

17. Two minutes

18. Food + Oxygen = Energy + Carbon dioxide + Water + Heat

19. The body taking in and using enough energy to continue producing energy

20. Creatine phosphate

21. The body when it is short of oxygen, due to working anaerobically

CHAPTER 6   EXAMINATION QUESTION ANSWERS

The examination questions can be found on page 43. These answers are taken from the actual examination board mark scheme to provide an insight into the types of answer required.

MEG 1997 Paper 1 Q1

d. Aerobic respiration: an activity carried out at a steady pace; oxygen needed usually comes directly from the air; the oxygen is usually required only at a leisurely rate. If sufficient oxygen is available the activity can be carried on almost indefinitely. Pyruvic acid is produced by breaking down glycogen; this is converted to carbon dioxide and water, which are then removed through the lungs. Glucose + Oxygen = Energy + Water + Carbon dioxide. Activities include long-distance running, long-distance swimming, cycling, canoeing, etc.

MEG 1997 Paper 1 Q2

e. Energy is required for muscular contraction. This is supplied by a substance called adenosine triphosphate (ATP). ATP is made and used in all cells. When a muscle fibre is stimulated to contract, myosin molecules act on ATP to cause the muscle contraction. ATP is broken down to adenosine diphosphate (ADP) by this reaction. As the supplies of ATP in the muscles are small it has to be reformed if further muscular contraction is to follow. ATP is reformed in one of three ways, depending on hardness and length of contractions:

1. Creatine phosphate system: anaerobic, ATP gives energy for contraction + ADP, ADP + CP gives ATP + creatine

2. Lactic acid system: aerobic and anaerobic, ATP gives energy for contraction + ADP, ADP + glycogen gives ATP + pyruvic acid, pyruvic acid with oxygen gives CO_2 + H_2O and without oxygen gives lactic acid

3. Aerobic system, ATP gives energy for contraction + ADP, ADP + glycogen gives ATP + pyruvic acid, pyruvic acid + O_2 gives H_2O + CO_2

The question asks the candidate to respond in two ways. First they must show knowledge of the anaerobic energy systems and, second, demonstrate an insight into how movement comes about.

1. The creatine phosphate (CP) system. This lasts for a short time only (up to 40 seconds) and is used to re-synthesise ADP to ATP. The lactic acid

From *GCSE Physical Education: A Revision Guide* by Tim Ferguson, 2002, Champaign, IL: Human Kinetics. MEG questions reproduced with the kind permission of OCR.

system works for a longer period of time. If sufficient oxygen is available the body uses the aerobic system (this is based on the intensity of the activity). However, with limited oxygen availability (anaerobic work), pyruvic acid is converted to lactic acid. As above, this system requires the breakdown of ATP to ADP. Glycogen is then used to re-synthesise the ADP to ATP.

2. Movement: muscle fibres contract maximally (all or none law). The strength of the contraction is dependent on the number of fibres stimulated. Actin filaments pull in the myosin filaments, and the muscle pulls on the bone to create movement. Lactic acid diminishes the efficiency of contraction; lactic acid eventually forces the cessation of activity.

AQA(NEAB) 1997 QA2

d. The short-distance event requires an immediate burst of energy so glycogen is released without oxygen through anaerobic respiration, but lactic acid accumulation limits prolonged activity. The long-distance event requires a long, slow release of energy so that glycogen is oxidised through steady state or aerobic respiration at 70 to 80 percent capacity

AQA(NEAB) 1995 QA2

c. i. Releasing energy with the use of oxygen; can work aerobically for a long period of time

c. ii. Releasing energy without the use of oxygen; can only work for short periods of time

d. i. Sprint (anaerobic): don't use oxygen to release energy; breathing takes place but not so that oxygen can be used; energy release is through the creatine phosphate or lactic acid system. This creates an oxygen debt. After the race breathing is heavy to get the necessary oxygen back into the system to repay the oxygen debt.

d. ii. Long-distance race (aerobic): oxygen is used to release energy, breathing is continuous and gradually over time increases in depth and speed to keep up with the oxygen requirement.

e. High altitude affects stamina because the air is thinner due to lower pressure, therefore every breath contains less oxygen so the body gets less oxygen through the process of diffusion, thus producing less energy. Stamina suffers and performance is hindered, reducing an athlete's ability in competition and training in terms of both intensity and duration.

AQA(SEG) 1999 Paper 2 Q3

d. Award up to two marks for each correct definition and one further mark for each correct example from a physical or game activity. Definitions: aerobic: respiration in the presence of oxygen, or summarised as Glucose + Oxygen = Carbon dioxide + Water + Energy; anaerobic: respiration in the absence of oxygen, or summarised as Glucose = Lactic acid + Energy

London 1999 Q23

a. Carbon dioxide; water
b. Lactic acid
c. Muscle cramps, stiffness, soreness, fatigue, aches, pains
d. Anaerobic

London 1998 Q22

a.   i. Submaximal work, keep going for a long time, uses oxygen
a.   ii. Maximal work, work flat out, does not use oxygen
b. Sprints; shot put; any intense, explosive example
c. Insufficient oxygen available
d. Performance begins to slow down or deteriorate

CHAPTER 7   QUICK TEST ANSWERS

Chapter 7 Quick Test questions are found on page 48. These are the author's own answers.

1. Go red; sweat; deep breathing
2. Simple aerobic and anaerobic energy equations
3. Increased heart rate; increased cardiac output; increased stroke volume; increased blood pressure
4. Increases to the breathing rate; tidal volume; minute volume; breathing becomes deeper
5. Bones become stronger; ligaments get stronger; cartilage becomes thicker
6. Heart increases in size; it gets thicker walls; during exercise the heart has a greater cardiac output, stroke volume, heart rate; during rest the heart has a lower heart rate; the heart can also return to resting HR quicker
7. The blood is pumped around the body more quickly
8. Capillary network increases around the alveoli; alveoli become more efficient; diaphragm becomes stronger, as do the rib cage and sternum; the diffusion rate increases
9. Muscles become larger, stronger, more toned, increase their stamina, tendons increase in strength; muscles tolerate higher levels of lactic acid; become better at burning fat stores
10. False
11. True
12. False
13. True
14. True
15. False
16. False
17. False

From *GCSE Physical Education: A Revision Guide* by Tim Ferguson, 2002, Champaign, IL: Human Kinetics. London questions reprinted, by permission, from Edexcel Foundation.

18. False
19. True

CHAPTER 7 EXAMINATION QUESTION ANSWERS

The examination questions can be found on page 49. These answers are taken from the actual examination board mark scheme to provide an insight into the types of answer required.

MEG 1999 Paper 1 QB2

e. Description of graph: oxygen is transported to working muscles; CO_2 is exhaled; all work requires an increased O_2 uptake; line A shows a gradual increase in the volume of air breathed in and out (10 litres to 40 litres per minute), as the body meets the demands for O_2 and exhales CO_2; between 3 and 10 minutes the volume of air breathed in and out remains the same because of oxygen supply equalling demand outlined by line C (steady state or homeostasis rate of breathing has increased, as has depth of breathing); tidal volume: to meet O_2 demand; due to the initial delay in satisfying the demand for O_2, an O_2 debt is built up. (b) there is a sudden fall in ventilation at 10 minutes when the exercise stops followed by a more gradual fall. (d) less O_2 required; the gradual fall allows for repayment of the O_2 debt. (d) incurred at the start. (b) O_2 uptake assists with removal of lactic acid.

MEG 1998 QB2

d. Line A: heart rate at start of run is 72bpm but quickly rises over the first three minutes as the body attempts to meet the demands of the working muscle. Part of this response is a rapid rise in HR as oxygen is carried in the blood to the working muscles. Line B: at three minutes the body has adapted to the work load and the heart maintains its speed, that is oxygen demand equals the supply. This is called homeostasis or steady state. The athlete maintains the same effort over the following seven minutes. This is shown by the straight line B. If more effort were put in, the HR would increase because of the need for more O_2; if less effort were put in, then the HR would decrease because of the reduced demand for O_2. Line C: exercise stops and the HR decreases. This is because the heart now reacts to the new reduced demands of the body; HR continues to fall over the next few minutes as the post-exercise oxygen replenishment (oxygen debt) takes place. This fall continues until normal resting HR is achieved and oxygen demands return to normal levels.

AQA(NEAB) 1997 QB1

Short-term effects of exercise: skin goes red; body becomes hot; body becomes sweaty or smelly; heart rate increases; breathing increases; may cough or wheeze; may get cramp; may get stitch; may get aching muscles or joints; may pick up an injury (slight, or serious and long-term); may become sick, dizzy, thirsty, tired; relieves stress or tension. Long-term benefits of exercise: improvements in physical

From *GCSE Physical Education: A Revision Guide* by Tim Ferguson, 2002, Champaign, IL: Human Kinetics. MEG questions reproduced with the kind permission of OCR. AQA(NEAB)/AQA examination questions are reproduced by permission of the Assessment and Qualifications Alliance.

fitness overall or for specific parts of the body; increased effectiveness or efficiency of components of fitness; improved performance in daily tasks or in sport; increased suppleness through increased range of movement and relaxation capability of muscles; increased speed of movement and of reaction; increased muscle tone, strength in muscle and connective tissue; increased muscular stamina; increased cardiovascular stamina through efficient respiration or metabolism and circulation; increased vital capacity; larger or stronger heart; increased cardiac output; reduced incidence of heart attacks, strokes and high blood pressure; reduced risk of injury; reduced obesity; enhanced body shape; enhanced weight and body composition; enhanced confidence, vitality and esteem; enhanced quality of life (but not longer life); more resistant to illness; less days off work.

AQA(SEG) 1997 Paper 1 Q7

a.   i. Heart rate increases

a.   ii. Breathing rate increases or becomes deeper

a.   iii. Body temperature increases and sweat appears on the skin, skin becomes reddened

a.   iv. Muscles may be feeling tired or heavy or even sore, increased blood flow or more flexible

b.   i. Improved body shape; helps relieve stress or tension; reduces the chances of illness and disease; gives a physical challenge; social aspects; improves posture; increases basic strength, stamina and flexibility

AQA(SEG) 1997 Paper 3 Q6

a.   i. Heart: main function is to act as pump to circulate the blood around the body, therefore supplying the body with oxygenated blood, and then removing the waste in the return cycle. Blood: functions are to transport oxygen, make clots and fight disease. Veins: transport blood back to the heart. Arteries: transport blood away from the heart. Capillaries: allow carbon dioxide, oxygen, nutrients and waste products to pass through their walls

a.   ii. Air passages: these could be the nasal cavity, mouth, pharynx, epiglottis, larynx, trachea, bronchus or bronchioles. Functions are to allow the oxygen to be taken in by the body. Lungs allow gaseous exchange to take place as oxygen is taken in and carbon dioxide is passed out. The diaphragm: assists with the process of breathing, seals off the chest cavity and contracts and relaxes in breathing action

a.   iii. Award up to four marks for why the efficiency of the systems would be an advantage and for up to four marks for a suitable and well explained example, maximum of 6. Example: greater capacity to take in oxygen as fuel and turn it into energy. This makes the muscular system more efficient as it receives the correct amounts. The heart and lungs have a greater capacity and greater efficiency, and you are therefore able to work harder and for longer. Recovery rates after exercise are quicker and you are less likely to be fatigued as quickly. Less prone to illness and injury if these systems are efficient. Note that an example must be given to qualify the answer and these may be many and various. Example: Marathon runner needs to be able to work for longer periods of time at

From *GCSE Physical Education: A Revision Guide* by Tim Ferguson, 2002, Champaign, IL: Human Kinetics. AQA(NEAB)/AQA examination questions and AQA(SEG) examination questions are reproduced by permission of the Assessment and Qualifications Alliance.

a constant pace so needs to be efficient in utilising energy. Needs to train hard so needs to be able to recover fairly quickly after training sessions and keep up training.

London 1999 Q26

Cardiovascular: drop in resting heart rate; increase in stroke volume; stronger heart or bigger, greater red blood cell production; drop in blood pressure; capillary increase; VO_2max increase. Respiratory: intercostal muscles; diaphragm gets stronger; more air (or O_2) taken in with each breath; more alveoli available for gas exchange; including capillarisation of alveoli; lung capacity increase; more efficient removal of CO_2.

London 1998 Q29

a. See figure A.2 for the accurately plotted graph of each athlete or player (two marks per athlete, lose one mark for each error).

b. B

c. i. No

c. ii. His or her heart rate had not returned to its pre-exercise level

d. i. B

d. ii. Recovered quicker or lower resting heart rate

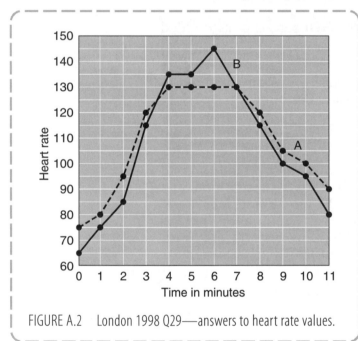

FIGURE A.2   London 1998 Q29—answers to heart rate values.

CHAPTER 8   QUICK TEST ANSWERS

Chapter 8 Quick Test questions are found on page 61. These are the author's own answers.

1. Strength; speed; stamina; suppleness; skill-related
2. Rugby scrum; hanging on a beam
3. Maximum force that can be exerted in one movement
4. Rowing or sit-ups continuously
5. Response time
6. Experience: better ability to anticipate
7. Bouncing to your limit may go too far
8. The heart and lungs continue supplying oxygen to the body
9. Cycle ergometer; rower; abdominal bleep test
10. Bleep test
11. Grab-ruler test
12. Partner stretching for you
13. Muscular strength of a person and their ability to keep going
14. Six seconds
15. Muscular; cardiovascular or cardio-respiratory

16. Hand grip dynamometer or tensionometer; time a "hang" on a beam
17. Explosive
18. Reaction time
19. Abdominal bleep test
20. Sit and reach test

CHAPTER 8   EXAMINATION QUESTION ANSWERS

The examination questions can be found on page 61. These answers are taken from the actual examination board mark scheme to provide an insight into the types of answer required.

MEG 1997 Paper 1 Q6

e. Each test should be viewed from the candidate's ability to set up the test, administer it accurately, collect data from the tests, plot results etc., draw conclusions and know the limitations of the test (conditions that can be tested, improved).

   i. Harvard step test: the HST tests pulse recovery rate. The ability to take an accurate resting pulse reading is essential. A bench 50cm high is required. A person steps on and off with both feet at a rate of 30 per minute, that is left foot-right foot to full standing in one second (on), left foot-right foot to full standing in two seconds (off). Continue step-ups for five minutes non-stop. Assistance can be used to judge the correct tempo. At the end of the test pulse counts are taken at intervals to plot recovery. This should be done one minute, two minutes, three minutes, four minutes and five minutes after ceasing exercise. These pulse counts should be recorded using pencil, paper, stopwatch, etc. Performance scores can be calculated using the formula: duration of exercise in seconds divided by 2 (sum of pulse counts after 1, 2, 3 minutes) × 100. Result matched with 90+ is excellent, 80 to 89 is good, 65 to 79 is average, 55 to 64 is below average, and below 55 is poor. The test is based in the fact that a quick recovery rate after strenuous exercise indicates a higher level of cardiovascular endurance.

   ii. National Coaching Foundation (NCF) multi-stage fitness test: a progressive shuttle run, also known as the bleep test, is often used as a training method because it is progressive and maximal. This means it starts easy and becomes more difficult as it progresses. The test is designed as a general test of endurance. It can test VO_2max, or maximum oxygen uptake. The test requires a tape cassette player and lines or cones to mark a 20m distance. The test consists of a recording with pre-recorded bleeps at various intervals. Test personnel do a series of shuttle runs to cover the 20m distance within the bleep times, thus running at a pace dictated by the bleeps. At the start the bleeps are a long time apart and running is at an easy, slow pace. Each minute the level changes and the bleeps occur more quickly. Performers still have to run the 20m shuttle run but at a quicker pace. In all, there are 25 levels, at the end of which candidates have long been sprinting. The longer the performer can run, the higher their score and the higher their level of endurance. Each runner must turn in time with the bleep. Three consecutive failures to turn on the bleep result in disqualification. Runners should not give in too early or at the first sign of discomfort.

iii. 12-minute run (Cooper): this is another test of aerobic capacity. Like the bleep test it tests VO_2max, or maximum oxygen uptake. The test requires very little equipment, simply a marked area and a stopwatch. The easiest course consists of ten cones at 10m intervals. The test consists of counting how many circuits of 100m can be completed in 12 minutes. At the end of 12 minutes, multiply the number of circuits completed by 100 (add two noughts) to give the total distance. A partner can record completed laps. Estimates of possible distance can be worked out according to time used or time left. Each time the test is completed an improved distance will show improved cardiovascular fitness. Performances are compared with rating charts. For example, 15 to 16 yrs: excellent = 2800 (M), 2100 (F); good = 2500 (M), 1900 (F); fair = 2300 (M), 1700 (F); poor = 2200 (M), 1500 (F). Subsequent attempts should be carried out in identical ways (for example, same surface).

MEG 1996 Paper 1 Q5

a. General fitness is the ability to participate in moderate activity without discomfort during or after exercise.

c. We need sufficient energy in the form of food and O_2 to enable the body to work effectively; we need muscles that are strong enough to support us and enable us to move ourselves and things about us; we need to be able to move our joints through their full range of movement and so use our body in the way it was designed to be used; we need to be able to act skilfully, work efficiently and use the minimum of effort; we need to be able to react and move quickly and so protect ourselves in potentially dangerous situations; we need to develop sufficient determination and motivation to see things through even if they become difficult.

AQA(NEAB) 1999 QA1

a. Heart, lungs or muscles

b. Two answers such as swimming, skiing, dancing, cycling, running, walking, aerobics, gymnastics, plus many games

c. Three answers such as boxing, racket sport, swimming, athletic throws, cricket, basketball, canoeing, rowing, golf, softball, baseball, football, sprinting, fencing, hockey, rugby

e. There will be a variety of responses depending on the choice of the activity. Expect the answers to contain the following common elements: analysis of the specific fitness in terms of the four S's and the five skill-related components; analysis of the specific fitness in relation to the body parts; analysis of the specific fitness in relation to the demands of the activity and the movement patterns and time. Note that the answer must name the component of fitness and a reason to get the mark. Aspects of physique are not credited.

From *GCSE Physical Education: A Revision Guide* by Tim Ferguson, 2002, Champaign, IL: Human Kinetics. MEG questions reproduced with the kind permission of OCR. AQA(NEAB)/AQA examination questions are reproduced by permission of the Assessment and Qualifications Alliance.

AQA(NEAB) 1998 QA1

a. One answer such as jogging, cycling, dancing, brisk walking, aerobics, or any listed on syllabus.

b. Two answers such as: slowing down of movements; aching muscles (build-up of lactic acid); reduction of skill; breathlessness; feeling "heavy"; pain; dizziness or feeling light-headed; collapsing; nausea; poor concentration.

c. Dynamic strength, explosive strength, static strength

d. The test could be for one of the three types of strength identified in c. using a dynamometer or a field test (e.g., pull-ups) as a general guide. Give no mark for the named test because there is no real consensus. The description should focus on: what is done on the test; how measures are taken; what is being tested. Possible points are: facility or equipment needed; any other people needed; instruction about what to do; how long test lasts; what type of measure is used; how score is recorded. The test could be for any part of the body.

e. Muscular stamina is best suited to football or hockey. This is because the games last for a considerable time. Stamina is the ability to withstand fatigue, particularly in the muscles of the legs. This is illustrated when the legs have to make repeated efforts lasting seconds interspaced with periods of low work rate and periods of rest and recovery, followed by periods of steady state work at a substantial level. Cardiovascular stamina is also well suited to hockey or football. Over the course of the game there is an overall demand on the heart and lungs to supply O_2 or energy. This is because both games have periods of maximum effort, steady state and "near rest". Also accept an answer that indicates both types of stamina are necessary for football and hockey; an answer that indicates not all football and hockey players need the same extent of stamina (for example, goalkeepers compared to outfield players). Note that both parts of the question (type and reasons) need to be answered for full marks.

AQA(SEG) 1996 Paper 2 Q6

a. One mark for each of the following: flexibility, suppleness, endurance, stamina, power, speed, agility, co-ordination, balance, reaction time

b. i. One mark for correctly identifying an activity requiring explosive strength and one further mark for stating how it is used. Example: sprinter using explosive strength to leave the starting blocks quickly

b. ii. One mark for correctly identifying an activity requiring static strength and one further mark for stating how it is used. Example: rugby when forward players push in the scrum

c. Award up to four marks for a detailed answer, which should make reference to: principles of training; specificity; overload; progression; frequency; intensity; duration

London 1999 Q28

a. *(a):* reaction time or agility; *(b):* power; *(c):* speed.

b. See table A.4 for answers.

From *GCSE Physical Education: A Revision Guide* by Tim Ferguson, 2002, Champaign, IL: Human Kinetics. AQA(NEAB)/AQA examination questions and AQA(SEG) examination questions are reproduced by permission of the Assessment and Qualifications Alliance. London questions reprinted, by permission, from Edexcel Foundation.

TABLE A.4 London 1998 Q28—Answers to Components of Fitness		
Component of fitness	Skill related or health related	Use of component
Agility	Skill related	Change the body's position and direction quickly
Strength	Health related	Support body weight, or other appropriate answer (e.g., power in service)
Flexibility	Health related	Increase range of movement
Co-ordination	Skill related	Accurate timing of movement of legs and hands

London 1998 Q27

a. i. Move whole body quickly with co-ordination, control, change direction.

a. ii. How quick the response is to a stimulus.

a. iii. Work = (force × distance) / time or = speed × strength

b. i. Side stepping; dodging; goalkeeping

b. ii. Getting a quick start or improve response to opponents

b. iii. Take off, approach run, force behind shot (for example, smash, serve, volley)

CHAPTER 9   QUICK TEST ANSWERS

Chapter 9 Quick Test questions are found on page 72. These are the author's own answers.

1. Age; sex; somatotype; disability; illness or injury
2. Diet; exercise; drugs; environment
3. Never
4. 30 percent
5. 20
6. 15 percent
7. Body type
8. Rugby
9. Vitamins; minerals; fats; proteins; carbohydrates; fibre
10. Fat
11. Provide energy
12. Meat; fish; milk
13. Two hours
14. Altitude; humidity; pollution; weather
15. Oils; butter
16. Severe chilling of the body
17. Training at an altitude of 1000m upwards

From *GCSE Physical Education: A Revision Guide* by Tim Ferguson, 2002, Champaign, IL: Human Kinetics. London questions reprinted, by permission, from Edexcel Foundation.

18. Increase exercise and eat a balanced diet

19. Build and repair cells

20. Rounded, lot of body fat, short limbs

21. Muscular, thin person

22. It reduces fitness

23. Helps keep the digestive system healthy

24. Increasing the body's carbohydrate stores

25. Calcium

26. Humid

27. Basal metabolic rate

28. Iron

CHAPTER 9 EXAMINATION QUESTION ANSWERS

The examination questions can be found on page 73. These answers are taken from the actual examination board mark scheme to provide an insight into the types of answer required.

MEG 1998 QB1

b. Endomorph and mesomorph

MEG 1996 Paper 1 Q5

d. Carbohydrates: provide energy for muscle use; proteins: provide building materials for cells, tissues, also amino acids not made by the body; fats: the main muscle fuel when resting or asleep, stored energy; dietary fibre: provides the bulky mass for the intestinal muscles to work on for food to be moved and expelled from the body; minerals: go directly into the bloodstream via intestinal walls and assist in bone repair, blood clotting, muscle function and nerve irritability; water: the most essential nutrient, without which there would be no building of body tissues or temperature regulations, food production seriously affected and sporting performance affected

AQA(NEAB) 1999 QA2

c. Three such as blindness; deafness; loss of organ; loss of limb; faulty organ; arthritis; paralysis; epilepsy; spina bifida; cerebral palsy; blood disorders

d. Illness affects performance: coughing creates a sore throat and affects breathing; high temperature reduces heat loss; a cold or flu can make you tired, lethargic, muscles and joints ache; headaches lead to a lack of concentration and slower reactions; stomach bugs lead to nausea; reduced muscle efficiency; reduced reactions; reduced concentration; restricted breathing; pain

AQA(NEAB) 1998 QA2

d. Assumption is that the question refers to "old age". Aging affects capabilities and hence fitness. Without specific training, aging has the following possible effects: redistribution of fats; weaker bones; reduction in muscle strength, stamina, suppleness, speed; rheumatism or arthritis; effect on movement; delayed reactions; poor circulation; poor cardiovascular stamina; increase in blood pressure; reduction in peak heart rate; reduction in O_2 uptake, or cardiorespiratory efficiency; more prone to injury, illness or heart disease; longer recovery from injury or illness

e. Physiological reasons: the basic skeleton, musculature and body size and composition (fat and blood volume) are different in women compared to men. This has a consequential effect on the "S" components of fitness, which in turn affects performance. This may be illustrated particularly well in power (strength and speed) activities such as field athletics where recorded distances are lower, and in stamina activities such as track athletics where recorded times are slower. It may be the case that women perform better in activities where suppleness is a major factor but this is not easily quantifiable. Sociological reasons: the history and evolution of women's involvement in sport has been behind that of men. Due to ignorance or prejudice and tradition there have been fewer opportunities for women to gain access, to be involved, to compete, to be coached, to receive support, to have achievements recognised.

AQA(SEG) 1998 Paper 2 Q2

c. Award up to three marks for considering a balanced diet: correct intake of the basic nutrients one mark; mention of carbohydrates, fats, proteins, vitamins, minerals, water and fibre (minimum of three award one mark); the need to have the correct energy intake award one mark; award up to a further four marks for correctly contrasting two different types of performer and considering their dietary needs. Answers should contain some reference to needs before, during and after a performance.

AQA(SEG) 1998 Paper 2 Q3

a. Endomorph; mesomorph; ectomorph

d. Award one mark for correctly identifying physiological factors as being those which directly affect the body (allow injury) or the body systems and one mark for correctly identifying psychological factors as affecting the state of mind. Award up to five further marks for giving correct examples for each and correctly describing the effect it can have. One mark for each example plus up to three marks for the description

London 1999 Q32

a. Vitamins, minerals, fibre or roughage, water

b.   i. Carbohydrates

b.   ii. Carbohydrates or fats

b. iii. Fats

b. iv. Fats, carbohydrates

b.   v. Fats, carbohydrates

London 1998 Q37

a.   i. Muscular

a.   ii. Circulatory, respiratory, cardio-respiratory, cardiovascular

b. Carbohydrates or fats

c. Specific requirements of sport, doesn't want to gain weight, that is intake should relate to demands of sport

d. Fats

e. Dangers to health, illegal, banned

CHAPTER 10   QUICK TEST ANSWERS

Chapter 10 Quick Test questions are found on page 78. These are the author's own answers.

1. To prevent injury; prepare body for action
2. Intensity; frequency; duration
3. Warm down
4. Overload; reversibility; specificity; progression
5. If training is stopped for a period of time fitness characteristics will decline
6. Age; sex; physique; disability; injury or illness; diet; smoking or drinking; which sport is being done; present level of fitness; experience; any special aims
7. To adapt to the stresses asked of it, so it will be better prepared next time
8. To improve the fitness characteristics through overload and progression
9. Soreness; aching muscles and joints
10. Become stronger; more powerful; improved muscular stamina; improved muscle tone
11. True
12. True
13. True
14. True
15. False
16. The amount of training required to have a beneficial effect
17. Training too often or too intensely
18. The point where performance does not improve even though training is continual
19. Training a particular aspect of fitness to meet an aim
20. To practise actions that will be used in the actual match or game

From *GCSE Physical Education: A Revision Guide* by Tim Ferguson, 2002, Champaign, IL: Human Kinetics. London questions reprinted, by permission, from Edexcel Foundation.

CHAPTER 10   EXAMINATION QUESTION ANSWERS

The examination questions can be found on page 79. These answers are taken from the actual examination board mark scheme to provide an insight into the types of answer required.

MEG 1996 Paper 1 Q5

e. Specificity: the effects of any training programme will be specific. If heavy weights are lifted with few repetitions, strength will be increased. Muscles will get bigger and stronger. Using lighter weights but many repetitions, dynamic strength will be increased. Muscles show little gain in size but better muscle tone. Explosive strength will be increased if heavy weights are lifted at speed. Only muscles that are stressed will be improved and they need to work in a similar way to the sporting situation. High-speed competition needs high-speed training to develop fast-twitch fibres.

Overload: muscles will become stronger if they are forced to work harder than they are used to. This can be achieved by increasing the intensity by using heavier weights or working faster. Duration will be increased by making muscles work for longer than they will need to. The frequency can be increased by training more often and with less recovery time in between.

Progression: it is important that any overload (stress) is increased progressively so that muscles, ligaments, tendons and other connective tissues have time to adapt to extra stress. The fitter a person becomes, the harder it is to keep on increasing fitness. Bones, ligaments and tendons take longer to adapt than the more responsive muscles of the body. Too much stress can cause breakdown and injury. Too little stress can lead to staleness and boredom.

Reversibility: in the same way that muscles adapt to any extra stress being placed on them by becoming bigger and stronger, they will also adapt to disuse or lack of stress by wasting away or atrophying. Muscles need stress to maintain their strength and efficiency. It takes only three or four weeks for the body to get out of condition. Deterioration is seen in aerobic activity as muscles quickly lose ability to use oxygen. Strength gains are lost at one-third of their rate of gain. Speed and strength are lost. As muscles become weaker and smaller they injure more easily. Weak muscles take longer to heal after injury.

MEG 1995 Paper 1 Q6

b. Cardiovascular fitness or stamina is the ability to exercise the whole body for long periods of time. It is the ability of the circulatory system (heart and blood) and the respiratory system (lungs and breathing) to withstand periods of hard work. It is the ability of a performer to maintain the fastest possible speed for the longest possible distance. It enables a performer to tolerate lactic acid.

c. Reversibility is the opposite of progression. Too little progress can lead to staleness or boredom. The body adapts to less strain or stress. It takes only a few weeks for the body to get out of condition. Deterioration can be seen most readily in aerobic activity. The muscles quickly lose much of their ability to use oxygen. Anaerobic activities are less readily affected by lack of training because the use of oxygen is not as crucial. Strength gains are lost at about one-third of their gain rate. If muscles are not used they atrophy or waste away. Both speed and strength are gradually lost. As muscles become weaker and smaller they become more prone to injury. Weak muscles take longer to recover from injury.

d.   i. Power is the product of explosive strength and speed or force; both must be mentioned to gain a mark.

d.   ii. Exemplar test (any explosive strength measurement using instruments or vertical leaps can be used). For example, standing broad jump: stand feet comfortably apart, toes immediately behind the start line; bend knees, swing arm forward and push off vigorously; jump as far as possible along the mat; your score will be taken from where your heels land; land with feet together and do not fall backwards.

AQA(NEAB) 1999 QA4

a. Overload (do not accept frequency, intensity or duration as separate answers); progression; specificity; reversal

d. Facilitates recovery; brings body systems back to normal; redirects the blood smoothly; re-oxygenates blood; removes lactic acid; prevents "pooling" of blood in veins; avoids muscle stiffness, soreness or tightening; prevents dizziness, light-headedness or fainting; keeps blood capillaries dilated; flushes oxygenated blood to muscles; helps muscles return to normal temperature slowly; reduces risk of injury; allows other parts to be reactivated (e.g., digestion)

e. There will be a variety of answers depending on the choice of activity; however the answers will probably involve warm-up; conditioning or physical fitness; mental preparation; skill practice; team practice (allow tactical practice); game or routine or event; warm-down or cool-down.

AQA(NEAB) 1998 QA4

e. The principle of overload involves putting the body functions under progressively increased stress to get a training effect (maximum two marks). In weight training this is done, depending on the required outcome for muscular strength or muscular stamina, by adjusting the intensity of the training session, the number of repetitions, the number of sets, the weight lifted, the rest period, the duration of the training session, or the frequency of the training session. Two marks only for saying simply "intensity, frequency, duration".

NB Both parts of question to be answered for full marks.

AQA(SEG) 1998 Q2

b.   i. Award up to two marks for stating that it increases the body temperature, increases the range of movement and reduces the likelihood of injury, psychological preparation. Warm up a muscle award no marks.

b.   ii. Award up to two marks for outlining a suitable warm-up which would include both stretching or mobility exercises and pulse raisers. Allow skill rehearsal; jogging must be qualified.

From *GCSE Physical Education: A Revision Guide* by Tim Ferguson, 2002, Champaign, IL: Human Kinetics. MEG questions reproduced with the kind permission of OCR. AQA(NEAB)/AQA examination questions and AQA(SEG) examination questions are reproduced by permission of the Assessment and Qualifications Alliance.

London 1999 Q29

a.   i. Time
a.   ii. Frequency
a. iii. Type
b. Overload / progression
c. Progression
d. Reversibility
e. Specificity

London 1998 Q28

a. See table A.5 for answers.
b. Type of activity

TABLE A.5 London 1998 Q28— Answers to Definitions of the Principles of Training	
Intensity	C. How hard you work during the session
Frequency	D. How often you train
Duration / time	A. How long you exercise
Progression	B. Start slowly and increase the amount of exercise

CHAPTER 11   QUICK TEST ANSWERS

Chapter 11 Quick Test questions are found on page 86. These are the author's own answers.

1. Aerobics; interval; circuit; long, slow distance; Fartlek
2. Weight; interval; circuit
3. Interval; circuit
4. Very adaptable; no special equipment required; suitable for all fitness levels within the same circuit session
5. No equipment required; burns fat stores; excellent aerobic training
6. Training designed to ensure athletes peak in fitness at certain times of the year
7. Maintain motivation; reduce boredom
8. Alter training methods
9. The degree of intensity an individual needs to be working at for training to be beneficial
10. An aerobic workout which allows for anaerobic bursts, similar to the type of exercise seen on a football or hockey field

11. Similar to Fartlek, involves a series of reps which could be short sprints intermixed with a series of rests

12. 220 minus your age

13. Aerobic training zone = 60 to 85 percent of maximum HR; anaerobic training zone = +85 percent of maximum HR

14. High working HR; low resting HR; large difference between resting and working HR; quick recovery rate

CHAPTER 11   EXAMINATION QUESTION ANSWERS

The examination questions can be found on page 87. These answers are taken from the actual examination board mark scheme to provide an insight into the types of answer required.

MEG 1996 Paper 1 Q6

a. Cardiovascular fitness is the ability to exercise the whole body for prolonged periods of time. Efficient heart, lungs, circulation.

MEG 1995 Paper 1 Q5

c. Muscular endurance emphasises non-stop activities of the whole body; local endurance is the ability of isolated muscle groups to resist fatigue and to keep working under the pressure of continuous, localised use such as press-ups, pull-ups, etc. Most people stop the activity because they are unable to stand the pain. The above is background information. Exemplar test, to measure abdominal muscular endurance; equipment: mat or mats, stopwatch (use abdominal bleep test). Instructions for the subject: sit on the mat, back upright, hands across chest; knees bent at 90 degrees, feet flat on floor (held by partner); lie on your back until shoulders touch mat and return so that elbows touch knees, keeping hands completely on chest; on "go" repeat this action as many times as possible for a given time (for example, 30 seconds or one minute); stop when told to. Instructions for tester: check starting position; allow practice; time accurately; count aloud each time a correct sit-up has been done.

d. Resistance training is trying to gain strength by making muscles work harder than they have been used to. The stress that the body is put under must be built up gradually. It is not necessary to have any special equipment. Partner work involving pushing, pulling, lifting, carrying involves overload or stress; running up and down steep hills, over sand, in mud, or into a strong wind all involve working against a resistance. This puts extra strain on the muscles, which will adapt and become stronger. Intensity and duration of a programme can be planned by building up to a maximum load whilst reducing the number of repetitions. It is important to ensure that as far as possible any resistance exercises match closely to the actual sporting movements, and to the speed of the event. The main difference between strength training and endurance training is the weight of the resistance and the number of reps.

From *GCSE Physical Education: A Revision Guide* by Tim Ferguson, 2002, Champaign, IL: Human Kinetics. MEG questions reproduced with the kind permission of OCR.

AQA(NEAB) 1999 QA4

b. Two such as athletics (middle distance or sprinting); invasion games; racket games

c. Three such as works the whole body; makes a demand on breathing; demand on the heart and circulation; demand on stamina of muscles; enable steady-state work, low intensity, long duration; not working beyond anaerobic threshold; improvement to various systems

AQA(NEAB) 1998 QA4

a. One such as improves performance (in terms of quality, quantity and consistency); improves fitness or skill; improves body shape; loses weight; helps feel-good factor

b. Two such as usually based on running: variable; periods of high-level work: speed, variable intensity or demand; periods of low-level work; periods of rest or recovery; variable total time involved, distances and terrain

AQA(NEAB) 1997 QA4

a. Stamina (accept endurance or cardiovascular fitness)

b. Two such as continuous; interval; Fartlek; circuit training; weight training; slow, long distance

d. i. The point at which the effect of exercising is beneficial or the point beyond which there is a training effect

d. ii. Maximum three points along the lines of: state maximum heart rate for age; formula (200 minus age or 220 minus age); calculate 60 / 70 / 80 percent; accept one mark for each, stating maximum HR, allowance for age, upper and lower percent age threshold

e. Consider: components to be improved: suppleness, stamina, speed, strength; parts of the body to be stressed; types of exercises that can be used (facilities, time, and cost in mind); arrangements of exercise stations; type of apparatus and arrangement; number of exercises; number of reps and laps; time allowances; number of people taking part; age and sex of people; level of ability, fitness, any illness or injury; disability of people taking part

AQA(SEG) 1997 Paper 3 Q3

a. i. Award up to two marks for a full answer which must refer to at least two body parts or areas. These must also be appropriate to the chosen activity; for example, long jumper: legs, notably hamstrings, calves and quads, and arms, notably shoulder mobility.

a. ii. Award up to two marks for a full answer which must consider more than one type of exercise to be used or the way the exercise would be performed for the named body areas; for example, stretches of the hamstrings by crossing feet over each other and bending at the trunk, keeping legs straight; also arm rotations at the shoulder to loosen shoulder.

From *GCSE Physical Education: A Revision Guide* by Tim Ferguson, 2002, Champaign, IL: Human Kinetics. AQA(NEAB)/AQA examination questions and AQA(SEG) examination questions are reproduced by permission of the Assessment and Qualifications Alliance.

a. iii. Candidates may choose to consider the time each phase of the warm-up should last or the overall time to be taken. There will be some variation in responses, depending on the activity chosen and the level at which the performer is performing. It would be expected that at least several minutes should be spent on the warm-up for each phase to be effective.

b. The training method chosen must be an accepted and relevant one and credit should be given where more than one method is stated to improve different aspects of performance; for example, weight training to improve strength and speed coupled with endurance training to improve stamina.

c. i. Motivating; instilling confidence; assisting the mental rehearsal of the performance; calming nerves, generally calming them down; stress control; reducing anxiety; psyching up. An explanation is asked for so there would need to be some understanding (for example, motivating would not be enough; must say motivating to go out and perform their best).

c. ii. Organise training; assist with diet; choose tactics and strategies and practice them; achieve and maintain fitness levels; analyse performances; help with skill acquisition

AQA(SEG) 1997 Paper 3 Q4

b. i. The number of times the weights are moved

b. ii. The number of times that the repetitions are performed

c. i. Give a full, detailed description of equipment available. This can be either multi-gym or machine station type equipment with details and examples, or both free-standing equipment with details and examples of both.

c. ii. General benefits: increase in strength, power and possibly local muscular endurance. Specific benefits which relate to the named activity: increase in explosive strength to help the sprinter due to performing exercise at speed. Examples would be required for full marks, general comments would not be sufficient.

London 1998 Q35

a. Fluctuating or up and down

b. Changes in the demands made on the body

c. Interval

d. Accept anything other than aerobic activities (for example, sprinting, high speed, football, explosive activities); must be specific situation.

e. Specificity

London 1998 Q36

a. i. Strength, muscular endurance, power

a. ii. Weight training, circuit, isometric, plyometrics (must be related to part i)

From *GCSE Physical Education: A Revision Guide* by Tim Ferguson, 2002, Champaign, IL: Human Kinetics. AQA(SEG) examination questions are reproduced by permission of the Assessment and Qualifications Alliance. London questions reprinted, by permission, from Edexcel Foundation.

b. Allows adaptation or progression to occur, stops reversibility, maintains current fitness (or relevant explanation; for example, a description of reversibility).

c. Individual needs

d. Isometric

e. i. Warm-up

e. ii. Cool-down or warm-down

CHAPTER 12   QUICK TEST ANSWERS

Chapter 12 Quick Test questions are found on page 97. These are the author's own answers.

1. Cramp in the diaphragm
2. One or more bones forced beyond their normal position
3. Treatment given by the first person to help
4. Open; closed; compound; simple; stress; greenstick
5. Painful to move; joint swollen; bruising appears
6. A small tear
7. When the broken bone has caused damage to other tissue
8. Support and immobilise; send for medical help; reassure them; keep comfortable and warm
9. Realign bones; put in plaster for length of time; physiotherapy
10. Rest, ice, compression, elevation
11. Stretch the muscle group, massage
12. A muscle that has been overstretched
13. Raise injured part above level of heart, this helps to drain excess fluid and reduce blood flow to injury
14. Inflammation of the tendon
15. Through repetition

CHAPTER 12   EXAMINATION QUESTION ANSWERS

The examination questions can be found on page 98. These answers are taken from the actual examination board mark scheme to provide an insight into the types of answer required.

MEG 1997 Paper 1 Q5

a. Being deprived of shelter or protection; open to the elements (heat, cold, wind or rain); being exposed to nature

d. i. First aid is that assistance given immediately by the first person on the scene until medical help arrives.

d. ii. Assess the situation to avoid further risk. Diagnose: ask questions, check breathing, bleeding, consciousness, finger tip search. Treat: according to circumstances—not breathing with pulse, mouth to mouth; not breathing, no pulse, mouth to mouth and resuscitation. Make comfortable. Seek further help: if 999 give location, who you are, nature of accident, pin-point place and number involved and severity, action so far, let them put phone down; record: findings, event, action taken as soon as possible after the emergency

e. Stitch: is a form of cramp affecting the diaphragm. It is common in running events where a sharp pain is felt in the upper part of the abdomen. It may be caused by lack of blood to the diaphragm, or the blood supply is reduced because of pressure from the lungs (caused by heavy breathing) above and the abdominal muscles below. Possible cause: irritation from eating before exercise with a full intestinal tract. Treatment: strengthening diaphragm and abdominal muscles, avoiding eating before exercise, effective warm-up; with stitch: slow down, bend forward, push clenched fist into area of pain, controlled breathing

MEG 1997 Paper 1 Q6

b. Cricket: gloves, pads, box, helmet; football: boots, shin pads; hockey: goalkeeper, boots, pads; rugby: scrum cap, gum shield, shin pads, padded posts, scrum machine; athletics: safety net, appropriate footwear

c. The body would not survive without water; temperature regulation: body overheats; performance is affected; dehydration; feeling faint, dizzy, weak, sick (generally unwell); thirsty; activity ultimately stops

d. A muscle cramp is a sudden, painful contraction of a muscle group or muscle: a relevant reference to warm-up. It can last seconds or hours. Cramps occur at any time; the most common times are during or after intense exercise. Common causes are chilling of body, lack of salt and other minerals, muscle injury, and prolonged muscular contraction without movement.

AQA(NEAB) 1999 QB2

Accept the following injury types (regardless of tissue) for one mark each: cut or graze; bruise; burn or blister; fracture (any type); sprain; dislocation or displacement; concussion; strain or pull; tear or rupture. Risks of injury may be reduced by better technique; better fitness; better preparation, training or rehearsal, warm-up or warm-down, escape routes (for example, outdoor education); having the correct attitude, determination, playing to the rules, not fooling about, no risks or short cuts; using better weather conditions, weather, surfaces; better equipment and facilities; wearing appropriate clothing (protective); better diet; health profile (medical check-up); better officials or coaches; playing at the appropriate age or standard; no jewellery; tie hair back.

NB Both parts of question must be answered for full marks.

AQA(NEAB) 1995 QA3

a. Tendon: pulled, torn, strained, ruptured or stretched; bruise; cut; blister or burn; ligaments: torn or pulled; cartilage torn

From *GCSE Physical Education: A Revision Guide* by Tim Ferguson, 2002, Champaign, IL: Human Kinetics. MEG questions reproduced with the kind permission of OCR. AQA(NEAB)/AQA examination questions are reproduced by permission of the Assessment and Qualifications Alliance.

b. Blue lips; feel cold and clammy; quick, shallow breathing rate; weak pulse; feel nauseated and concussed

c. i. Loss or lack of body fluid

c. ii. Severe chilling of the body

c. iii. Overheating of the body

d. i. Fracture

d. ii. Fracture: send for medical help; stop any bleeding; do not move; keep warm and comfortable; talk and reassure them; no food or drink

e. Example: hockey; warm-up or warm-down (thorough, at least 15 minutes including a full stretch); training (regular and specific): prepare the body and mind for competition, increase fitness; skill level: improve skill and knowledge to help avoid injury; competition: at appropriate level for standard including age; environment (consider conditions): icy, hot, cold or wet, etc.

AQA(SEG) 1998 Paper 2 Q2

a. R: rest; I: ice; C: compression; E: elevation

London 1999 Q37

i. Tendon

ii. Brain

iii. Friction

iv. Protects

v. Crack

vi. Water

London 1998 Q38

a. Break, fracture, strain, torn ligament, torn tendon, dislocation

b. Rest; ice; compression; elevation

NB one mark for RICE

c. Danger; response; airway; breathing; circulation

d. Dial 999 or get help

CHAPTER 13   QUICK TEST ANSWERS

Chapter 13 Quick Test questions are found on page 107. These are the author's own answers.

1. Something that is learned, efficiently done, smooth, looks good, controlled and goal directed

2. Born with

3. Strength, stamina, speed, agility, suppleness, balance, timing

4. Cognitive; perceptual; perceptual-motor

From *GCSE Physical Education: A Revision Guide* by Tim Ferguson, 2002, Champaign, IL: Human Kinetics. AQA(NEAB)/AQA examination questions and AQA(SEG) examination questions are reproduced by permission of the Assessment and Qualifications Alliance. London questions reprinted, by permission, from Edexcel Foundation.

5. A skill involving a large muscle group

6. Open: a skill that is done in a changing environment; closed: a skill that can be repeated in the same environment

7. Basketball free shot: a distinct beginning and end

8. Tennis serve: the performer controls the rate of the action

9. Basketball free shot: the environment is always the same

10. A skill involving co-ordination

11. A skill involving a small muscle group

12. Self-paced: performer controls the rate of the action; externally paced: performer has no control of the rate of the action

13. Cycling has no obvious beginning or end

14. Closed skill, self-paced skill, serial skill

15. Making a pass in a game of football

16. Sensory input; decision making; motor output; feedback

17. Process of filtering information and focussing on the important information

18. Eyes; ears; touch (proprioception)

19. After any action is carried out, the news whether success or failure is fed back to the memory

20. Long- and short-term memory stores

21. Feedback from someone else

22. Knowledge of results

23. Extrinsic

24. Immediately

25. Reaction; movement time

26. Grab ruler test

27. Time taken from the signal (starter's gun) till the first movement is initiated

28. Viewing information and sorting out the relevant or important information

29. Speed; trajectory; colour; size; starting point

30. Muscles receiving and carrying out instructions

31. Knowledge of performance

CHAPTER 13   EXAMINATION QUESTION ANSWERS

The examination questions can be found on page 108. These answers are taken from the actual examination board mark scheme to provide an insight into the types of answer required.

MEG 1998 Q9

Decision making: making decisions; output: doing the movement; feedback: getting information about the movement.

From *GCSE Physical Education: A Revision Guide* by Tim Ferguson, 2002, Champaign, IL: Human Kinetics. MEG questions reproduced with the kind permission of OCR.

MEG 1998 QB1

c. i. Closed skill is a pattern of movements that has been learned by the performer and that can be produced without the environment having any effect on the movement. This includes stable, predictable, a movement that is always the same and not affected by anything else, habit, control (maximum two marks).

c. ii. Examples such as activity is basketball, closed skill is a free shot; activity is gymnastics, closed skill is forward roll (2).

MEG 1997 Q3

b. Performers process information after performance. This information about the actual performance is fed back from a variety of sources. Feedback can be internal: a performer feels or senses that an action is carried out in a particular way (proprioceptive). Feedback can be external: a performer hears or sees whether they were successful or not; knowledge of results; knowledge of performance; intrinsic or extrinsic; negative or positive.

d. Candidates should relate their answers to closed and open skills. Some sports are won by doing the same skill the same way because the situation is always the same. This allows the performer to repeat a movement as close to perfection as possible. Improvement is then possible by increasing strength, power, speed, etc., above that of rival competitors. Some activities are won by adapting skills, often to fit either an unpredictable series of environment requirements or a very exacting series, whether predictable or unpredictable. Opponents must be overcome as well as the environment. This could imply out-thinking or outwitting adversaries. Appropriate examples should be rewarded.

MEG 1997 Q4

a. Fine motor skills, precise movements

b. Any suitable explanation that involves eliminating the difference between a performer's intention and what actually happens

c. Individuals can only handle limited amounts of information at any one time. This is called limited channel capacity, selective attention. To avoid this, coaching should be well guided, well organised and well demonstrated. Performers should learn where and when to look and what to look at. Appropriate information messages should be grouped together. Automatic responses should be learnt. This frees the brain to concentrate on elements vital in performance (for example, tactics). Performers are also able to gain from experience.

e. Information stored in memory is the result of previous experiences, games, opponents, situations, etc.; its value to performance is in its comparative use during practice and performance; in STM information is quickly lost; STM does not entail detailed coding of information, practice or concentration; it is an initial comparative store and retrieval is only temporary; when information is coded and practised it enters the LTM; effective retrieval is based on the initial efficiency of the coded storage; STM receives information once meaning and interpretation have occurred; the amount that the STM (and subsequently LTM) can handle is limited at any

From *GCSE Physical Education: A Revision Guide* by Tim Ferguson, 2002, Champaign, IL: Human Kinetics. MEG questions reproduced with the kind permission of OCR.

one time; STM is important in the learning of complex skills; the components of the skill are assembled and practised until the whole skill is developed; a reasonable time span is required for practice and coding; once this has been achieved information can enter the LTM with fewer interference processes inhibiting retrieval.

MEG 1996 Paper 1 Q3

a. Motor skills are movement skills used in everyday life, or they are often specific to a particular activity and in specific movements; motor skills are physical skills.

b. Individuals can only handle limited amounts of information at any one time; if they receive too much information they become overloaded and confused.

d. To become an expert in open skills (for example, team and racket games, fencing, boxing), learn how to deal with a variety of situations; learn how to control this variety of situations; make up for deficiencies in technique through constant practice, break down skills; make up for deficiencies in physique through appropriate methods of training; avoid mental fatigue by constantly spending time in training simplifying and clarifying cues for action; to become an expert in closed skills an individual must acquire well-timed muscular co-ordination; perfect them; build up strength, power, endurance, mobility with appropriate example; remove any deficiencies or faults in skill techniques; overcome deficiencies in physical attributes.

AQA(SEG) 1999 Paper 2 Q4

d. Three marks for correctly describing feedback. The following points may be made: information received about how good a performance was; this may be internal feedback (knowledge of performance); may be external feedback (knowledge of results); two further marks for examples from actual games or physical activity situations which must be suitable and acceptable examples appropriate to the activities chosen.

AQA(NEAB) 1999 QB1

Definition: The learned ability to bring about a predetermined result with maximum certainty and efficiency / minimum time or effort. Skill is founded on the physical components of agility, balance, co-ordination, reaction and timing. Award one mark for each component that is described—award one mark only if components are just named. Acceptable answers: a combination of mental and physical abilities; a combination of physical ability and decision making; the application of technique; patterns of movement; something that you do well. Allow one mark for each of the following: gross and fine; closed and open; simple and complex.

Effects on performance: All other factors (e.g., fitness, motivation, conditions) being equal, the level of skill determines the level (or quality) of performance. The higher the skill, the higher the performance because athletes are better at using available energy (more efficient, less waste); are in better control of actions (smoother); don't feel as tired; make fewer mistakes; are able to see what's happening, to anticipate; make the right decision at the right time, quickly; have

From *GCSE Physical Education: A Revision Guide* by Tim Ferguson, 2002, Champaign, IL: Human Kinetics. MEG questions reproduced with the kind permission of OCR. AQA(SEG) examination questions and AQA(NEAB)/AQA examination questions are reproduced by permission of the Assessment and Qualifications Alliance.

more "tricks" in their "armoury"; have increased unpredictability through more variety; have increased interest, motivation, satisfaction and confidence; reduce the effects of chance or luck; are in the right place at the right time; are less likely to cause injury. Acceptable answers: The more skilful you are, the more likely you are to be successful, consistent, able to repeat or perform at a higher standard.

NB The question is not about how skills are learned.

NB Both parts of the question must be answered to gain full marks.

AQA(NEAB) 1998 QA2

b. Sight or vision; sound or hearing; touch or feeling

c.   i. To raise performance; to gain an advantage; for safety

c. ii. Goalkeeper at a penalty kick; racing driver at the start grid, for example

CHAPTER 14   QUICK TEST ANSWERS

Chapter 14 Quick Test questions are found on page 118. These are the author's own answers.

1. Intrinsic; extrinsic
2. Drive to achieve
3. Need to learn; drive generated to satisfy need; action takes place; if success then there is a drive reduction
4. Motivation from external sources
5. Something that is a certificate rather than praise
6. Intrinsic
7. Can get the best out of their athletes
8. Yes
9. Certificate; badge; medal; trophy
10. Money; other material goods
11. No
12. True
13. Yes
14. Make training fun, enjoyable; give success; make it challenging, exciting; give variety; set a goal or target

CHAPTER 14   EXAMINATION QUESTION ANSWERS

The examination questions can be found on page 118. These answers are taken from the actual examination board mark scheme to provide an insight into the types of answer required.

MEG 1999 QB1

e. The desire to do well is based around motivation. This answer should be based around intrinsic motivation. A definition of this could gain reward.

Reference to extrinsic motivation, with an example equals one mark. Continued motivation (desire to do well) can be achieved through setting goals, which motivates you to work hard, helps you prepare mentally, provides you with success (could be extrinsic), and raises your confidence; being totally focussed on their own performance; training to maintain fitness levels; training to maintain skill levels. The performer should also insure that the goals are good goals. This is achieved through goals being Specific, Measurable, Agreed, Realistic, Time phased, Exciting, Recorded (SMARTER). With detailed explanation, one mark each, SMARTER on its own one mark only.

MEG 1998 QB2

e. i. Motivation is difficult to define, but if the candidate implies it is a condition where the performer has needs, wants, drives or interests that can be stimulated either from within or from the outside, give credit.

e. ii. Success or winning; praise: from coach, teacher, parent or friend (extrinsic motivation); reward (for example, self-satisfaction from winning money; through good teaching or coaching; through competition) provides a standard to aim for; intrinsic motivation: desire to succeed, win or be the best; through progression, the performer can see progress; realistic objectives that ensure success; keeping results so that success can be monitored; respecting the teacher or coach; fear of being left behind or not being as good as the others; the feel-good factor; fear of criticism; emulate role model; media; music. (SMARTER is related to target setting and should be credited with only one mark).

CHAPTER 15   QUICK TEST ANSWERS

Chapter 15 Quick Test questions are found on page 127. These are the author's own answers.

1. Football Association; Hockey Association; Lawn Tennis Association
2. National Coaching Foundation
3. Central Council for Physical Recreation
4. Increase participation; quality and quantity of facilities; increase standards of performance; provide information
5. Define rules; organise leagues; settle disputes; provide coaching; promotion; selection of representative teams
6. Improve or develop sport; support the NGBs; advise the Sports Council
7. Sports Council; media rights; corporate sponsorship; ticket sales; membership fees
8. Facilities; coaching; advertising or promoting; events; grants
9. Corporate sponsorship; Sports Council grant; donations from members
10. UK Sport; SC for England; Scotland; Ireland; Wales
11. True
12. International relations and major events; ethics and anti-doping; producing winners; UK sports institute

From *GCSE Physical Education: A Revision Guide* by Tim Ferguson, 2002, Champaign, IL: Human Kinetics. MEG questions reproduced with the kind permission of OCR.

13. Research has shown that if you play sport in school you are more likely to play sport throughout your life.

14. False

15. Judge; umpire; referee; linesman; referee's assistant; scorer

16. Laws; regulations; codes

17. Rugby players shaking hands at the end of the game

18. National governing bodies

19. Verbal warning; sin-binned; sent off; yellow card; penalty

20. Fined; suspended; banned; community service; imprisoned

21. Pass back: football; support in the lineout: rugby union; 40m to 20m rule: rugby league; offside rule: hockey

22. Photo finish: horse racing; video referee to adjudicate try in rugby league; third umpire to adjudicate run outs in cricket using a camera

23. An unwritten code of conduct

24. Maintain safety; make sport exciting to watch and to play

25. Football Association; Lawn Tennis Association

26. Safety; excitement; increase number of spectators; incorporate the advanced technology

CHAPTER 15 EXAMINATION QUESTION ANSWERS

The examination questions can be found on page 128. These answers are taken from the actual examination board mark scheme to provide an insight into the types of answer required.

MEG 1999 QB3

e. Physical benefits are: look better; feel better; improved muscle tone; posture improved; improved skill levels; bones and joints become stronger; reduces body fat (excess weight); improved fitness; improved health. Social benefits are: mixed games playing; join a team or club; meet people with similar interests; make new friends and enjoyment; learn about co-operation and teamwork; can make a career out of activity; raise self-confidence; reduces risk of boredom, credit for mental well-being, such as stress, anxiety, extrinsic rewards (excluding money). Maximum eight marks.

MEG 1995 Paper 2 Q2

a. ASA: Amateur Swimming Association; FA: Football Association; LTA: Lawn Tennis Association; BAGA: British Amateur Gymnastics Association

c. Raise participation in sport nationally; raise standards; educate people regarding the value of sport and physical recreation; improve facilities; maximise use of current facilities

d. PE teachers could spend more time during lessons with the pupil; give extra-curricular time; verbally encourage pupil; give individual training programmes; enter the pupil for county teams; direct the pupil to good local clubs; ensure the pupil does not get carried away with his or her success; put facilities at pupil's disposal. The PE programme could offer a variety of activities (for example, major games; minor game; individual activities; access to outside clubs; outdoor pursuits; water sport); parents could encourage or support their child (for example, monetary measures and promote enjoyment; attend practices and games or events; transport the child to events; take an interest in the sport as a whole; have contact with the PE staff).

e. Leisure is that time available for the individual which is free from any working, domestic, or social commitment; unfortunately, leisure trends have to include TV, pubs, etc. Unemployment has to be a key issue in terms of raising the amount of leisure time. The jogging craze or running boom is a recent trend; examples are marathons, fun runs. Reasons include awareness of health needs. Aerobics and step aerobics: in fashion, awareness of health needs. Health clubs and private gyms: people are willing to spend money on healthy pursuits; such clubs are still fashionable and continuing to expand. Rambling and walking: to get away from the city, smog, hustle and bustle. Countryside commission: developing and maintaining footpaths which further encourage walking as a leisure pursuit. There will be many more examples of leisure trends. Allocation of marks when correct and relevant points made.

AQA(NEAB) 1999 QA6

d. Providing publicity materials (e.g., magazines, billboards, TV posters, newspapers); on the Internet; award schemes; centres of excellence and sport colleges; junior competitions; marketing merchandise; negotiating TV and media rights, or sponsors; give money for capital projects; employing development officers and resources; producing educational programmes and resources; using role models or celebrities to promote (new) ventures; working with the Youth Sports Trust or Sport England.

AQA(NEAB) 1998 QA6

a. National Coaching Foundation

e. The Sports Council promotes sport by providing: information and advice to the public; publicity and promotional material; promotional campaigns (a list of campaigns award one mark); grants; national sport centres or academies; advice to the government and CCPR; back-up services such as a drug-testing service, sport medicine; coaching courses; sponsored events and services.

AQA(NEAB) 1997 QB3

Examples of what and how. Football: professional foul in the box, sent off; rugby league: high challenges, sin-bin; tennis: racket abuse, warning and points; athletics: two false starts, disqualification; basketball: five personal fouls, disqualified; cricket: limited bouncers per over; football: proven allegations of match rigging: banned; weight lifting: proven use of prohibited drugs: banned; rugby union: last ditch tackle on player chasing ball: penalty try; horse racing: interfering with the contacts: disqualification; boxing: hitting below the belt, warning plus.

NB Off the field incidents must have a consequence on the field (for example, to say that Tony Adams (Arsenal) was taken to court for drunk driving, found guilty, fined, banned and sent to prison is not enough: it is the effect on sport [Arsenal lost his services for "X" games]) that is the punishment. It is not that Gazza is an alleged woman beater but that if this behaviour continues Hoddle will not pick him for England; reasons—foul behaviour on the field breaks the rule of the activity and is cheating; off the field breaks the law and is criminal; punishments for culprits range from a quiet word or official cautions to disqualification, with the victims receiving a variety of bonus points or plays. Without fair play and good sportsmanship the game descends into chaos: ill feeling and meaninglessness result. Victory through intimidation is hollow; foul behaviour brings shame to individuals or the sport into disrepute; foul behaviour is punished to set an example and to prevent repetition. It is punished to maintain safety and standards. Both parts of the question must be answered for full marks.

AQA(NEAB) 1995 QA6

d. Use examples. Rules ensure safety of the players (for example, high tackle in rugby not allowed; footballers must wear shin pads to prevent or reduce the number of broken legs; spectator safety-barriers in motor racing and appropriate stadia; some sports such as rugby stop players playing in the next game if they have a concussion; boxing forces fighters to have regular medical tests by neutral doctors).

e. Examples: unsure decision: drop ball in football or ice hockey; snatch in netball; tip off in basketball; technology: video referee in rugby league to decide try; in cricket to decide run outs; in gymnastics and diving to replay to give aesthetic scores; sprinting and horse racing: cameras to decide winners and runners up.

AQA(SEG) 1998 Paper 2 Q5

c. i. One mark for each benefit: finance received in entry fees; buying merchandising materials; support and encouragement for the team; some volunteer help and assistance.

c. ii. One mark for each disruption or problem correctly identified: possible hooliganism; police and stewarding costs; segregation arrangements; abuse or taunting of players or affecting the image of the organiser.

AQA(SEG) 1997 Paper 2 Q1

a. i. One mark for any named official (for example, referee, umpire)

a. ii. One mark for each named responsibility: checking kit and equipment; checking correct number of players; timing the event or match; interpreting rules and enforcing them

a. iii. One mark for each clearly identified item: whistle; notebook or scorebook; pen or pencil; counting stones; watch or stopwatch; coloured cards (for example, yellow or red); distinctive kit or uniform

From *GCSE Physical Education: A Revision Guide* by Tim Ferguson, 2002, Champaign, IL: Human Kinetics. AQA(NEAB)/AQA examination questions and AQA(SEG) examination questions are reproduced by permission of the Assessment and Qualifications Alliance.

AQA(SEG) 1996 Paper 2 Q1

a. One mark for each correctly named marking or area (for example, 18-yard line or penalty area for football). Do not accept field placements.

b. i. Two marks for correctly identifying the rule or regulation and for describing what it is (for example, basketball, double dribble: the player dribbles the ball using two hands at the same time or dribbles, stops and then recommences the dribble).

b. ii. Two marks for the action the official takes. Candidates should identify that play is stopped, the breach is pointed out and the appropriate action taken (for example, for double dribble the official blows the whistle, signals with alternate movement of hands up and down, opposition has possession at the sideline).

CHAPTER 16   QUICK TEST ANSWERS

Chapter 16 Quick Test questions are found on page 138. These are the author's own answers.

1. Compulsory competitive tendering
2. Management bids to run sport facilities
3. Local authorities; Sports Council; private enterprise; voluntary
4. Population; access; demand; competition; flexibility
5. Excellence
6. Bisham Abbey; Lilleshall; Plas y Brenin; Holme Pierrepont; Crystal Palace
7. Holme Pierrepont
8. For profit
9. Village hall; scout hut
10. Outdoor activities
11. Someone who does not get paid for playing sport
12. Someone who gets paid for playing sport
13. Lack of time; lack of money; resources; poor facilities; no coach or trainer
14. Pressure from their club or team, from the public, from the media; difficult private lives; loss of confidence though variety of pressures
15. So the players from the North could be given the money they missed from lost earnings from work when they played rugby
16. A fund set up so individuals can concentrate on sport but still get an education
17. True
18. Boxing
19. Bring the best athletes together to compete in a friendly atmosphere helping to unite the world
20. Tennis
21. Government; corporate sponsorship; media; private individuals; tickets and merchandise; charity

From *GCSE Physical Education: A Revision Guide* by Tim Ferguson, 2002, Champaign, IL: Human Kinetics. AQA(SEG) examination questions are reproduced by permission of the Assessment and Qualifications Alliance.

22. TV; radio; newspapers
23. Publicise; provide money; increase profile; boost sponsorship opportunities; create personalities; help with analysis and technology
24. Lack of coverage can be damaging; criticism of players, etc. can go too far; pressure caused by "spotlight"; rewards provided by media cause problems
25. Support in a variety of forms in return for wearing a "label"
26. Clothing; transport; equipment; accessories; training
27. Advertising; tax benefits; promotion
28. Limited company: shareholders, etc.
29. National lottery
30. Promotion; facilities; equipment; wages; scholarships; training; shareholders; events
31. Under soil heating; synthetic turf: Astroturf for all weathers; padded gym or martial arts floors
32. Waterproof; breathable; warmer or cooler
33. Energy return system; improved grip
34. Shin pads; gum shields; scrum caps; helmets
35. Run outs in cricket; a try in rugby league
36. Magic eye machine; tennis ball machine; sensor on the net: net faults on service
37. Collecting information for analysis; giving statistics from information for analysis
38. Make safer; improve standards, improve coaching and analysis
39. Skiing: quick release binding for safety of skier, don't break legs when they fall; football: shin pads reduce number of broken legs

CHAPTER 16   EXAMINATION QUESTION ANSWERS

The examination questions can be found on page 139. These answers are taken from the actual examination board mark scheme to provide an insight into the types of answer required.

MEG 1998 QB3

    d. Amateur games player: participate in sport because of the enjoyment and satisfaction they get; taking part is more important than winning; they train and compete in their own time and when they want; it is outside their work time; money paid into trust funds. Professional games player: are paid to compete and sport is their work; winning is important and they have to compete to gain money; they usually train full time; better facilities, coaches, equipment, medical support. There is a blurring between the amateur and professional performer, and candidates may offer the following responses (one mark); no agreement between governing bodies as to what constitutes an amateur; basketball is becoming more popular and the "importing" of American players has encouraged the growth of professional players; thus

From *GCSE Physical Education: A Revision Guide* by Tim Ferguson, 2002, Champaign, IL: Human Kinetics. MEG questions reproduced with the kind permission of OCR.

basketball has become "mixed", with professionals, semi-professionals and amateurs; rugby union, a traditionally amateur game, has moved toward professional status and is now very mixed; the amateur rugby union player can still receive very generous expenses which, over a season, amount to a large sum of money; to compete with the professional the amateur has to train more, often giving work up to train; activity may be specified as amateur, professional or open, and restricts entrants; lottery funding for amateurs.

MEG 1997 Paper 2 Q2

a. A park; sport centre; swimming pool; tennis court; gym.

b. Sport For All; Sport For All: Disabled People; 50+ All to Play For; Ever Thought of Sport; What's Your Sport; Women: Milk in Action for Women; Year of Sport; Sport For All: Come Alive.

c. i.

TABLE A.6 MEG 1997 Paper 2 Q2 National Sport Centres	
National Centre	**Activity**
Holme Pierrepont	Water sport
Plas y Brenin	Mountain activities

c. ii. Answers related to excellence: provide opportunity for talented sport people to train; allow use of top class facilities; top class equipment; build up sporting tradition in UK; win medals, events or competitions internationally; centres of excellence

e. It can lead to an increase in general sponsorship, raised awareness, team sponsorship or individual sponsorship; lead to increased income (for example, gate money; more money pays for facilities, equipment, training); better performance; giving sport a better name; ultimately leads to an increased audience; leads to greater participation; leads to improved standards; local newspapers, radio and magazines can all encourage participation at grass-roots level; acceptable role models are created.

MEG 1995 Paper 2 Q1

b. Cheaper if existing facilities can be used for more than one purpose, then new facilities need not be built; schools can be dual use and are usually located in the heart of the community therefore more convenient; increased bonding between school and community; more respect for school property; greater range of facilities for school children during the day; maximise use of facilities; school receives money for hiring

c. Draft the rules and laws of the game; organise local and national competitions; select teams and coaches for international competitions; keep players and participants informed; maintain relationships with the media; promote the sport, or marketing; devise award schemes; aim to improve facilities;

support and minimise pressure on individuals, emotional and financial; CCPR and SC provide feedback

d. Positive factors: better climate to train in; better facilities; equipment; trainers or coaches; competition; train full time, still leaving time to continue education; the above could lead to improved technical ability; improved performance (times or distances); could lead to British athletics on the world stage; promoting British athletics abroad and at home; increased attendance at athletics meetings in the UK; increased participation (desire to emulate); increased sponsorship of individuals, meetings; new coaching ideas

AQA(NEAB) 1999 QA6

a. Education; leisure or recreation; community services; parks and amenities; sport development group.

b. Swimming or diving pool; weight-training room; fitness suites; sport halls or gymnasiums; parks; golf courses; pitches; tennis courts; greens; dry ski slopes; athletics tracks; cycle tracks; ice or roller rink; tenpin bowling; outdoor basketball rings.

AQA(NEAB) 1998 QA6

b. Local professional club; centre of excellence; national sport centre; specialist school or college

c. Local council policy; finance; traditions; lack of demand or support; lack of natural environment or resources; safety regulations; planning regulations; accessibility; private provision

d. Emphasis on "non-playing" volunteer; names of voluntary posts (treasurer, secretary, chairman) just one mark; serving on committee; organising fixtures or teams; publicity, communication or PR; transport or kit; fund raising; marking, mowing ground; coaching and training; officiating; running meetings; arranging social events; providing refreshments; controlling finances; providing first aid

AQA(NEAB) 1997 QA7

e. Advantages: award and coaching schemes; ground improvement; event staging; kit or clothing; training opportunities; travel costs; campaigns and other publicity that raise the sport profile; accommodation; use of equipment or hire of facilities; buy players and pay wages. Disadvantages: short-term alliance; threat to minority sport if TV sponsor pulls out; product association; stealing the limelight (distractions); determining policy decisions; only famous team or individuals get top sponsorship

AQA(NEAB) 1997 QB2

Yes, because TV gives access to a wide audience at home and abroad; provides a good medium for public relations; it communicates and informs; educates; brings news, results and reports; publicises and promotes; advertises; does this through broadcasting events and related programmes (teletext or videos); camera evidence

From *GCSE Physical Education: A Revision Guide* by Tim Ferguson, 2002, Champaign, IL: Human Kinetics. MEG questions reproduced with the kind permission of OCR. AQA(NEAB)/AQA examination questions are reproduced by permission of the Assessment and Qualifications Alliance.

used to facilitate decisions; support penal appeals, third eye in cricket and rugby; TV footage used for coaching; increases awareness; interest; enjoyment; popularity; increased participation; provides entertainment at home (plus action replays and opinions); access to those who cannot attend live through illness, work commitments, simultaneous events, distance, expense, tickets sold out; enables money to go directly to sport for televising rights; through sponsors. No, because TV concentrates on top or élite performers, teams and events; resources directed disproportionately; TV live detracts from attendances at the gate (revenue); cheaper and easier to stay at home ("couch potato"); loss of atmosphere; reducing active participation; limited perspective (only see what you are shown); TV dictates the programme (times and commercial breaks); can influence rules; replays pressurise officials (criticisms, trial by camera)

AQA(NEAB) 1996 QA7

a. A person or group who gives support in return for something
b. Provide: clothing; equipment; training; money; transport; accessories
c. SC; media rights; private individuals; tickets and merchandise; charity
d. Paid for doing what you enjoy; more time to train; high wages; prestige; fame and popularity
e. National curriculum: schools and PE departments have to teach certain activities by law; certain number of periods per week; subjects laid out; all have to learn to swim; must have gymnastics; games; athletics; outdoor activities; dance; give examples; international: politics used sport (boycotted Olympic Games, banned sport tours, allowed individuals to compete for our country [Zola Budd]; provided facilities to get chance to host major events)

AQA(NEAB) 1995 QA5

a. Conserve environment; provide access; information about places of interest
b. Two such as Snowdonia National Park; Peak District National Park
c. Bisham Abbey; Lilleshall; Plas y Brenin; Crystal Palace; Holme Pierrepont
d. Dual use in school: soccer, rugby or hockey pitches, indoor netball or basketball courts, weight-training or fitness rooms; sport centres: similar but may have swimming pools, greens for bowling; ice or roller rinks, squash courts; golf clubs; parks
e. Advantages: could be used every day for all sport; cost effective; give the nation a sense of pride; feeling of a home; our venue; place on the world stage; having one first- or world-class venue or facility. Disadvantages: only one place in the country would have the facility, whereas the alternative is to spread good facilities around the country; which sport would have priority; conflict between sport; which day to host which event or contest

AQA(NEAB) 1995 QA8

a. Someone who does not get paid for playing
b. Football; tennis; golf

From *GCSE Physical Education: A Revision Guide* by Tim Ferguson, 2002, Champaign, IL: Human Kinetics. AQA(NEAB)/AQA examination questions are reproduced by permission of the Assessment and Qualifications Alliance.

c. Bribing officials, players, clubs, coaches; players taking drugs; spectators behaving as hooligans; coaches or players arguing with the officials; players or coaches behaving illegally outside of the sport (for example, Tony Adams' drunk driving)

d. Sponsorship deals will be more prolific and larger; possibility of turning professional if not already; kudos or fame from the popularity gained from winning; with the fame comes "personality" (money from doing interviews and shows; glory and honour); feeling of self-satisfaction and success of achievement

e. Increase: because more sports are applying to join the movement for the kudos, prestige, to enhance their sport, increase the numbers of people wanting to watch, play and be involved in their sport; future ruling allowing all professionals to compete in every sport at the games. Decrease: IOC turns down sport or removes current sport from the movement; possible future changes disallowing any professionals from competing or going back to their roots, future host cities not having the ability to host more sports due to the already massive increase in the number of athletes and sports involved in the Games

AQA(SEG) 1998 Paper 2 Q5

a. Television or satellite TV; Internet and CD ROM; radio; newspapers

b. One mark for the following and one mark for a correct description: equipment; clothing; accessories; transport or travel; money; training; entry fees and expenses; food

AQA(SEG) 1997 Paper 2 Q10

a. i. Sport where people are paid to take part in terms of prize money or pay; people taking part do so as a full-time job with no other source of income; the sport is run as a business enterprise with paying customers attending.

a. ii. People taking part do not get paid for competing and are not allowed to collect prize money above a certain level; all those taking part have other full-time jobs and sources of income; the sport is not always run at a profit and spectators usually do not pay to watch.

a. iii. Both professional and amateur sport people are allowed to compete at the same time; amateurs compete for fun but the professionals compete for prize money; there are usually paying spectators at these events.

AQA(SEG) 1996 Paper 2 Q9

a. i. One mark for a harmful effect and two marks for a described example: e.g., loss of privacy: press hounding individuals for statements, plus constant photographs and requests for statements and press conferences; smear campaigns: claiming information of illegal payments, drug abuse or similar, and printing damaging articles

a. ii. One mark for identifying a beneficial effect and two marks for the described example; positive image: sport portrayed as clean and healthy with the benefits of fair play and the reward of taking part; exposing

From *GCSE Physical Education: A Revision Guide* by Tim Ferguson, 2002, Champaign, IL: Human Kinetics. AQA(NEAB)/AQA examination questions and AQA(SEG) examination questions are reproduced by permission of the Assessment and Qualifications Alliance.

bad practice: disclosing and publicising possible cheating or even foul play (TV evidence)

a. iii. One mark for each way sponsors and media may affect plus one mark for each example. For example, promotion or advertising: increasing participation; changing timings of events: Olympic events and boxing matches; advertisers time outs: allowed in American football broadcasts; dictating competitors: golf tournaments and tennis; obtrusive advertising: hoardings around stadiums, logos on shirts

AQA(SEG) 1996 Paper 3 Q7

a. i. Lighter materials for outdoor pursuits and therefore less bulky; more aerodynamic for speed skaters, skiers, swimmers; artificial surface materials such as Astroturf, tartan tracks, etc.; graphite; Teflon treatment of clothing materials

a. ii. Better designs (for example, aerodynamic, larger head rackets); better use of materials (for example, graphite rackets, fibreglass poles, etc.); high-tech equipment such as electronic timing devices, magic eyes on lines (Wimbledon); more availability (for example, safety helmets and safety equipment)

a. iii. Many now purpose-built for specific sport: indoor tennis centres; recessed gymnastics areas; multi-use facilities; improved design and use of space; better materials mean improved surfaces

CHAPTER 17   QUICK TEST ANSWERS

Chapter 17 Quick Test questions are found on page 146. These are the author's own answers.

1. Doping
2. Any chemical substance which alters the biochemical balance of the body
3. Social
4. Stimulants; anabolic steroids; analgesics; tranquillizers
5. True
6. Reduces reaction time; causes muscular co-ordination problems; slurs speech and hearing; blood pressure increases; heart rate increases; cirrhosis of the liver
7. Liver
8. Nicotine
9. Removing a volume of blood and then replacing this at a later date to temporarily increase the blood volume
10. Reduce fatigue
11. Valium; beta blockers
12. Cycling; other stamina-based events
13. Painkiller
14. Testosterone; nandrolone
15. Heart disease; high blood pressure; infertility

From *GCSE Physical Education: A Revision Guide* by Tim Ferguson, 2002, Champaign, IL: Human Kinetics. AQA(SEG) examination questions are reproduced by permission of the Assessment and Qualifications Alliance.

16. Increase the volume of water that is eliminated
17. False
18. 1988, Ben Johnson, Seoul Olympics, for example
19. Urine
20. Increase in the number of deaths of athletes from drug taking

CHAPTER 17   EXAMINATION QUESTION ANSWERS

The examination questions can be found on page 147. These answers are taken from the actual examination board mark scheme to provide an insight into the types of answer required.

MEG 1999 QB1

c. i. High blood pressure; body hair or facial hair; become aggressive; male breasts; infertility; deeper voice for females; heart disease; excess testosterone; addiction; acne

c. ii. International agreement, banning guilty parties from competition, all-year testing; regular updates of banned substances; governing bodies work independently to reduce abuse (for example, media; removal of records or medals)

AQA(NEAB) 1999 QA2

a. A drug designed or manufactured to arouse; accept a drug; a chemical or hormone

b. Two such as by coughing or wheezing; through pain; destroys cilia; reduces stamina; tar in the lungs; reducing vital lung capacity; reducing oxygen supply; build up of mucus; takes up the place of oxygen in the blood; through shortage of breath

e. May steady nerves, calm emotions; may adversely affect judgement, agility, co-ordination, timing; may cause loss of balance; slow down reactions; opens the bladder; upsets the body fluid balance, dehydration; increases aggression; improves confidence; causes erratic behaviour; increases risk of injury; blurred vision; long-term effects (for example, liver damage, addiction, obesity)

AQA(SEG) 1996 Paper 3 Q6

a. i. Social drugs are controlled drugs usually taken to heighten feelings or emotions and performance-enhancing drugs are taken by sport performers specifically to improve their performance.

a. ii. Stimulants; narcotics; diuretics; peptide and glycoprotein hormones and analogue; alcohol; marijuana; local anaesthetics; corticosteroids; beta blockers

a. iii. Side-effects in three categories. Liver disease and heart failure: jaundice; liver failure; tumours; bleeding of the liver; increased fatty sub-

From *GCSE Physical Education: A Revision Guide* by Tim Ferguson, 2002, Champaign, IL: Human Kinetics. MEG questions reproduced with the kind permission of OCR. AQA(NEAB)/AQA examination questions and AQA(SEG) examination questions are reproduced by permission of the Assessment and Qualifications Alliance.

stances; cancer; increased risk of heart attacks, strokes, blood pressure. Sexual and physical problems: stunted growth; reduced sperm count; sterility; shrinking and hardening of the testicles; impotence; growth of breasts (men); disrupted menstrual cycle; changes in sex organs; balding; acne; growth of facial hair; miscarriages; still birth; deepening of voice (women). Behavioural effects: increased moodiness; aggression.

b. More likely to contract cancer of the throat, mouth, lungs; greater chance of heart disease, nicotine and carbon dioxide; damage to heart and blood vessels; increased chance of contracting bronchitis; these factors should be linked to the fact that the sportperson's cardiovascular or respiratory system would be adversely affected and would therefore decrease performance levels.

London 1999 Q34

a. Alcohol, smoking or nicotine or tobacco
b. Kidney or liver damage; male secondary characteristics on women; heart disease; cancer; high blood pressure; infertility
c. Increase training potential; to win; gain wealth; to increase aggression; improve power, strength, endurance; enhance performance; to aid speed of recovery
d. They may ignore the pain due to injury and therefore incur injury

CHAPTER 18   QUICK TEST ANSWERS

Chapter 18 Quick Test questions are found on page 153. These are the author's own answers.

1. Very popular amongst the masses
2. Separateness
3. South Africa
4. Commonwealth countries, 1977, cut links with South Africa
5. For example, 1980, Moscow, USA boycotted over the Soviet invasion of Afghanistan
6. Retaliation for the 1980 Olympics, USA boycotted
7. Olympics is on the world stage
8. 1991
9. True
10. Won several gold medals, the star of the games, he was black

CHAPTER 18   EXAMINATION QUESTION ANSWERS

The examination questions can be found on page 154. These answers are taken from the actual examination board mark scheme to provide an insight into the types of answer required.

From *GCSE Physical Education: A Revision Guide* by Tim Ferguson, 2002, Champaign, IL: Human Kinetics. AQA(SEG) examination questions are reproduced by permission of the Assessment and Qualifications Alliance. London questions reprinted, by permission, from Edexcel Foundation.

MEG 1999 Paper 1 Q3

d. Some believe that many games can harm women (for example, rugby, football); successful performance often requires determination, high fitness levels and commitment, this is unfeminine and clashes with social mixing; few role models; this is changing with Laura Davies, Jane Sixsmith, encouraging participation; women's sport has little media attention; prize money is less for women, therefore it is more difficult to earn enough money to live on; sponsorship, most sponsors opt to sponsor men's sport, this also leads to financial difficulties; time; transport such as only one car per family or inaccessible venues; traditional attitudes (cooking, washing, etc.); poor crèche facilities; religion or culture; few women administrators.

MEG 1996 Paper 2 Q1

e. Question concerned with how sport has been used for political purposes, individual, party, national and international, and requires a degree of explanation to gain marks. Raise the game: party political statement; candidates may respond from the "cold war" perspective, that is building centres of excellence in eastern bloc countries, young children taken from their homes to train, etc., all to give the communist system credibility; may also opt to put more stress on apartheid events: rugby tours, cricket tours, western government intervention in these cases (for example, the Commonwealth relation to apartheid: Gleneagles treaty). Reference could be made to any number of Olympic Games (for example, 1936, Berlin, Hitler's desire to show the superiority of the Aryan race through sport, it backfired; 1956, Melbourne, Chinese withdrawal to bring attention of the world to its claims on Taiwan; 1960, Rome, South Africa competed with an all-white team; 1964, Tokyo, South Africa invitation withdrawn; 1968, Mexico, black power movement, USA black athletes; 1972, Munich, Israeli athletes murdered by Palestinian terrorists; 1976, Montreal, black nations boycotted over New Zealand rugby tour to South Africa; 1980, Moscow, USA boycotted over Soviet invasion of Afghanistan, then in 1984, USA, eastern bloc countries boycotted in retaliation).

MEG 1995 Paper 2 Q2

b. 1936: Berlin; 1948: London; 1956: Melbourne; 1968: Mexico; 1972: Munich; 1976: Montreal; 1980: Moscow; 1984: Los Angeles; 1988: Seoul.

AQA(NEAB) 1997 QA8

a. One of potentially many; from one of matches to periodic sport festivals such as the Olympics, Commonwealth games, world cups.

b. Promote new sport; show off; acclaim, status, honour, recognition; prove to be the best; challenge or better competition; improve standards; improve relationships or unite countries.

c. Boycotting Olympic Games to force action about South Africa; banning South Africa from international competition due to apartheid; prohibiting countries from entering the Olympics; proposals to introduce ID cards; rais-

From *GCSE Physical Education: A Revision Guide* by Tim Ferguson, 2002, Champaign, IL: Human Kinetics. MEG questions reproduced with the kind permission of OCR. AQA(NEAB)/AQA examination questions are reproduced by permission of the Assessment and Qualifications Alliance.

ing awareness about inequality through "black power"; instigating terrorism in Munich or at the grand national; promoting Nazism.

d. Yes, reflects the priority sport is given; importance of sport; ability of the competitors; support of coaching, resources and facilities. No, because medal tables do not explain underlying features about: how many competitors there are per percentage of the population participating; how much money, resources put into sport; how much progress has been made; representatives of a country may not actually live or train in that country; consistently appearing in positions just outside medals; countries successful in non-Olympic sport.

e. Exercising sportsmanship might contribute by: showing responsibility; exercising choice; making and accepting decisions; understanding the need for laws and rules; understanding concepts such as fairness and justice; recognising the rights of others; knowing right from wrong; fair play; promoting co-operation and teamwork; learning to cope with competition (success and failure); keeping a sense of value; keeping a sense of proportion or context; a conscience.

AQA(NEAB)   1996 QA8

a. Los Angeles, London, Munich, Mexico City, etc.
b. i. International Olympic Committee
b. ii. British Olympic Association
c. 1968: Mexico City, 200 Mexicans died in riots over demonstrations regarding poverty; 1972: Munich, nine Israeli athletes killed in a botched kidnap attempt by terrorists; 1976: Montreal, 20 African countries boycott the games; 1980: Moscow, United States boycott the games because of Soviet Union's invasion of Afghanistan.
d. Cost: can't afford to host the games, provide the facilities or do not have the existing facilities (including airports, hotels, road system transport, etc.); political reasons such as poor human rights record (China, political unrest; North Korea); games also not given to a country from the same continent twice in a row.
e. Increases the support through increased coverage of the sport; increased participation and increased finance of the sport through worldwide advertising; acts as a shop window to show off a sport; increases interest to participate, support, organise, officiate, administer the particular sport; maybe the sport does not have its own major world cup or championship.

AQA(SEG) 1997 Paper 3 Q8

b. Five marks for a full, detailed answer; note problems must be stated and these must be qualified by examples: acts of terrorism; financial disasters; media interference; boycotts and political interference; apartheid issues; security problems; drug taking; crowd disorders and problems.

Glossary

ADP (adenosine diphosphate)—see ATP.

aerobic energy—energy produced using oxygen over a long period of time.

agility—the ability of an individual to act using speed and flexibility to change body position.

alveoli—tiny air sacs in the lungs. The process of diffusion takes place here.

amateur—someone taking part in sport without receiving payment.

amino acids—substances which link together to form larger protein molecules.

anabolic steroids (androgenic anabolic)—performance-enhancing drugs based on the male hormone testosterone, which help the body to repair and build muscle tissue.

anaerobic energy—energy produced in short bursts without using oxygen.

anatomy—the structure of the body.

anorexia nervosa—an eating disorder (illness) characterised by insufficient food intake.

antagonistic (pair of muscles)—two muscles working as a pair but in opposition to each other (e.g., the biceps relaxes whilst the triceps contracts).

anxiety—caused by worry about a situation and can lead to stress.

aorta—the largest artery in the body, which carries oxygenated blood from the heart to the body.

arterioles—smaller blood vessels that branch off the arteries and help to distribute the blood to the body.

articular capsule—strong fibrous tissue surrounding synovial joints.

ATP (adenosine triphosphate)—the substance used to help facilitate energy production. Once used, it forms ADP (adenosine diphosphate); this can be converted back to ATP later.

atria (singular form is atrium)—the upper chambers of the heart. They receive blood from the veins.

atrophy—muscle wastage, usually through lack of use.

autonomous stage of learning—the third stage, where a skill becomes automatic, thus allowing the performer to concentrate on other tasks such as tactics / strategies and position of teammates.

balance—maintaining the equilibrium of the body.

basal metabolic rate (BMR)—the minimum rate of energy required to keep all the life processes of the body functioning whilst at rest. The BMR is the amount of energy burnt whilst doing nothing.

body composition—the relative proportions of fat and lean body mass.

bronchi—the two main tubes in the lungs that branch off the trachea to each lung.

bronchioles—the smaller tubes that branch off the bronchi in the lungs.

calorie—a unit that measures heat or energy production in the body (joule is the metric equivalent).

carbohydrate loading or carboloading—a legal technique enabling the body to store increased amounts of carbohydrate before a competition or event.

carbohydrates—one of the main nutrients of the body; carbohydrates are energy-rich substances (e.g., bread, pasta and rice).

cardiac output (Q)—the amount of blood pumped out of the heart in one minute (heart rate × stroke volume).

cardiovascular endurance—the ability of the heart and lungs to supply oxygen to the body.

cartilage—a tough, shiny substance that covers the ends of bones. It protects the bone by acting as a buffer or shock absorber where two bones meet and also allows frictionless movement.

CCPR (Central Council for Physical Recreation)—an advisory body to the Sports Council and the national governing bodies of sport.

CCT (compulsory competitive tendering)—the forcing of local authorities to allow private groups or consortia to bid for the management rights to sport centres and other facilities.

cholesterol—a fatty substance that can build up on the inner walls of arteries, reducing blood flow.

circuit training—a training method using different stations of exercise; usually lasts 40 to 60 minutes.

closed skill—a skill performed in a stable environment. The skill should be the same each time it is executed.

cognitive stage of learning—the first stage of learning, when beginners have to understand what to do.

concentric contraction (dynamic contraction or isotonic contraction)—the muscles shortening as they contract.

concussion—an injury to the head which can cause a player to become unconscious.

co-ordination—the ability to control body movements.

cramp—a sudden, uncontrollable and painful contraction of a muscle. Treat by massage and stretching. Loss of body salts can cause cramps.

creatine phosphate (CP)—an energy reserve stored in the muscles; it is used to convert ADP to ATP.

decision making—part of the information-processing chain. Once information has been collected a decision needs to be made.

dehydration—loss of water from the body.

diastolic pressure—blood pressure when left ventricle relaxes.

discrimination—distinguishing between people because of their sex, race, or disability.

distributed practice—training sessions or practice with rest breaks.

dual use—sharing of facilities to maximise the usage. This is common with schools and sport centres.

dynamic contraction—see **concentric contraction**.

dynamometer—a hand grip meter used to measure strength.

eccentric contraction—the muscle trying to contract whilst lengthening (e.g., the thigh muscle while running down hill).

ectomorph—a somatotype; an individual with thin arms, legs and body.

endomorph—a somatotype; an individual with thick arms, legs and body.

endurance—stamina, or the ability to keep going for long periods of time. This is also known as cardiovascular fitness, cardio-respiratory fitness and muscular endurance.

etiquette—an unwritten rule or code of convention, which is not enforceable but is expected.

exhale—to breathe out, expiration.

expiration—see **exhale**.

extrinsic feedback—information given to the performer from a source other than the performer.

extrovert—personality type; sociable, loud and confident.

Fartlek—"speed play", a type of training going slow and fast over differing terrain.

fast-twitch fibre—muscle fibres that contract quickly but tire quickly.

fats—one of the main nutrients, an energy-rich substance such as butter and oil.

feedback—any information a performer receives about an action they have carried out.

fine motor skill—involving small muscle groups to carry out a skill or action.

first aid—treatment to someone by the first person to arrive at an accident scene.

fitness—comprises several factors that help define the abilities of a sportsperson.

flexibility (or suppleness)—the range of movement at a joint.

gastric juices—the substance which breaks down proteins in the stomach.

gender—sex of a person.

glucose—sugar found in carbohydrate; it is stored in the body in the form of glycogen.

glycogen—see **glucose**.

gross motor skill—a skill or action performed using large muscle groups.

haemoglobin—the substance found in red blood cells that combines with oxygen to form oxy-haemoglobin.

heart attack—when the heart muscle is starved of oxygen, usually caused by a blockage to the blood supply.

heart beat—one contraction and relaxation of the heart.

hormone—a chemical messenger used by the body (e.g., adrenaline).

information processing—a model to explain how we take in and deal with information before carrying out an action.

inhale—to breathe in; inspiration.

inspiration—see **inhale**.

interval training—a type of training when there are intervals of rest and work.

introvert—a personality type; quiet, withdrawn and insecure.

inverted U theory—theory regarding arousal levels and performance, helpful to a coach wanting to motivate an athlete.

involuntary muscle—muscles not controlled by the body; they work automatically (e.g., the heart).

isometric contraction—a muscle contraction where the length of the muscle does not change.

isotonic muscle action—normal muscle action where the muscle shortens as it works.

joule—a measure of energy; 4.2 joules is equivalent to 1 calorie.

knowledge of performance (KoP)—a type of feedback giving the performer information about how the performance was.

knowledge of results (KoR)—a type of feedback giving the performer information about the results of his or her actions.

lactic acid—an acid produced whilst working anaerobically. It builds up in the muscles and eventually leads to muscle fatigue.

lactic acid system (anaerobic)—the system used to break down glucose (glycogen) for energy without oxygen; lactic acid is the waste product.

learning curve—a graph of learning against time.

ligaments—strong fibrous bands of tissue used to hold bones to bones at the joints.

long-term memory—the permanent memory store. Information needs to be rehearsed before it can enter the LTM.

manual guidance (mechanical)—physically helping someone to perform a skill.

massed practice—a training or practice session where there is no break for rest.

mechanical guidance—see **manual guidance**.

media—term describing the various forms of broadcasters and reporters, such as TV and newspapers.

mesomorph—a somatotype; an individual with muscular arms, legs and body.

motivation—the drive or determination people have to do what they do.

movement time—the actual time taken to move once the muscles have received the message to move from the brain.

muscle tone—the tension in the muscles even at rest; muscle definition.

muscular endurance—the ability of the muscles to continue working over a period of time.

National Curriculum—the programmes of study laid down by government; schools have to meet these requirements.

nerves—the passageways of the body to carry messages. A state of anxiety that can affect performance, leading to anxiety and eventually stress.

neurotic—a personality type; someone who is anxious and insecure.

obesity—extreme overweight.

oesophagus—the food pipe connecting the mouth to the stomach.

open skill—a skill performed in an ever-changing environment; each open skill is performed slightly differently from the last.

overload—one of the four principles of training; to tire the body through training.

oxygen debt—when the body uses more oxygen than it can gain from the outside environment it continues to produce energy without oxygen, causing a debt. This can only continue for a short period.

part learning—breaking down a skill into parts to make learning easier.

passive stretching—flexibility exercises in which partners work together to stretch muscles.

perception—part of the information-processing model; understanding what the information collected actually means.

performance-enhancing drug—an illegal drug which is beneficial to an athlete whilst in competition or training.

personality—a person's unique traits (characteristics); this is what makes us individuals.

physiology—how the body functions.

physique—a person's body type.

plateau—when a person's learning stops improving and levels out.

platelet—a small blood cell that helps with clotting.

power—a combination of speed and strength; = work/time or (force × distance)/time.

professional—someone who gets paid for playing sport.

progression—one of the four principles of training; after a training session it is important to slightly increase effort in the next session, thus progressing.

protein—one of the main nutrients; important in helping the body repair and build muscle tissue.

pulmonary artery—the only artery which carries de-oxygenated blood. It carries blood from the heart to the lungs.

pulmonary vein—the only vein that carries oxygenated blood. It carries blood from the lungs to the heart.

pulse—located in several places, such as the wrist or neck; the number of times the heart beats per minute.

Q—see **cardiac output**.

reaction time—the time taken for the brain to receive information, make a decision and tell the muscles what to do.

response time—reaction time plus movement time; it is the total time for the brain to receive information and the muscles to carry out the action to completion.

reversibility—one of the four principles of training; if someone stops training over a period of time his or her fitness declines. This is known as the reversal of fitness effect.

saliva—a digestive juice found in the mouth.

selective attention—the process of focussing on relevant information and blocking out the noise.

sensory input—information is received from the eyes and ears.

short-term memory—a temporary information store. If information is not rehearsed it is forgotten.

skill—the ability to carry out a predetermined action with minimum effort and maximum certainty.

slow-twitch fibre—muscle fibre that contracts slowly but has the ability to work for long periods of time.

somatotype—an individual's body type.

specificity—one of the four principles of training; when training it is important to practise the skills used when competing (e.g., a runner would not gain much from rowing to help increase his or her stamina).

speed—a factor of fitness; the ability to move quickly.

sphygmomanometer—device used for measuring blood pressure.

sponsorship—the giving of money or other aid to an athlete, usually in return for advertising a product.

stamina—a factor of fitness; the ability of the body to keep working.

standing broad jump—a two-footed jump forward; a measure of explosive strength.

stitch—a specific muscle cramp affecting the diaphragm.

strength—a factor of fitness; the amount of force that can be produced by the muscles.

stretching—exercises carried out to improve flexibility, lengthening then holding the muscles.

stroke volume—the volume of blood pumped out of the heart in one contraction.

suppleness—a factor of fitness; see **flexibility**.

synovial joint—joints in the body which allow free movement.

systolic pressure—the blood pressure when the heart contracts.

tendon—fibrous tissue connecting the muscles to the bones.

tidal volume—the amount of air breathed in and out during normal breathing.

training—a set of conditions the body is put under to improve any factors of fitness.

vein—blood vessels which carry deoxygenated blood from the body to the heart.

vena cava—the largest vein in the body; carries blood from the body back to the heart.

ventricles—the lower chambers of the heart.

verbal guidance—helping a performer by telling him or her what to do.

visual guidance—helping a performer by showing him or her what to do.

VO$_2$—the total amount of oxygen the body needs and takes in at any time.

$\dot{V}O_2$max—the maximum amount of oxygen the body can take in and use.

voluntary muscle—muscle that is under our control, such as the biceps and triceps.

whole learning—learning a skill or action without breaking it down into parts.

Credits

AQA(NEAB)/AQA examination questions are reproduced by permission of the Assessment and Qualifications Alliance.

AQA(SEG) examination questions are reproduced by permission of the Assessment and Qualifications Alliance.

London questions reprinted, by permission, from Edexcel Foundation.

MEG questions reproduced with the kind permission of OCR.

References

Bandura, A. 1969. *Principles of behaviour modification*. New York: Holt, Rinehart and Winston.

Baron, R.A. 1977. *Human aggression*. New York: Plenum Press.

Cattell, R.B. 1967. *The scientific analysis of personality*. London: Pelican Books.

Eysenck, H.J. 1947. *Dimensions of personality*. London: Routledge & Kegan Paul.

Gill, D.L. 1986. *Psychological dynamics of sport*. Champaign, IL: Human Kinetics.

Hull, C.L. 1943. *Principles of behaviour*. New York: Appleton-Century-Crofts.

Seyle, H. 1976. *The stress of life*. New York: McGraw-Hill.

Sheldon, W.H., Stevens, S.S. and Tucker, W.B. 1940. *The varieties of human physique*. New York: Harper.

Index

Figures and tables are indicated with an italic *f* or *t*.

About the Author

Tim Ferguson holds a degree in sport science and a PGCE in physical education and has more than five years of teaching experience. He is also a qualified basketball, rugby, soccer, tennis and squash coach and has recently qualified as a climbing instructor.

Tim owns and runs High Adventure Outdoor Education Centre. In his free time he concentrates on his favoured sports of mountain biking, snowboarding and climbing.